Recent Developments and Applications of

Natural Language Processing

Recent Developments and Applications of Natural Language Processing

UNICOM

APPLIED INFORMATION TECHNOLOGY REPORTS

Editor **Jeremy Peckham**

KOGAN
PAGE

First published in Great Britain in 1989 by
Kogan Page Limited, 120 Pentonville Road, London N1 9JN
in association with Unicom Seminars Limited

British Library Cataloguing in Publication Data
Recent developments and applications of
 natural language processing. – (Unicom applied
 information technology reports)
 1. Man. Natural language communication with
 computer systems
 I. Peckham, Jeremy II. Series
 006.3′5

 ISBN 1-85091-682-9

Printed and bound in Great Britain by
Billings & Sons, Worcester

CONTENTS

RESEARCH

PREFACE

This book is a collection of papers presented at the UNICOM seminar on Recent Developments and Applications in Natural Language Understanding in December 1987. The purpose of the seminar was to draw together both users and developers of Natural Language Processing (NLP) technology and the chapters of this book reflect that aim. I have divided the material into just two broad headings, Applications and Research. Such a division, although convenient in directing the reader to his or her broad interests, will inevitably not be a completely clean one and some "applications" may still appear to be of a research nature.

The field of natural language processing is as broad in its application as it is diverse in the theoretical approaches to the problem. Applications for natural language processing span areas such as text processing aids, machine translation, database query, text summarising and scanning, message generation for explanation and help both in expert systems and conventional computing, and interactive dialogue as well as speech understanding.

Research into NLP was given a significant spur with the establishment of the Alvey Programme in the UK and the ESPRIT Programme in Europe. Both were set up with the aim of promoting collaboration between companies and universities in pre-competitive IT research. It is not surprising therefore that a number of the papers described in both the applications and research sections in this book derives from these initiatives.

In the first chapter Johnson sets the broad application field for NLP into context by giving a realistic analysis of the markets for Natural Language Processing taking account of real capabilities. Specific coverage is then given to intelligent text processing, machine translation, speech based NL systems, and the use of natural language in Knowledge-based-Systems (here a synonym for Expert Systems!).

Most users of word processors will be familiar with the use of spelling checkers but perhaps less so with the current developments in style critiquing. In the Text Processing section, Dale discusses the use of NLP in the development of such 'intelligent' editorial aids and describes in particular IBM's EPISTLE system.

i

Machine translation is covered from both a commercial and research point of view. Medhurst addresses machine translation from the perspective of providing a commercial document translation service using existing products, whilst McGee Wood and Arnold describe some of the latest research and developments in this area. Although of a more research nature, the papers by McGee Wood and Arnold have been placed in the Applications section in order to restrict the Research section to matters of more general applicability.

Speech Technology occupies a large field in its own right in terms of both applications and research, but in the last several years has begun to increasingly overlap with the field of natural processing. The reason for this is principally that speech signals, once transformed into symbols such as phonemes or words, require very similar processing to text in order to achieve understanding of the sentence. Peckham describes a Voice Operated Database Inquiry System (VODIS) for train timetable enquiries which incorporates an intelligent dialogue manager to handle the human-machine interaction in a graceful fashion. Steer's paper covers a different application for speech recognition, that of translating spoken phrases into another language over the telephone. The final paper by Newell in the Speech and Natural Language section presents the results of a series of experiments carried out to discover the responses of users to a listening typewriter with and without a simulated natural language interface.

Oakley, a former director of the Alvey Programme, introduces the section on research with an overview of the initiatives in Natural Language Processing forming part of the overall Alvey Programme set up by the UK government in 1983.

The following papers in the research section are grouped under three main headings according to their main thrust. The section on Theoretical Issues is largely concerned with the formal treatment of NL semantics; problems of intensional logic and belief representation are dealt with by Ramsay and the semantics VP modifiers by Pulman.

Boguraev's paper in the subsection on Tools describes experience gained working with an on line version of a large dictionary and the usefulness of its syntactic and semantic information in NLP. It also discusses the usefulness of phonemeic transcription s in a speech understanding project.

The final subsection on Discourse Structure and Dialogue Design covers aspects of the design of natural language dialogues. Wachtel describes a dialogue system which embodies many of the pragmatic features observed in human dialogue. Reilly, on the other hand, discusses the design of a dialogue program capable of handling instances of communication failure.

After a couple of decades of research, NLP may appear to many to be still very much in its infancy and dominated by ongoing research directed towards achieving the ultimate goal of unrestricted or general language coverage, rather than successful commercial applications. It is hoped that this collection of papers will help to illustrate what can be achieved in the way of practical systems as well as those areas still requiring further research.

Jeremy Peckham, September 1988.

BIOGRAPHIES

Doug Arnold has taught at the University of Manchester Institute of Science and Technology, and the University of Essex where he has taught Theoretical and Computational Linguistics since 1981. His main research interests are in these fields, with special emphasis on Machine Translation where he has published several papers.

Louisa Sadler has been a lecturer in the Department of Language and Linguistics at the University of Essex since 1985. She teaches courses in Theoretical Syntax, Morphology and Computational Linguistics. She was previously a lecturer in Linguistics at the University of East Anglia. Apart from Machine Translation, her main interests are in Computational Linguistics generally and Syntax. She is the author of 'Welsh Syntax: a Government and Binding Approach' (Croom Helm, 1987). Arnold & Sadler are co-leaders of the Machine Translation research group at Essex and have played a central role in the EEC's Eurotra project for a number of years.

Branimir Boguraev is an SERC (UK Science and Engineering Research Council) Advanced Research Fellow at the University of Cambridge. He has been with the Computer Laboratory since 1975, and completed a doctoral thesis on the Automatic resolution of linguistic ambiguities in 1979. He has worked in the area of natural language interfaces; more recently, under grants awarded by the UK Alvey Programme in Information Technology, he has been involved in the development of computational tools for natural language processing. His current interests focus on issues of software support for large scale grammar and lexicon development, and making computational sense of on line lexical resources.

Robert Dale currently works as a researcher in artificial intelligence for Syntek Ltd, a London based software house. He has worked on projects in the publishing industry for several years, and is currently completing a PhD in computational linguistics at the University of Edinburgh. His main research interests are in natural language generation and in the use of natural language processing techniques to develop powerful tools for text processing.

Dan Diaper is a senior lecturer in the Psychology Section of the Department of Combined Studies at Liverpool Polytechnic. He manages an Alvey Project (MMI/098 - The Human-Expert System Interface), which he originally started when a research fellow at the Ergonomics Unit, University College London. Dr Diaper has been an executive member of the British Computer Society Human-Computer Interaction Specialist Group for the last three years; in 1987 he was programme chairman of the Specialist Groups' Annual conference and he is to be Editor-in-Chief of a new international journal in the field of Human-Computer Interaction.

Tony Shelton is presently involved in a research project at Liverpool Polytechnic on the use of interactive video and expert systems for applications for sports coaching. This work is being undertaken in collaboration with the British Lawn Tennis Association. His interests lie in the area of expert system applications and also in the nature of the human-computer interface.

Jackie Fenn is a consultant in knowledge-based systems at Logica Cambridge Ltd. Since joining Logica four years ago with a degree in computational linguistics from UMIST, she has worked on the development of expert systems in a variety of applications. She is currently project managing Logica's involvement in the ESPRIT project 'An Expert Assistant for Electomyography'.

Simon Garrod is Reader in Psychology at Glasgow University. He was trained at Oxford and Princeton and briefly held a Fellowship at the Max Planck Institut fur Psycholinguistik in Nijmegen. His major areas of research are text comprehension, semantics and dialogue. He is currently an editor of the Journal of Semantics.

Tim Johnson is Chairman of Ovum Ltd, a company which specialises in published studies and consultancy on advanced computer technology and telecommunications. He is the author of Ovum's report on the commercial applications of natural language computing, which remains the leading source on these markets. He is also active as a consultant on markets and future developments in other applications of artificial intelligence research, including expert systems and object oriented programming. Tim Johnson read Physics at Imperial College London and began his career as a science journalist, first on the

Daily Telegraph and later as Technology Correspondent of the Sunday Times. From 1975 to 1982 he worked for Logica, the leading UK consultancy and systems house.

Christine Guilfoyle is a Consultant with Ovum Ltd, and was recently responsible for a project to update Ovum's forecasts of NLP markets in the USA. She is also lead author of a new Ovum report on "Expert Systems in Banking and Securities", to be published early in 1988. Before joining Ovum she was Editor of Expert Systems User. She graduated from Cambridge in English, but transferred to computer science and has carried out research in artificial intelligence at Bath University and worked on expert systems development for Helix.

Mary McGee Wood is temporary lecturer in Computational Linguistics in the Centre for Computational Linguistics at the University of Manchester Institute of Science and Technology. From a background in theoretical linguistics, she joined CCL in 1984, contributed to the design and implementation of the Ntran prototype, and for its third year was project director. Her research interests include categorial grammars and parsers, and specialized applications of machine translation.

Marian Medhurst is the Translations Manager of ESC, the first commercially operated machine translation group established outside the North American continent. She has been involved in the machine translation environment for many years and has been active in the translations business for over thirty years. She has also had considerable experience as an interpreter, author of language courses and as a language teacher.

Alan Newell is Professor of Electronics and Microcomputer Systems at Dundee University and Director of the University's Microcomputer Centre. His major research contribution has been in communication systems for the disabled. He has also developed a speech transcription system based on a Palantype shorthand machine. This is now commercially available as a simultaneous speech transcription system for the deaf and for use in verbatim reporting environments such as the law courts. He is currently investigating the human factor aspects of speech using this system as a simulated recogniser. His other research interests are in the man-machine interface field including the use of microcomputers in the electronic office, in rehabilitation and in therapy.

Brian Oakley was a civil servant for many years, until his retirement in 1987. He worked for most of that time in Computing. For the last four years he was Director of the Alvey Programme of Advanced Information Technology. He is now the chairman of Logica (Cambridge) the research arm of Logica and in October 1988 became President of the British Computer Society.

Jeremy Peckham joined the Royal Aircraft Establishment in 1972 and worked in the field of applied optics and scientific photography. He graduated with a first class honours in Applied Science (Physics Major) in 1977. From 1977 to 1980 he carried out research on the effects of stress on pilots and air traffic controllers' speech. During this period he was also responsible for work on Direct Voice Input (DVI) to avionic systems, covering both technology and human factors aspects. In 1980 he joined Logica, an international professional services company working in the broad field of information technology, as a senior consultant specialising in speech technology. His responsibilities have included the design and development of Logos, one of the world's first continuous speech recognition systems, which won the British Computer Society award for Technical Achievement in 1982. He provides consultancy internationally on speech technology and applications and currently manages the speech and natural language group in Logica Cambridge, which provides the main international focus within the company for Research in Knowledge Based Systems, Speech and Natural Language Technology and Human Computer Interaction.

Steve Pulman is a lecturer at the University of Cambridge Computer Laboratory. His research interests include syntax and parsing, word meaning, and formal semantics and pragmatics.

Alan Ramsay is a lecturer in Artificial Intelligence at the University of Sussex. His main research interest is in computer processing of natural language, with particular concern for the rational use of language in the service of non-linguistic goals. He is co-author of two books on the use of the programming POP-11 as a general purpose language for AI, and sole author of a forthcoming book on the use of formal logic in AI.

Ronan Reilly is a Research Fellow at the Educational Research Centre in St Patrick's College, Dublin. He is manager and project leader of ESPRIT Project P527 (CFID), the aim of which is the development of a robust natural language dialogue interface to a database. Apart from doing conventional AI research in natural language, he is also involved in research on connectionist models of language understanding.

Martin Steer joined British Telecom as a student in 1981, and spent one year of industrial training before attending university. He graduated with an honours degree in Electronic Engineering from Southampton University in 1985 and joined the Speech Technology and Language Processing division at British Telecom Research Laboratories, Martlesham Heath. Since then he has been working on the design of speech recognition hardware and the design and development of speech driven language translation systems. He is an Associate Member of the Institution of Electrical Engineers.

Tom Wachtel was Senior Lecturer in Linguistics at the University of Warsaw from 1979. Since joining Scicon Ltd in 1984, he has been working on the LOQUI natural language interface, and in particular on parsing, generation and discourse. This is part of ESPRIT Project 107. He is currently technical coordinator of the natural language work in the project.

ABSTRACTS

APPLICATIONS

1. Commercial Markets for NLP Products

T Johnson and Christine Guilfoyle (Ovum Ltd)

The paper reviews current commercial developments in the seven main applications of natural language processing - mainframe interfaces, micro interfaces, dialogue interfaces, machine translation, content scanning, text editing, and the talkwriter. Progress has been slower than hoped in most areas but even so sales of NLP products in the USA have doubled between 1985 and 1987. Estimates of current sales and projection to 1995 are provided.

2. Computer-based Editorial Aids

R Dale (Syntek Ltd)

This paper surveys some applications which, by embodying knowledge about natural language, can provide intelligent text processing facilities. The paper describes the limits of the techniques embodied in simple spelling correction and style critiquing programs; it then goes on to describe twosystems, IBM's EPISTLE and Syntek's Editor's Assistant, which aim to use NPL techniques to provide the basis of sophisticated text processing systems.

3. (Non)-Compositionality and Translation

Doug Arnold and Louisa Sadler (University of Essex)

The aim of this paper is to describe a notation for automatic translation (a 'translation machine'), and discuss its application to a class of problematic phenomena, collectively characterised as being 'non-compositional'. The discussion focuses on the treatment of idioms as typical exemplars.

4. Japanese for Speakers of English: The UMIST/Sheffield Machine Translation Project

M McGee Wood (UMIST)

This paper describes a Japanese-English machine translation project undertaken jointly at UMIST and the University of Sheffield under the Alvey programme. Both prototypes, Japanese to English (Aidtrans) at Sheffield and English to Japanese (Ntran) at UMIST, are designed for use by a monolingual English technical writer. The functions and formats of interaction with such a user in the two systems are compared in some detail.

5. Machine Translation in the Commercial Environment

M Medhurst (ESC)

Machine Translation has been proved to be a commercially viable proposition in the correct environment. In this paper we discuss the environment currently required and indicate areas where further development would be beneficial to enable large volumes of high-quality, consistent translation to be produced by a machine-assisted process at a commercially acceptable price.

6. Using a Knowledge Base for Automatic Text Classification

J Fenn (Logica)

This paper presents a text classification system in the medical field of electromyography. A major feature of the system is that it makes use of an existing knowledge base developed for an expert system. A review of other text scanning systems shows that the frame-based hierarchies of this knowledge base form a suitable basis for semantic analysis and a design is outlined which incorporates the knowledge base as part of its semantic component.

7. Natural Language Requirements for Expert System Naive Users

D Diaper and T Shelton (Liverpool Polytechnic)

The 'Wizard of Oz' simulation technique is used to allow expert system naive users to believe that they are interacting with an intelligent expert system capable of understanding full natural language. The purpose of the research is to discover how little natural language may actually be required. This paper analyses the syntactical usage of the users with a data-driven, sequential, left to right parse. The results suggest that the syntactical options required for real systems to understand user inputs may be computationally less complex than might be predicted from theory alone.

8. VODIS - a Voice Operated Database Enquiry System

Jeremy Peckham (Logica)

Logica, British Telecom and Cambridge University are jointly working on the Voice Operated Data Base Inquiry System (VODIS) research project which is sponsored by the Alvey Directorate. In this paper the scope as well as the method of investigation are discussed in broad terms. The system architecture is described and issues covering dialogue management, linguistic processing, speech recognition, message generation and human factors are considered.

9. Speech Language Translation

M Steer (British Telecom Research Labs)

This paper describes the design and development of a speech driven language translation system. Keyword spotting techniques are used to overcome the inaccuracies of speech recognition and the uncertainties of natural language. Commercially available hardware and software have been combined to implement a prototype demonstration system based on two personal computers.

10. Speech Simulation Studies: Performance and Dialogue Specification

A Newell (Dundee University)

Natural language and speech input systems have very close links; they also share the common problem that the current level of technology is not adequate for most realistic applications. It is therefore not easy to predict users' reactions to systems for which this technology is recommended. This paper describes a simulation technique for analysing users' responses to a 'listening typewriter'.

Results obtained from an implementation both with and without a simulated 'natural language interface' will be discussed.

11. Alvey Initiatives in Natural Language processing

B. Oakley (Alvey Directorate DTI)

Natural Language theme straddles a number of research topics which are part of the Alvey Programme. In this paper some of the major investigations supported by the Alvey Directorate are summarised and the positioning of these investigations in relation to industry's needs are discussed.

12. WH-questions and Intensional Logic

A Ramsay (University of Sussex)

AI treatments of natural language borrow from a number of sources. It is becoming apparent that there is considerable tension between the requirements of three current approaches, namely the use of AI planning techniques to situate language use within other rational activity, of formal logic for reasoning about the knowledge possessed by participants in a dialogue, and of notions from formal semantics for dealing with the linguistic content itself. This tension can be seen particularly clearly when we try to deal with questions, either answering them or asking them. The current paper attempts to clarify exactly where the problem lies, rather than offering a putative solution.

13. Events and VP Modifiers

S Pulman (University of Cambridge Computer Lab)

This paper describes and develops Davidson's theory of adverbial modification as predications of events. The theory is extended to some non-extensional adverbials and it is suggested how the introduction of states as individuals on a par with events might allow further development in order to cover some types of aspectual modification.

14. On-line Lexical Resources for Natural Language Processing

B Boguraev (University of Cambridge Computer Lab)

This paper is an attempt at a retrospective analysis of the collective experience stemming from the use of the machine- readable version of the Longman Dictionary of Contemporary English for natural language processing. It traces the relationships between specific requirements for lexical data and issues of making such data available for diverse research purposes. A particular model of on-line dictionary use is presented, which promotes a strong separation between the processes of extracting information from machine-readable dictionaries and using that information within the pragmatic context of computational linguistics. The paper further analyses some characteristics of the raw lexical data in electronic sources and outlines a methodology for making maximal use of such potentially rich, but inherently unreliable, resources.

15. Discourse Structure in LOQUI

T Wachtel (Scicon)

This paper describes parts of the LOQUI system, a natural language interface to databases and other software. The emphasis of this project is on providing a system that has a good dialogue capability. The approach adopted in LOQUI to matters relating to discourse structure, reference resolution, and so on, is outlined, preceded by briefer outlines of other parts of the system that are related to discourse.

16. Communication Failure in Dialogue; Implications for Natural Language Understanding

R Reilly (St Patrick's College)

The purpose of this paper is to highlight some of the theoretical and technical issues involved in getting computers to engage in non-spoken natural language dialogue with a user. An additional concern is the issue of robustness in natural language communication. The paper's main theoretical assumptions are (1) that the best medium for robust natural language understanding is dialogue, and (2) that the best basis for a computational dialogue system is a plan-based one. A typology of dialogue miscommunication is presented. Finally, a dialogue model is outlined which is intended to form the basis for a robust natural language understanding system.

17. Conceptual and Semantic Co-ordination in Dialogue: Implications for the Design of Interactive Natural Language Interfaces

S Garrod (University of Glasgow)

Human dialogue depends upon the participants' ability to co-ordinate their use and interpretation of language within particular domains. In this paper we explore various mechanisms which people employ to do this and use the analysis and simulation of human design principles for Human-Machine interfaces capable of dynamic interaction.

Chapter 1
Commercial Markets
for
NLP Products

T JOHNSON AND C GUILFOYLE,
Ovum Limited

1   INTRODUCTION

In 1985 Ovum researched and published a report on the commercial applications of natural language processing (NLP) (Ref 1). The report reviewed the work then being done to commercialise NLP in both the USA and the UK. An important feature was that it identified seven different application areas for NLP, and developed forecasts for the potential market in each case. Recently we have had the opportunity to talk again to most of the suppliers covered by the earlier report. We have been able to review their progress to date and develop a new set of forecasts for the USA.

This paper presents an outline of progress to date in each of the seven application areas, and a summary of the revised forecasts for the USA. The NLP market is still small - about $33m altogether in the USA this year. It is doubling in size every two years and continues to offer a very exciting long-term potential, but our revised forecasts are substantially lower than the earlier ones. The 1985 report recognised many of the obstacles to commercial NLP applications, but in practice the rate of progress has been even slower than expected.

We have not been able to re-do our UK market forecasts, but there is no doubt that they would show essentially the same trends as in the US, only on a much more limited scale. There are a few significant natural language developments in Britain with commercial application, mainly in areas related to voice recognition, but it is too early to talk about a market in the UK in any meaningful sense.

2   MARKETS BY APPLICATION

Mainframe Interfaces

This application is defined as the use of natural language technology to provide a user interface to database applications running on mainframes or minicomputers.

In 1985 a number of vendors were seeking to enter this business in the USA; now many of them have dropped out. Natural Language from McDonnell Douglas (formerly sold under the Microdata name), and Natural Link from Texas Instruments have been withdrawn. Frey Associates never achieved significant sales with its Themis product and has disappeared from the scene, Intelligent Business Systems has withdrawn Easylink, and is developing a successor product.

The remaining mainframe db interface suppliers (Artificial Intelligence Corporation, On-line Software, Carnegie Group) are selling slowly. This leaves the market leader, Artificial Intelligence Corporation, in a relatively strong position. One result has been a sharp rise in the average price per sale in this sector, so that the value of the market has increased even though the number of units sold has fallen. Even so, the value of sales in 1987 is expected to be no more than two-thirds the level forecast in 1985.

With over 500 installations, AI Corporation has achieved a substantial customer base, including some enthusiastic large-scale users. Like other vendors, AI Corp emphasises integrating natural language either with applications or with other technologies, such as expert systems. It seems mainframe and mini interfaces will develop in two ways:

- application-specific interfaces, integrated with other technologies, and

- 'new generation interfaces', with substantially improved quality and speed of performance.

A key point made by suppliers still interested in the business is that an NL product needs to be of first-rate quality in its own right, with the implication that many of those which failed were not.

Micro Interfaces

Micro interfaces are personal computer packages which provide low level natural language access to applications such as databases and spreadsheets.

Some products in this sector have had reasonably good sales - although they have made little impact in the UK as yet. The figures are swelled by Lotus's HAL (which is barely an Nl product), but other more Nl-ish packages have also done well. Symantec's Q & A has been successful, as has MDB's Guru. Microrim's Clout is still selling and reportedly is used by application developers for third party packages. The key point seems to be that these are good polished products anyway, with natural language as the icing.

The level of sales now estimated for 1987 is about what was previously forecast for 1986. However, the original forecasts predicted a sharp leap in sales in 1987, with NL becoming a key selling point for one or more big selling packages. This now seems unlikely, and the new forecasts project more steady growth.

As micro packages increasingly provide flexible and friendly interfaces, a menu-based or limited free-form natural language interface is likely to be a common option, increasingly with powerful 'WIMPS' interfaces.

Dialogue Interfaces

Sophisticated new-generation software such as expert systems or intelligent computer-aided instruction (ICAI) require more flexible and responsive interfaces to be used successfully. The applications of natural language processing to this requirement are what we classify as 'dialogue interfaces'.

The 1985 forecasts saw this as essentially a market for the future, but the new figures take a rather different view. They now categorise some of the work already being done under R&D contracts by companies like Cognitive Systems and BBN in the USA as being dialogue interface developments. However, the experience of the last two years suggests that unit prices will be higher and growth slower in future. This gives higher sales figures for 1987 - $4 million rather than zero - but a forecast of lower sales from 1988 onwards.

Machine Translation

Attempts at machine translation, using computers to convert text from one language to another, go back more than 30 years, but only in the last few years has the price-performance begun to approach that required for widespread usage.

The leading suppliers of two years ago - ALPS, Logos and Weidner on minis and PC's Systran on mainframes - are still on the scene but making little progress. A number of new companies have entered the market, but they do not seem to have expanded it significantly as yet. It may be that the technology needs to be taken in hand by a large supplier with marketing muscle before it can show rapid growth.

The change of strategy by ALPS may prove significant in this context. In mid-1987 the company returned to an earlier policy and is now aiming to be a 'total translation services' supplier rather than a vendor of stand-alone translation software. This reflects frustration at the difficulty of building a significant sales volume in translation software, but it remains to be seen whether the new approach will be any more successful than previous attempts to create a substantial business in a notoriously fragmented market.

For the moment, the market appears to be static, and we estimate that the growth which was forecast to appear by now may be postponed by as much as five years.

Content Scanning

If machine translation uses computers to facilitate communication between people, content scanning can be seen as a technology to improve communication between people and computers. Typically it entails computer reading and reformatting of messages sent by people so they can be loaded into a computer database and processed automatically.

There is a big potential market here in aiding international telex and electronic mail communication, but here again, earlier optimism has not been justified by actual sales, and the new forecasts are some two years behind the earlier ones in market growth. However, Cognitive Systems has been able to demonstrate cost-effective results with the Atrans system in Citibank, which re-formats international money transfer telexes.

The forecasts assume there will be an extensive role for Atrans-like systems in future. Cognitive may sell the rights to an established computer vendor with the marketing power to exploit it more successfully. Sumitomo Bank has also reported a successful telex reading system developed with DEC Japan.

Text Editing

Spelling-checkers have become commonplace adjuncts to word processing systems. Clearly this raises the possibility that style and grammar checkers - text editors - should provide the next generation of support for document preparation.

A number of low-level style checkers are indeed available. They make crude checks on such matters as sentence length and the use of the passive, but they do not parse the texts they process. True - that is, parsing - text editing systems have not yet appeared in product form, and are not expected to do so for several more years. Instead, the market has been split between some high-value custom development contracts and simple checkers for PC word processors and computer-aided instruction.

ALPS is one company with a foot in both these markets. In 1985-86 it had major contracts with IBM to develop its 'Document Revision Facility', worth over $2million in 1986. It also sells a low-level style checker for the Mackintosh called Mac-Proof, but as with other products in this category, the sales are not included in these market estimates.

As with dialogue interfaces, the new forecasts show some earlier ALPS custom development contracts in particular, but reflect slower growth in future. The forecasts still assume there will be a shift of emphasis from custom development to product sales in the early 1990, but the uncertainties are particularly large in this area. It remains to prove whether there is a significant demand for text editing as such.

Talkwriters

Without any doubt the biggest prize in view for the application of natural language processing is the development of a machine which can take dictation - sometimes known as the 'talkwriter' by analogy with the typewriter. At the same time, it will be extremely difficult to develop systems which can accept continuous speech dictation of anything like the complexity which an audio-typist handles as a matter of course.

Pioneering suppliers in this field - companies like Kurzweil, Speech Systems and Dragon Systems - have tackled this problem by producing talkwriters able to take dictation in limited domains; medical specialities are a favourite target. As a result some business has developed earlier than the previous forecasts allowed for, but penetration of the mainstream dictation market is likely to be delayed and overall growth projections have been reduced.

Application-specific systems are easier to develop than general purpose talkwriters, and have been brought to market more quickly, but their niche is more limited. The forecasts also incorporate estimates for 1000-word vocabulary voice recognizers (but not for those with more limited vocabularies) which were not included previously.

Current application-specific systems are in medical domains; others, in legal for example, are expected to follow. The predictions continue to assume that genuine general purpose machines will become available in the mid-1990s.

3   MARKET FORECASTS

Table 1 shows what the assessments above imply in terms of market forecasts. The totals are compared with the figures produced two years earlier, and they show a big reduction in the short to medium-term projections. However, there are two important positive conclusions for any company active in this market, or planning to enter it:

1 Total sales are expected to double every two years, based on much more history than was available when the earlier forecasts were prepared.

2 In the longer term, the total potential for NLP applications is as great as it ever was; the future has been postponed rather than cancelled.

Figures for the UK are also shown for comparison. They indicate the relative scale of the two markets, and should be scaled down by a similar factor to reflect the development of the past few years.

4   REFERENCE

1 Johnson T, Ovum Ltd (1985), Natural Language Computing: the commercial applications, 459pp, #275.

Table 1 Forecasts for Natural Language products by application in the USA ($'000s) Source: Ovum Ltd

	1985	1987	1989	1991	1993	1995
MAINFRAME INTERFACES	9.0	11.8	18.9	42.5	64.9	108.5
MICRO INTERFACES	3.0	5.9	11.0	12.9	46.7	97.9
DIALOGUE INTERFACES	0.2	4.0	6.4	9.0	25.8	48.0
MACHINE TRANSLATION	2.3	1.7	2.9	8.2	9.6	14.4
CONTENT SCANNING	0.7	1.7	5.1	11.0	20.4	39.1
TEXT EDITING	0.5	2.0	2.0	9.4	25.4	90.0
TALKWRITERS	0.0	5.7	22.0	68.8	177	306
TOTALS (1987 ESTS)	15.7	32.6	68.3	162	370	704
TOTALS (1985 ESTS)	15.5	97.0	307	593	1017	1466
UK FORECASTS (1985)	1.1	7.0	39.0	73.0	143	229

Chapter 2
Computer-based Editorial Aids

R DALE,
Syntek Ltd

1   INTRODUCTION

This paper surveys some applications that lie in the fuzzy area between text processing and natural language processing (NLP). The systems discussed are not straightforward text processing applications such as formatters and editors, but neither are they mainstream NLP applications such as database interfaces and machine translation systems. Rather, they are systems which, by embodying knowledge about natural language, can provide more intelligent text processing facilities. Style critiquers and grammar checkers fall into this category, along with any other applications whose purpose is to increase the quality of the written output of human beings. Given the limited understanding of language they embody, some of these systems are still best described as performing text processing rather than natural language processing, but this is set to change as our understanding increases; as we will see, there already exist impressive uses of NLP techniques in this area.

In this paper, we begin by looking at the most obvious aid to improving the quality of text, the spelling checker. There are two reasons for making this our starting point: first, it shows how even apparently simple tasks need access to knowledge about language; and second, it demonstrates the importance of the user interface. We go on to discuss simple style checking programs: the lesson here is that results can be quite impressive without invoking NLP techniques. We then move on to the more sophisticated issue of grammar checking, and end by describing a project whose long term goal is to marshal all these techniques to aid the professional copy editor.

2   SPELLING CORRECTIONS

Existing Technology

Of all the tasks where computers can help in the editorial and writing processes, the automatic detection and correction of spelling errors is the most developed in terms of available techniques. Existing systems fall into two broad camps: those that identify misspelled words by their absence from a dictionary, and those that identify misspelled words on the basis of their containing sequences of letters infrequently used in the language. There are advantages and disadvantages to both approaches: a good survey of the technology is provided in [7].

There is an important distinction to be made between spelling error detection and spelling error correction: error detection involves identifying misspelled words, whereas error correction involves indicating possible corrections for a given error. Error detection is usually much easier than error correction, an important point which recurs throughout this field. In recent years, a great deal of attention has been directed towards the issues involved in spelling error correction. The problem here is to try to guess, for each error found, what the writer meant to type. Research on the kinds of keyboard mistakes people typically make can help. For example, Damerau [1] found that 80 per cent of all spelling errors are the result of four basic error types: transposition of two letters, addition of an extra letter, one letter missing, or one letter wrong. Running rules of this sort in reverse means that, for a given word that does not appear in the dictionary, it is possible to hypothesize a number of 'nearby' words that are in the dictionary. These can then be offered to the user as possible corrections for the error.

It is also useful to distinguish errors of execution and errors of intention. An error of execution occurs when the user has the correct spelling in mind, but due to some intervening circumstance (such as accidentally hitting the wrong key on the keyboard), does not succeed in transferring this to paper; an error of intention, on the other hand, occurs when the user actually believes that the way he or she spells a particular word is correct when it is not. The rules just discussed are primarily useful for errors of execution; a different approach, used by Yannakoudakis and Fawthrop [8, 9], embodies knowledge about errors of intention (in particular, misspellings on the basis of the way words sound).

Existing systems typically claim 80-90 per cent success in detecting errors and suggesting appropriate corrections, although it's never clear how such figures are derived.

Limitations

Although systems based on techniques like those just described can help a great deal, there are many cases where spelling errors will still not be detected. The most problematic cases are those where words are misspelled as other words. Some problems of this sort can be solved by using context-dependent or document-specific dictionaries, where only the words most likely to occur in that domain are listed in the dictionary: for example, a dictionary oriented towards sport might not include the word 'shim', and therefore would be able to detect this as a misspelling of 'shin' in a book about football injuries. Ultimately, however, the best dictionary to use is the dictionary which contains exactly those words which are supposed to be in the text and no others, since this reduces the possibility of words misspelled as other words to the theoretical minimum. There is, of course, no way of working out in advance, for any given text, what this dictionary would contain.

But even such a dictionary, were it possible to construct , would not permit detection of all words misspelled as other words. The next step is to make an appeal to syntactic information. Consider, for example, the misspelling of 'sail' as 'sale' in the sentence 'Branson will sale across the Atlantic'. Because 'sale' will be marked in the dictionary as a noun, a system which includes a parser of English will find this sentence to be ungrammatical: no verb will have been found. It would be possible to construct a mechanism which could hypothesise the nature of the error in this particular case. In general, however, detecting an error is one thing; determining the appropriate correction is something else altogether. To see this, take another example of where we might try to appeal to syntax in correcting spelling errors: consider the misspelling of 'there' as 'their' in the sentence 'There dogs bite postmen'. We might hope that a system which can carry out syntactic analysis would be able to determine that the word 'there' is the wrong part of speech, and should instead be a determiner. This might then lead the system to hypothesise that there is in fact a misspelling of 'their'. However, it is not so easy to determine that this is the cause of the sentence's ungrammaticality. In this particular example, the sentence may not be ungrammatical at all, but may contain a different kind of error: it may only be missing a comma, as in 'There, dogs bite postmen'.

Things can get much worse: often, the detection of spelling errors requires an appeal to semantic and pragmatic issues. Consider, for example, the sentence 'I threw the bull at the wall', where the writer intended to type 'ball' instead of 'bull'. Even a system which made use of reasonably sophisticated semantic restrictions on the kinds of objects that can be thrown and there are no currently available spelling checkers which do have this degree of sophistication would get this wrong in more unusual contexts, for example in a description of a dream. Humans, however, would still be able to pick up the error.

The Importance of the User Interface

Despite the limitations, spelling correction technology is now sufficiently robust to be useful, and yet there is still a reluctance in some quarters to use spelling checkers. There are a number of possible reasons for this, but a principal reason is the difficulty of use. There is a lesson to be learned here that is relevant to all text error correction tasks.

The earliest systems for checking spelling, such as the UNIX spell program, would process a complete file of text and then provide information about the errors found, typically in the form of an alphabetically sorted list of the errors. In the environments offered by early operating systems and editors, the user would have to either memorise these errors or write them down on a piece of paper, and then edit the file accordingly.

Somewhat more advanced editing facilities would allow the user to display the errors on one part of the screen and the file to be edited on another, thus removing the need to memorise or write anything down. However, it is only more recently that systems which operate in an interactive fashion have become available: these highlight the misspelled words on the screen one at a time, in each case displaying alternatives as a menu on another part of the screen, allowing the user to select the correct spelling with a single keystroke or mouse click so that it automatically replaces the misspelled word. The advent of these sophisticated user interface techniques is the catalyst that is now making the error correction task necessarily a co-operative task because of the machine's lack of intelligence a feasible application. It cannot be over-emphasised just how much additional leverage is provided by interfaces of this sort.

3   STYLE CHECKERS

The Writer's Workbench

The next step beyond spelling checking is 'style checking'. There are already a number of programs which perform some kind of style checking on the market: the most well known of these is the UNIX Writer's Workbench (WWB) software [2,3,6], with most of the other systems available using techniques derived from this system. The creators of the WWB system would probably not want to call it an NLP application crucially, it does not incorporate a parser and Bell Labs do not view it as an AI product. The system, although widely discussed in the text processing literature (and in literature related to the teaching of writing), is rarely mentioned in the computational linguistics literature. Nevertheless, it is useful to examine how it works both to see just how much can be done without proper linguistic processing, and also to see the limitations of the simpler approach used.

All programs of this sort use the same basic technique. The system makes use of a table of 'incorrect' strings and suggested replacements, and a simple string search routine is used to identify the locations in the text of instances of the incorrect strings. The programs are constructed on the basis of principles of good writing style as found in various 'style guides'. These include rules like:

- avoid hackneyed, empty, or frequently misused phrases

- use definite, specific, concrete language in preference to vague and abstract language

- do not use words that are infrequent in normal use of the language

- use correct punctuation and grammar

- use active voice rather than passive voice

- avoid nominalistions (i.e., nouns formed from verbs)

12

There are a vast number of books that urge the use of such rules as a means to improving writing style. In practice, constructing a program that assists in enforcing rules like these properly is not easy, since in many cases our theoretical understanding of natural language is not yet up to the task; however, the WWB system goes some way in the right direction using quite simple mechanisms.

In keeping with the UNIX toolkit philosophy, the WWB system consists of a large number of specialised programs that can be fitted together in a variety of ways. Some of the component programs address proofreading issues, such as detecting spelling errors, consecutive occurrences of the same word, punctuation errors, cliches and undesirable phrases, and split infinitives. Other programs in the system are concerned with what might be described as stylistic issues: these provide statistical information on word and sentence lengths, grammatical types of sentences (simple or complex), the proportions of passive verbs and of nominalisations, the proportions of different parts of speech used to start sentences, usage of abstract nouns, and identification of sexist words and expressions.

The WWB programs are increasingly widely used, which attests to their usefulness, and yet they are not particularly sophisticated: the system does not incorporate a parser, and, except for a small number of words such as determiners and prepositions, does not even have knowledge of the parts of speech of words: this is worked out using statistical information and heuristics.

Limitations

The major point of note here is just how much can be done without using natural language processing: of the programs described above, only the identification of split infinitives, sentence types and passives could be said to involve linguistic processing, and even then only of a very elementary type. Everything else in the system uses tricks that effectively treat a text as no more than a string of characters, instead of as a complex entity made up of words in sentences. As a result, the 'stylistic analysis' is really a sham: the programs embody no semantic theory of style, resulting in stylistic advice that can be useless or incorrect. The documenters of WWB are honest about this, but the promotional material for derivative systems is less scrupulous.

A real problem in this area is that the terms 'style checker' and 'grammar checker' are used very loosely, and often without justification. At the time of writing, there are no commercially available systems that carry out real grammar checking, while 'style' is a word that means different things to different people. In the remainder of this paper we will consider one system which does perform limited grammar checking, and one system which starts from a more well-defined sense of the term 'style'.

4   GRAMMAR CHECKERS

IBM's EPISTLE system [4,5] is a much more ambitious project than the UNIX WWB software. The long term objectives are to provide office workers, particularly middle-level managers, with a variety of application packages to help them interact with natural language texts. In its current form, the EPISTLE system addresses only the tasks of grammar, spelling, and style checking of English texts.

The Interface

The interface provided by EPISTLE is a major improvement on that offered by WWB and its derivatives, detecting and offering corrections for errors interactively (note that the use of the term 'interactive' here does not mean that the system detects errors while the text is actually being typed; rather, by 'interactive' I mean that the system enters into a dialogue with the user each time it detects what it considers to be an error), where the other systems generally favour a batch mode of operation. The file to be checked is presented to the user within a screen editor; the user selects the type of checking required (spelling, grammar or style) from a menu, and the system then proceeds to highlight any text it considers to be in error. For each such error, a menu is displayed, allowing the user to select one of a number of alternative actions, such as replacement of the highlighted text by a corrected form, using a pointing device. Further information can be requested on the kind of error diagnosed. Quite apart from the more sophisticated capabilities of the system, as described below, this interactive interface in itself makes EPISTLE much more convenient to use than the systems described above.

Style Checking

Because the system includes a parser, the style checking capabilities offered by EPISTLE are superior to those offered by the systems described earlier. The program is capable of diagnosing stylistic problems that involve syntax: for example, too much qualification of a noun, as in 'the disk pack holder mount flange tip'; too much separation between a subject and its verb; and a much wider variety of split infinitives.

Grammar Checking

The most impressive aspect of EPISTLE is its grammar checking capability. The mechanism used to detect grammatical errors is as follows.

The system parses text in a left-to-right, bottom-up fashion, using grammar rules written using an augmented phrase structure grammar (APSG). In APSG, each grammar rule looks like a conventional context-free phrase structure rule, but may have arbitrary tests and actions specified on both sides of the rule (this is not unlike the facility for attaching arbitrary code to grammar rules offered by definite clause grammars (DCGs) in PROLOG). So, for example, we might have a rule like the following:

NP

VP (NUMB.AGREE.NUMB(NP))

-- VP(SUBJECT = NP)

This rule states that a noun phrase followed by a verb phrase together form a VP, provided the number of the NP and the original VP agree. The resulting VP structure then has the original NP as the value of its SUBJECT attribute.

Using rules like these, the system attempts to parse a sentence as if it were completely grammatical. Then, if no parse is found, the system relaxes some conditions on the rules and tries again; if a parse is now obtained, the system can hypothesise the nature of the problem on the basis of the particular condition that was relaxed. Thus, if the above rule was used in analysing the sentence 'Either of the models are acceptable', no parse would be obtained, since the number of the NP 'Either of the models' is singular, whereas the number of the VP 'acceptable' is plural. However, if the number agreement constraint is relaxed, a parse will be obtained; the system can then suggest that the number of the verb in the input text is wrong.

Using this and related techniques, EPISTLE can detect errors of the following sorts:

- lack of number agreement between subject and verb

- wrong pronoun case (as in 'The report was written by Fred and I')

- noun-modifier disagreement (as in 'These report must be checked')

- nonstandard verb forms (as in 'The report was wrote by John')

- nonparallel structures (as in 'This will save time, money, and provide more control')

There are, of course, various kinds of grammatical errors that the program cannot detect; however, by careful analysis of a considerable quantity of business correspondence, the EPISTLE team have managed to handle the more common grammatical errors.

5   COPY-EDITING ASSISTANCE

In the previous sections, we have described applications primarily aimed at the author who is his or her own editor. In the publishing world, however, there is a much stronger distinction between the originator of a text and the individual responsible for the editing of that text. In this section, we describe a system, currently being developed by Syntek Ltd, whose specific purpose is to assist the copy editor.

The professional editor's job often involves extensive rewriting and high-level reorganisation of a text, but the most time consuming tasks are copy editing and proofreading, where the major concern is with the checking of lower-level detail. Publishers insist on their output conforming to a house style, which will often provide precise specifications covering not only matters like the use of punctuation and spelling, but also matters which to the uninitiated seem to be no more than nit-picking details: for example, the format and punctuation of dates, numbers and numerical values; the punctuation and use of abbreviations; and the typefaces and abbreviations to be used for words from foreign languages. In matters like these, there is often no right or wrong way of doing things: what is important is consistency, and so different publishers may develop different house styles. In some publishing environments, an editor may be responsible for as many as twenty or so manuscripts in various stages of production, with different style sheets for each manuscript.

The Editor's Assistant is a rule-based system which assists a copy editor in massaging a text to conform to a house style. The central idea is that publishers' style rules can be maintained as rules in a knowledge base, and a special inference engine that encodes strategies for examining text can be used to apply these rules. The program then operates by interactively detecting and, where possible, offering corrections for those aspects of a text which don't conform to the rules in the knowledge base.

Some of the things with which the Editor's Assistant is concerned are also dealt with by the UNIX WWB programs and IBM's EPISTLE. However, these systems are not concerned with the specific notion of house style used in publishing, and, more significantly, do not make use of a rule-based approach. In the Editor's Assistant, the aim is to provide a general language where the user can easily specify new rules or modify existing ones, in much the same way as this is done in current expert system shells.

The User's View

The interface to the Editor's Assistant is very like that used in EPISTLE, as described in the previous section. The text file to be proofed is loaded into the editor and displayed on the screen; the rule application mechanism then applies the rules in the rule base against the text. If a sequence of words causes a rule to trigger, the words in question are highlighted on the screen, and a menu of alternative actions appears. Using a mouse, the user then chooses the option to be executed and the screen display is updated appropriately. There are always at least four options on the menu:

17

- replace the highlighted string of words by something else: sometimes there may be more than one replacement option

- ignore the rule on this occasion, so that it has no effect on the text currently highlighted

- disable the rule that has fired: this is appropriate when you realise that a particular rule is not applicable to the text you are currently dealing with

- apply the rule automatically for the rest of the text, so that on subsequent occasions when the rule fires, substitution will happen without the user being asked for confirmation.

Style Rules

The rules used by the system are of various types. The simplest are those which match single words or sequences of words in the text, and specify one or more possible alternative words or phrases, much as is done in style critiquers like those discussed earlier. However, the capabilities of the approach used here go far beyond rules of this sort.

- More complex rules match patterns found in the text, and specify replacements on the basis of these patterns. For example, one rule finds any sequence of two identical words (a common error introduced in text input at screen line breaks), and suggests replacing them by a single instance of the word; another rule identifies any date specified in the form 'Day Month Year' and suggests the form 'Month Day Year' as a replacement (a typical house style requirement). Similar pattern-based rules identify misspelling of 'their' as in 'their are' and misuse of 'a' as in 'a onion'.

- yet more complex rules can perform arbitrary operations on the basis of the words that trigger them. For example, one rule detects any measurement specified in kilometres and offers a converted measurement in miles; another offers to insert the expansions of little known abbreviations, provided, of course, the system knows what the expansion should be: if it does not, it can prompt the user to supply one.

18

Since the rule bases are separate from the mechanism that applies those rules, new rule bases can be constructed and used as required.

How it Works

Text Preprocessing

Before we can apply the rules to the text, we first build an internal representation of the text as a hierarchical structure consisting of paragraphs, sentences and tokens. Each token is represented by an object that maintains information derived from the analysis of the word it corresponds to. We analyse each word into three parts:

- the root form of the word, after it has been analysed;

- a list of syntactic features (such as word class and number) and their values;

- a list of typographic features (such as casing and font style) and their values.

So, for example, the first word in the sentence 'Is this the best solution?' would be analysed as having the root 'be', with the syntactic features of present tense and singular number, and the typographic feature of capitalised casing. The value of this kind of analysis will be seen below.

The Structure of the Rules

Each rule in the rule base contains the following information:

Application Mode: this can be one of three values, Query Apply, Auto Apply, or Ignore, and determines how the rule operates, as described above.

Trigger: This determines whether or not the rule applies in a given situation, by specifying a set of conditions that must be true for the rule to apply.

Replacements: The Replacements slot specifies a set of one or more replacements that may be made for the text string that was being considered when the rule triggered.

19

Rule Application

Once analysed, a text can be viewed as a string of tokens. Rules operate on substrings of this token string. Because of the prior analysis of the text, a single rule can match a large number of possible token substrings by specifying only those features that are relevant.

The token specifications held in the Replacements slot may be of two types: each may be simply a pointer to a token in the source string, indicating that the original token is to be used, or it may be a specification for the construction of a new token. In order to produce a replacement for the token substring that caused the rule to trigger, this specification may have to be fully instantiated by inheriting data from the corresponding token in that substring.

This simple mechanism allows us to vastly reduce the number of rules that are required in the system. Any slots may be inherited by the new token substring. So, for example, suppose we want a rule that specifies that the first word following a colon should not be capitalized: the rule will look like the following ($1 and $2 refer here to the first and second tokens respectively).

```
Trigger:        $1:Contents = ": "
                $2:Case     = capitalized
Replacement:    $1          = $1
                $2:Case     = lower
```

When the second token in the replacement string is constructed, everything but the Case feature will be inherited from the corresponding token in the input string.

Each sentence in the text may go through a number of changes as rules are applied to it. Changes made to the text are never destructive: when new tokens are added to the text, a new version of the sentence in question is created. This allows the effects of rules to be undone.

20

6   CONCLUSION

We have looked at a number of systems which make use of various types of knowledge about language to provide assistance in detecting and correcting errors in text. We saw that on the one hand, even a task as apparently simple as spelling correction can benefit from NLP techniques, but that, on the other hand, a great deal can be accomplished without recourse to these techniques, as in the WWB programs. We then examined two more advanced systems, EPISTLE and the Editor's Assistant, which aim to use NLP techniques to provide the basis of sophisticated text processing systems.

There are a wide range of errors that can be made in texts, all the way from simple typing mistakes to gross errors of logic and consistency in argumentation: we can still only deal with the lowest levels of errors, but progress is slowly being made. Pulling these techniques together will relieve the editor (professional or otherwise) of having to worry about lower level details, and allow more time to be spent on those parts of the job the computer is not suited to, but we are a very long way from systems that can even begin to understand the unrestricted forms of language we read every day.

7   REFERENCES

1   Damerau, FJ (1964), A technique for computer detection and correction of spelling errors. Communications of the ACM, 7, 171-176.

2   Frase, LT (1983), The Unix Writer's Workbench Software: Philosophy. Bell System Technical Journal, 62, 1883-1890.

3   Gingrich, PS (1983), The Unix Writer's Workbench Software: Results of a Field Study. Bell System Technical Journal, 62, 1909-1921.

4   Heidorn, GE, Jensen, K, Miller, LA, Byrd, RJ and Chodorow, MS (1982), The Epistle text-critiquing system. IBM Systems Journal, 21, 305-326.

5 Jensen, K, Heidorn, GE, Miller, LA and Ravin, Y (1983), Parse fitting and prose fixing: getting a hold on ill-formedness. American Journal of Computational Linguistics, 9, 147-160.

6 MacDonald, NH (1983), The Unix Writer's Workbench Software: Rationale and Design. Bell System Technical Journal, 62, 1891-1908.

7 Peterson, JL (1980), Computer Programs for Spelling Correction: An Experiment in Program Design. Berlin: Springer-Verlag.

8 Yannakoudakis, E J and Fawthrop, D (1983), The Rules of Spelling Errors. Information Processing and Management, 19, 87-99.

9 Yannakoudakis, EJ   and Fawthrop,D   (1983), An Intelligent Spelling Error Corrector. Information Processing and Management, 19, 101-108.

Chapter 3

(Non)-Compositionality and Translation

D ARNOLD and L SADLER,
University of Essex

1   INTRODUCTION

The aim of this paper is to describe a notation for automatic translation (a 'translation machine'), and discuss its application to a class of problematic phenomena, collectively characterised as being 'non-compositional'. The discussion focuses on the treatment of idioms as typical exemplars.

Section 1 introduces the basic principles of the machine and the associated linguistic theory, and gives some examples of its application to non-idiomatic cases. In section 2 we provide background on the linguistics of idioms, describe their main characteristics, and introduce a condition (the 'headedness' condition) which idioms seem to satisfy. Section 3 discusses the application of the machine to idioms, showing that typical features of idioms can be handled straightforwardly, and that the most characteristic properties of idioms, including the headedness condition, are naturally related to the properties of the machine. Thus, the machine appears rather well suited to the practical treatment of idioms, and other similar 'non-compositionalities', and has some interest as a descriptive linguistic notation. Section 4 discusses problems and counterexamples, with some suggestions as to how they may be overcome [1].

2   THE BASIC MACHINE

The task is multilingual translation, and we assume that a transfer based architecture is appropriate for the machine. In such a system, translation involves relating source language (SL) text to an abstract, but still in some way source language oriented, representation language (RL/s), 'transferring' expressions of this abstract representation to expressions of a target language (TL) oriented representation (RL/t), which is then related to the target language text. Minimally, the transfer process involves replacing the SL lexical items, which are the leaves of RL/s, with those of the TL.(cf. Figure 1).

(1)

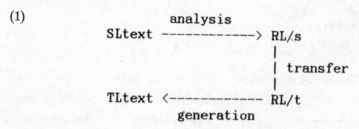

```
                        analysis
            SLtext  ------------>  RL/s
                                    |
                                    |  transfer
                                    |
            TLtext  <------------  RL/t
                        generation
```

We call expressions in these representation languages Interface Structures (ISs), and take the basic idea to be one of semantic dependency or argument structure. Each construction is assumed to consist of a governor, or head, with a number of dependents (arguments or modifiers). Dependents are said to fill 'slots' in the 'frame' of the head. Notice that this makes ISs linguistic, rather than more general knowledge representations.

(2)   The rats ate each other

(3)

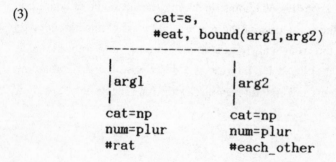

```
                    cat=s,
                    #eat, bound(arg1,arg2)
            ------------------
            |                   |
            |arg1               |arg2
            |                   |
            cat=np              cat=np
            num=plur            num=plur
            #rat                #each_other
```

24

For exemplification, we have omitted attributes such as definiteness, tense/time reference, person etc., and simplified in other small ways. In a dependency framework, constructions are assumed always to have a lexical head, here indicated by '#', and marked on the mother node. Branches are labelled to indicate dependency relations to the head. Node labels are feature bundles in the normal way. The anaphoric relation between 'the rats' and 'each other' is represented by means of the annotation 'bound (arg1, arg2)'.

On this view, the basic 'translation relation' becomes a relation between two linguistic representations: IS and IS'. This differs most notably from so-called 'direct' approaches (which omit the intermediate levels of representation), and 'interlingual' approaches in which the pair < IS/sl, IS/tl > is replaced by a single representation. The direct approach is not really feasible in the multilingual case (in effect N languages can require N*(N-1) separate direct translation systems). As regards interlingual approaches, we believe that translation is an irreducibly linguistic relation (in contrast with e.g. the more general relation of paraphrase), so that non-linguistic (e.g. 'knowledge based') interlinguas are simply inappropriate, and we are not convinced that existing proposals for linguistic interlinguas (e.g. those based on semi-natural languages) are effective in simplifying the task of MT.

A transfer architecture decomposes the problem of translating texts into the problems of Analysis and Generation, and the problem of 'translating' abstract representations. Two difficulties arise:

First, consider the task of writing a generation component for a language (L) in such a situation. In the worst case, the input to generation would be defined by the union of all other analysis components, and all transfer components that have L as their target. This seems to make the task impossible. There should be some independent, and linguistically well-motivated, definition of the class of ISs that are input the generation component of L, some definition of the notion 'well-formed expression' in IS of L. Moreover, it is natural if the input to generation should be the same as (or at least very similar to) the output of analysis (cf. Krauwer & Des Tombe 1984). Thus we are led to introduce a 'constructivist' principle: each IS/i is given an independent definition by means of a 'grammar' (G), which generates IS/i in the conventional sense. We take a G to consist of (i) declarations defining the notion 'well-formed feature bundle', and (ii) sets of 'constructors' (0 place constructors are also called 'atoms'), which correspond to lexical frames or argument structures, specifying the requirements that a lexical head puts on its dependents.

(4)

```
eat = {cat=s}.[ arg1 = {cat=np},
                arg2 = {cat=np},
                *mod ]
```

For example, (4) would be the (simplified) lexical entry for the verb 'eat': 'eat' has two obligatory arguments, both NPs, and any number of modifiers, of any category at all [2]; the category of a construction headed by 'eat' is s. A representation such as (2) can be generated by applying (3) to representations built by the constructors #rat, and #each_other, and filling in various features.

The second problem is finding a systematic basis for the translation relation (considered as an ISxIS relation). Here we think two ideas are useful. First, the idea that the translation relation is generally 'reversible' in the sense that 'expression2' is a translation of 'expression1' just in case 'expression1' is a translation of 'expression2'. Second, the idea that the translation relation is basically 'compositional'. Intuitively, compositional translation of a simple, unanalysable SL expression involves finding the corresponding TL item. Compositional translation of a complex SL expression involves translating its parts, and combining the translations together in a way that reflects the way the parts were combined in the SL. Given the constructivist idea just described, this has a natural interpretation. For an SL expression E, constructed by applying a constructor C0 to sub-expressions C1,...CN, the translation of E can be found by translating C1,...CN, and applying the corresponding TL constructor to the translations:

(5)   If E is an expression C0 : C1,....,CN, then

        Trans(E) = Trans(C0) : Trans(C1),....,Trans(CN).

This would give the following general format for translation rules,

(6)   sl_constructor: arguments < = > tl_constructor: arguments'

When constructors are taken to be lexical dependency frames, compositional translation involves simply relating those frames, e.g. translating between English and French as in (7)a and b involves a rule like (8).

(7)   a. John likes Mary.

        b. Marie plait a Jean.

(8)

```
t_like/plaire  =     {#like}.[ 1!arg1,
                               2!arg2,
                               3!*mod ]
                   <=>
                   {#plaire}.[ 2!arg1,
                               1!arg2,
                               3!*mod ]
```

#like and #plaire are the names of English-IS and French-IS constructors, and arg1, arg2, and mod are slots in their frames. The rule indicates that the arg1 of 'like' corresponds to the arg2 of 'plaire', and vice-versa. One can think of one side of the rule as an instruction to decompose a source language structure, and the other side as an instruction to build a target language structure. For example, from English = French, it could be read as: (i) take a structure built by the #like constructor, decompose it into 3 parts: whatever fills the arg1 slot, whatever fills the arg2 slot, and whatever things fill the mod(ifier) slot; (ii) translate these parts; and (iii) recombine the translations by applying the #plaire constructor, in such a way that #like's arg1 becomes #plaire's arg2, and vice-versa.

Notice that this interpretation incorporates the constructivist principle: the target language side of a translation rule is essentially a call to the target language G to build a structure. So translation rules are guaranteed to produce only structures which are well-formed according to the independent definition of the target G.[3]

We think analysis and generation are simplified and made more coherent if further levels of representation are recognised. We assume the relation between these levels is handled by the same apparatus as is used for relating ISs (i.e. the idea of 'translation' is generalised slightly). In addition to IS, we currently assume the following levels of representation (the optimal number and nature of 'other' levels is an empirical (or 'practical') matter, of course).'Eurotra' Relational Structure (ERS): a level of representation based on the idea of syntactic dependency. It is inspired by, and broadly analogous to, LFG f-structure (Kaplan & Bresnan 1982). There are two main differences: (a) Where f-structures are in effect simply features, an ERS structure is a tree with labelled nodes and branches. There is consequently a formal distinction in ERS between the representation of hierarchical relations (expressed via labelled tree geometry), and inherent properties (e.g. attributes for number, person, tense, etc.) expressed as features labelling nodes. This distinction is of no consequence in what follows. (b) We assume different analyses in certain cases, e.g. we assume, contra LFG, that auxiliary verbs are not ERS governors (= LFG PREDs) and are absent at this level, being replaced by appropriate values of tense, aspect and voice features. The effect of this is that ERS structures sometimes have a 'flatter' hierarchical structure than the corresponding f-structures (cf. the example below).

'Eurotra' Configurational Structure (ECS): a level of constituent structure (i.e. not based on ideas of dependency) analogous to LFG c-structure. The main differences are that (a) ECS nodes lack annotations indicating the configurational-functional structure mapping (the mapping is given separately by the translation rules that take ECS structures into ERS structures) and (b) ECS nodes are labelled with feature bundles (the possibility that c-structure categories should be feature bundles is forseen in LFG, but in practice they seem to be treated as if they were atomic). Since ECS is not a dependency level, the normal apparatus of constructors corresponding to lexical frames is not directly applicable. Instead, we take constructors to correspond to phrase structure rules; a constructor will be identifiable by means of its rule name, its 'slots' will be the branches that connect the mother to the daughters, and apparatus for indicating linear precedence (LP) between branches is added.

The following representations will make this more concrete.

(9)   The rats have been eating the cheese.

(10)   ECS (omitting some feature specifications)

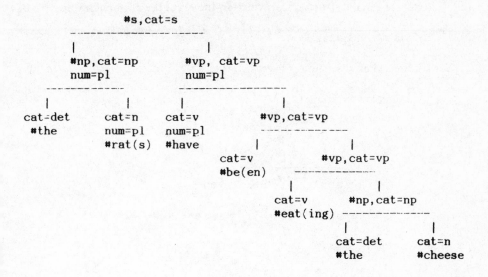

(11)   ERS

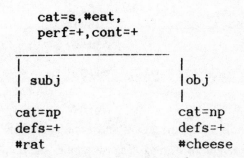

The major problem with the view of translation given above is that many cases appear to be only partially compositional according to the definition. There are many cases where it is not plausible to analyse source and target structures as having the same kind of 'constructor-to-constructor' structure, or where such an analysis distorts and undermines the linguistic basis of the representation languages.

29

For example, consider the relation between the Dutch and English sentences in (12), whose structures are represented in (13) [4], or the relation between the ECS and ERS structures given above. In both cases there are radical differences between the structures provided by the Gs of the different levels.

(12)   a. Jan zwemt graag.

        Jan swims 'likingly'

        b. John likes to swim.

(13)

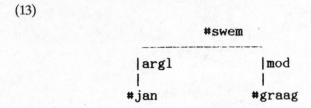

```
                    #swem
          ----------------------------
          |arg1              |mod
          |                  |
          #jan               #graag
```

(14)

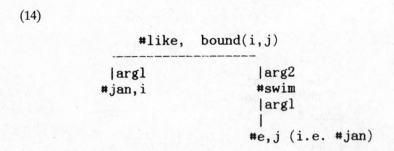

```
          #like,   bound(i,j)
          ----------------------
          |arg1              |arg2
          #jan,i             #swim
                             |arg1
                             |
                             #e,j (i.e. #jan)
```

What we can see in the 'graag-like' case is that English and Dutch 'invert' the relations between 'like/graag' and 'swim/zwemmen': where Dutch applies the frame of #zwemmen to #graag, English applies the frame of #like to #swim. This relation cannot be stated in a constructor-to- constructor system. In the case of (10) and (11), several things happen: the parts of the ECS structure built by s, and vp rules are all 'collapsed' in translation, part of the ECS structure of the form (15), presumably built by one of the vp rules, translates as a feature 'perf= +', and something similar happens with the translation of '[vp [be] ...]' into 'cont = +'.

(15)

```
                           #vp1
            -------------------------
            cat=v              vp2
            #have
```

To cope with this sort of problem, we propose to relax the definition of compositionality. The basic idea is this: it is often possible to split a problematic structure up into an 'exceptional' part, and a 'regular' part, in such a way that translating the 'regular' part is a strictly compositional process, and then to recombine the translations in some appropriate way 'licensed' by the target G. For example, as a first approximation, if 'graag' is removed from the Dutch representation (13), the remainder ('Jan zwemt') can be translated compositionally into 'John swims', which can then be combined with the 'likes (to)' (the translation of 'graag') so as to fill its arg2 slot, and give a structure like (14). The process for English to Dutch translation is analogous.

For the translation of (10) into (11), the solution is similar. First, consider the translation of the lowest vp. This can be found compositionally, by applying the translation of 'eat' (the ERS constructor (16)) to the translation of [np the 'cheese'] in such a way that the latter fills the object slot of the former (17).

(16)

```
    eat(ERS)  =          {#eat}.[ subj={cat=np},
                                  obj={cat=np},
                                  mod* ]
```

(17)   Translation of vp: 'eat the cheese'

```
    {#eat}.[ subj={cat=np},
             obj={#cheese,cat=np,defs=def}.[],,
             mod* ]
```

The translation of the vp dominating 'be' can be found by dividing it into 'be' and its sister vp, and 'injecting' the feature 'cont = +' into the translation of the vp. Similarly the translation of the vp dominating 'have' can be found by splitting it into 'have', and the sister vp, and injecting 'perf = +' into the translation of the vp, giving (18).

31

(18)   Translation of vp: 'have been eating the cheese'

```
{#eat,perf=+,cont=+}.[ subj={cat=np},
                       obj={#cheese,cat=np,defs=def}.[],
                       mod* ]
```

Finally, the translation of s can be found by splitting it into np and vp, and recombining in such a way that the translation of the np fills the subject slot of the translation of vp1, giving (11). ERS to ECS translation (i.e. generation) is the straightforward reverse, e.g. one step involves splitting (11) into 'subject', and a remainder, and combining them together in such a way that the translation of the subject fills the np slot, and the translation of the remainder fills the vp slot in the constructor that builds ECS s-nodes (assuming this to be equivalent to s-> np vp). Another involves a split into 'cont = +', and a remainder, using an ECS vp rule to build a vp consisting of 'have', plus an empty vp slot, and filling the vp slot with the translation of the remainder.

The following will exemplify the syntax of translation rules [5]:

(19)   Translating to/from [s [np] [vp]]

```
!{#s}.[ 1!np, 2!vp ]
<=>
2!{!cat=s}.[ 1!subj ]
```

(20)   Translating to/from [vp [have] [vp]]

```
!{#vp}.[   !v={#have},
           1!vp ]
<=>
1!{cat=s,!perf=+}.[]
```

(i.e. in analysis: translate 'have' and a sister vp by injecting the feature perf= + into the translation of the vp; in generation: translate an s with the feature perf= + by creating a structure with the vp constructor applied to the verb have, and the translation of the rest of the sentence under vp).

32

The relaxed definition of compositionality thus allows structures to be decomposed and built in ways that do not exactly mirror the analyses provided by the relevant Gs. There are still important restrictions on the power of translation rules, however. We will mention two.

First, there are restrictions on the 'slot filling' process which mean that the full path of nodes from the root of a target structure to the slot must be specified on the target language side (so (19) will not result in subject slots at arbitrary depth in a target language structure being filled). Thus, e.g., it is not possible to use translation rules to perform unbounded movement.

Second, the target G still provides the only basic constructors, and the process of building is restricted to (i) 'slot-filling' (the translation of one part fills a slot in the translation of another), or (ii) 'feature injection' (the translation of one part is a feature that is injected into the other). Since 'slot filling' can only put appropriate items in slots which are specified in the lexical frame of the head of a structure, only 'coherent' structures (in the sense of LFG) can be built into the target language. Moreover, well-formedness of feature bundles is checked automatically as structures are built up, and there is a global check that all obligatory slots are filled (thus, all structures are ultimately checked for 'coherence' in the LFG sense). Thus, the 'constructivism' of the system is not affected: it is still the case that the only structures which can be produced are those which can be generated by the target language G.

In addition, to this basic machine there are a number of extensions, to deal with phenomena which do not fit naturally into a framework of (relaxed) compositional translation.

It often happens that a structure can be translated in several ways. In particular, it may be that it can be translated by a relaxed compositional rule, and also translated strictly compositionally. Sometimes this reflects a genuine ambiguity. But in other cases it is undesirable, e.g. in the domain of morphology, Dutch 'kenner' should be translated as 'someone who knows', not as 'knower', which is what a normal compositional translation rule would give. For this reason, the basic machine is provided with a rudimentary control mechanism, which allows the user to state that if one rule applies, other rules must be prevented from applying (they must be 'suppressed'). E.g. the 'kenner' 'someone who knows' rule would suppress the strictly compositional translation rule.

The text ECS structure mapping is not performed by translation rules. The current implementation contains a bottom-up parser, distantly based on the work of Matsumoto et al (1983), and a simple table-driven morphological analyser which deals with inflectional morphology. Parsing consists essentially of applying the ECS grammar to the output of the morphological analyser.

Anaphoric relations (wh-trace, control, np-trace, pronominal) are not handled by the ordinary translation or G apparatus. Instead, there are anaphora 'specialists', which operate on the output of the translation rules, at different levels. They work by checking items that stand in certain structural relations (e.g. a subject of a control verb, and an unfilled subject slot in a complement clause), and assigning an indication of binding, and by giving certain features identical values in anaphorically related nodes. (We do not have apparatus for full 'sharing' of structures, or copying, though this could be simulated in part). The basic idea is that anaphoric relations are preserved in translation, so at any level, new annotations may be added, and existing ones may be checked for validity. However, the important point here is that though the application of translation rules may be sensitive to the presence/absence of anaphoric relations, they cannot directly affect anaphoric relations.

3   THE TREATMENT OF IDIOMS

In this section we will discuss the basic properties of idioms, give a brief review of some existing approaches, and propose a definition of the notion 'possible idiom'.

Much of the literature on idioms is concerned with the question of definition (cf. Chitra and Flavell (1981), Rose (1978), Wood (1985), etc.). For the purpose of this paper, however, our view can be rather pragmatic: idioms are typically syntactic constructions which translate as items without internal syntactic structure.

We can distinguish between the monolingual idioms in (1) and cases which are only idiomatic from a bilingual point of view (2):

(1)   John has kicked the bucket.

       Mary turned the tables on us.

       The police kept close tabs on them.

       They gave Mary a hand.

       They are pulling Mary's leg.

       They gave us a run for our money.

(2)   (Sp) madrugar   < = >   (Eng) to get up early

       (It) adagiare   < = >   (Eng) lay down with care [6]

       (NL) meelachen   < = >   (Eng) join in the joke

Though we will discuss some cases of expressions that do not fit the definition given above, we intend to exclude a number of things from consideration. We have nothing to say at present about morphological noncompositionality, hence we exclude cases like (3) and the interaction of idioms with morphological processes as illustrated in (4):

(3)   manhandle (does not mean 'to handle a man') rarity ('something that is rare'; compositionally should mean

       'the fact/degree to which something is rare', cf. Pesetsky 1985)

(4)   blind-eye approval (from 'turn a blind eye')

       John's a great one for leg-pulling (from 'pull X's leg').

In general, we will not attempt a treatment of the kind of case discussed in Pulman (1986) of idioms showing extreme degrees of variability with respect to syntactic and morphological form, and even lexis:

(5)   That's a case of chicken counting.

        That's got a feline among the pigeons.

        The excrement will encounter the rotary cooler at any moment [7].

There is no discussion here of collocations (6): taking lexical frames as a basis provides an obvious account of collocations imposed by heads on dependents, but it goes beyond the immediate concerns of this paper.

(6)   rancid butter, sour milk, rotten eggs

        (cf. *rancid milk, *sour eggs, etc.)

We also exclude genuine, or 'live' metaphors (6), which differ from idioms mainly in their degree of novelty; for the moment, we assume that metaphors are universal, and thus translated literally. This is a good approximation given similar cultures, and gives reasonable expectations about quality of translation.

(7)   Harry blew the final whistle on the proposal

        (meaning, perhaps: Harry signalled the final rejection of the proposal).

Perhaps the most striking property of idioms is what might be termed their 'surface regularity': from the point of view of surface form, idioms are completely indistinguishable from literally interpreted phrases. In particular:

(a) They show no inflectional irregularities: e.g. if an idiom involves the verb 'give', its past tense will involve the normal past tense form 'gave', and if it passivises, it will contain the past participle form 'given'.

(b) They have regular phrase structure properties: e.g. there are no idioms of the form 'determiner-verb-adjective', any more than there are literal expressions of this form (cf. Chomsky (1980: 149ff, 277f)).

(c) They are anaphorically regular: where idioms contain anaphorically related items, these relations satisfy binding conditions in the normal way.

There are, however, at least two sources of irregularity. It is well known that the behaviour of idioms with respect to syntactic processes such as passivisation, dative shift, topicalisation and clitic doubling is idiosyncratic, and a variety of proposals have been made in the literature to account for some of this variability (cf. Newmeyer (1973), Chomsky (1981), Jaeggli (1981)):

(8)   John gave Mary the finger.

        $John gave the finger to Mary.

        John gave Mary a raspberry.

        $John gave a raspberry to Mary.

        Peter kicked the bucket.

        $The bucket was kicked by Peter. [8]

A further way in which idioms are apparently unpredicatable concerns the extent to which they permit internal modification. Certain idioms seem to resist all internal modification, whilst others allow it if it is interpretable as modification of the whole idiom. We return to this issue below.

Intuitively, it seems clear that idiom formation is subject to some sort of locality condition. This intuition is reflected in many places in the literature (see, for example, the debate concerning the possibility of subject verb idioms: Marantz (1984), Bresnan (1982), Chomsky (1981)), and a number of different proposals have been made. For example, Chomsky (1980:149-153 and 1981:146:fn 94) suggests a re-analysis account which permits an idiom to be treated as a unit at some level of representation. In this account, an idiom rule re-analyses 'take advantage of' as a V with roughly the meaning of 'exploit'. Since re-analysis simply provides a further bracketing for independently generated strings, the surface regularity of idioms can be accounted for.

It is clear, however, that 'unit' at a given level cannot be defined straightforwardly as contiguity (which is what a re-analysis treatment invites), since an idiom may be separated by non-idiomatic parts (for example, cases of internal

37

modification), and may require the presence of free arguments internal to the idiom:@A TAB = (9)John pulled Mary's leg.

It is difficult to imagine a level of representation at which a local construction involves 'pull' and 'leg' but not 'Mary's'.

The clearest recent suggestion for a locality constraint is made by Pesetsky (1985) in a discussion of idiomatic interpretation in morphology [9]. Pesetsky proposes to account for the availability of idiomatic readings of complex words in terms of a restriction on the rule of idiosyncratic interpretation, which is involved in the interpretation of idioms and non-compositionalities in general. Pesetsky suggests that X and Y may receive idiomatic interpretation if they are sisters, or Y is the head of X's sister. Although Pesetsky limits his discussion to two levels of structure, it is clear that such a locality statement could be generalised to permit further levels of embedding. Such idioms do occur:

(10)   John rammed the theory down Pete's throat.

         Pete laid his failure at Mary's door [10].

Although Pesetsky is working within a framework in which all the levels of representation are basically configurational, the locality condition may be give a natural and straightforward interpretation in a dependency model:

(11)   Each local construction involved in an idiom

         must contain a head which participates in the idiom

In what follows, we refer to this condition as the 'headedness condition', and show that this condition is closely related to the design of the basic machine.

4   IDIOMS AND THE BASIC MACHINE

We assume that treating an idiom involves relating a complex structure to a simple expression (e.g. a word) with the same interpretation [11]. When the direction is complex-simple, we will speak of 'recognising' the idiom, when it is simple-complex, we will speak of 'generating'. Recognising and generating idioms are typically tasks for translation rules.

We will begin with some characteristic examples.

(1)   John gave Mary a hand   < = >   John helped Mary

       John pulled Mary's leg   < = >   John teased Mary

       John lost his temper   < = >   John became angry

(2)   John gave Mary a hand < = >   John helped Mary

       give[1, 2, a_hand]   < = >   help [1,2]

The surface syntactic structure is not distinguishable from a literal expression (in fact, ambiguity is the normal state of affairs). However, it seems clear that 'a hand' is not a semantic argument of 'give' on the idiomatic interpretation, so that a unit interpretation should be assigned at IS (it is not crucial if this interpretation involves 'help' or an abstract unit 'give_a_hand', but it clearly simplifies the transfer component if it is the former). Thus, the following rule should be part of the ERS-IS translator:

(3)

```
        !{#give}.[ 1!subj,
                   2!obj,
                   !obj2{#hand,!def=indef}.[],
                   3!*mod]
           <=>
        !{#help}.[ 1!arg1, 2!arg2, 3!*mod ]
```

That is: to translate a structure built by (i.e. headed by) #give, where the obj2 is an indefinite phrase headed by #hand, build a construction using the IS frame for #help. The (translation of the) subject of #give becomes the arg1 of #help, and the (translation of the) object becomes the arg2. Modifiers remain modifiers. In generation, structures headed by #help will be decomposed into arg1, arg2, and modifiers, and a structure will be built where #give has an obj2 built from the lexical entry for #hand, with a feature marking it as indefinite injected. As it stands, the rule requires that the construction headed by #hand is empty (so 'John gave Mary a left hand' will not get treated as an idiom). However, some modifiers of #hand are allowed; specifically the adjective 'helping' (e.g. 'John gave Mary a helping hand'). This can be accommodated by allowing this modifier with this head as an optional part of the construction. This rule is presumably in addition to a strictly compositional translation rule for 'help', relating its ERS and IS frames. Consequently given an IS like 'helped[John, Mary]' it will be possible to generate the text 'John gave Mary a hand' (and 'John gave a hand to Mary'). If this is undesirable, it can be stated that the strictly compositional rule should 'suppress' the idiomatic rule in generation.

(4)   John pulled Mary's leg < = >   John teased Mary

       pull [1, leg[2]]   < = >   tease [1,2]

(5)

```
!{#pull}.[ 1!subj
            !obj={#leg}.[ 2!poss ]
          3!mods ]
<=>
!{#tease}.[ 1!arg1, 2!arg2, 3!mods ]
```

Here the ERS possessive modifier, occupying the poss slot, corresponds to an argument of 'tease' at IS, occupying the arg2 slot of its frame.

(6)   John lost his temper < = >   John became angry

       lose [1, 1's temper]   < = >   become [1, angry]

40

(7)

```
!{#lose}.[ l!subj,
            !obj={#temper}.[ 2!poss ],
            3!*mod ]
  bound(1,2)
      =>
{#become}.[ l!argl, !arg2={#angry}.[], 3!*mod ]
```

This example is straightforward (and similar to (4)) apart from the issue of anaphoric relations. In analysis, the indication of anaphoric relatedness between subj of #lose, and the possessive modifier of #temper will ensure that 'John lost np's temper' will only be translated as 'John became angry' if it has been possible to establish an anaphoric relation between John and the possessive, e.g. if np is 'his', not if it is 'Mary's' etc. However, this rule is not reversible as it stands: because there is no indication of the lexical content of the possessive slot on the ERS side, there is no way to construct a filler for this slot. One solution would be to introduce an obligatorily bound ERS pronoun unmarked for person, number, etc. into the ERS side of the t-rule. The anaphora rules which operate at ERS will bind this pronoun, giving it the number/person features of its antecedent. The ECS <- >ERS translation rules will relate this neutral pronoun to different actual pronouns.

These examples show that at least 'typical' cases of idioms can be handled straightforwardly within the framework we have described. Such a demonstration that the framework is sufficiently powerful is not in itself particularly impressive, of course. What is more interesting is that it seems to be ONLY sufficiently powerful, in that the only kinds of structure that can be treated as idioms are those that show the main characteristics described in section 2. Thus, taken as a machine for practical machine translation, the framework displays an interesting degree of 'appropriateness' or 'problem orientation'. Seen as an abstract tool for linguistic description, it has some 'explanatory' interest.

The linguistic coherence of Gs means that if an expression has an internal structure at some level, that structure has to be 'regular' in terms of that level. For example, if an expression has any syntactic relational structure, it will be a regular relational structure; if it has a semantic structure, it will be a regular semantic structure. A natural consequence of the coherence of the Gs is that there is no

41

provision for any kind of 're-analysis' within a level. Hence the idiosyncracies of idioms will relate to their translational behaviour: as already suggested, typical cases of idioms will be structures at one level that translate as single units at another.

Since the text-ECS mapping is not translational, but simply under the control of the ECS grammar (and the inflectional morphology component), there is no provision for translational behaviour, and no provision for idioms to display irregularity with respect to inflectional morphology, phrase structure, and lexis. Likewise, since assignment and checking of anaphoric relations is non-translational, but done within each level considered in isolation, there is no provision for anaphoric irregularity in idioms: if an idiom contains anaphoric items, their relations to their antecedents have to observe normal restrictions.

Finally, only idioms that observe the 'headedness condition' can be treated in this framework. This is best seen by considering what an example that would violate this constraint would look like. Suppose there were an idiom 'to leave X the lurch', with X a preposition, meaning perhaps, to abandon in a particular spatial relation (e.g. 'to leave in the lurch' would contrast with 'leave outside the lurch' in terms of the kind of predicament that results for the 'leavee'). Note that such an idiom would violate the headedness constraint.

Generating (or analysing) such an idiom would involve a t-rule with the idiomatic side along the lines of:

(8)

```
!{#leave}.[   1!subj,
              2!pobj={*?*}.[ !obj={#lurch, !def=def} ],
              .... ]
<=>
....
```

(*?* is intended to draw attention to the fact that the lexical head of this construction is not identified). In cases like this, idiom recognition would be unproblematic: the rule will apply irrespective of the head of the pobj. However, when this is the rhs of a t-rule, that rule will always fail, because the system is unable to generate a construction to fill the pobj slot of #leave. More generally, it will only be possible to generate idioms where each construction which is involved contains a head which is part of the idiom. This framework thus provides the basis of an explanation of the absence of idioms which violate the headedness condition: such idioms are impossible because they cannot be generated.

5   PROBLEMS

This section discusses some problem cases in a general and rather tentative way, indicating changes which could be made to accommodate them.

A minor problem is the following: idioms are translational phenomena on this view, and there do indeed appear to be examples of ERS-IS idioms, and IS-IS idioms (cf. Section 2). However, given the levels we assume, we would also expect there to be ECS-ERS idioms, that is, idioms whose recognition depends crucially on configurational properties such as word order. There are such idioms, but they are relatively rare. Handling them is no problem:

(1)

```
aid and abet:
!{#co-ord}.[1!#aid, 2!#and, 3!#abet,(1>2>3)]
<=>
!{a#aid-and-abet}.[]
```

(Where the annotation (1 >2 >3) is an linear precedence (LP) statement which ensures that only the correct word order is recognised and generated). But we have no principled account why all such cases appear to be co-ordinate (rather than dependency) structures.

We will deal with some more important problems under two headings: (i) 'modification of idiom parts', and (ii) 'challenges to the headedness condition'.

(i) Modification of idiom parts.

As well as containing free argument slots, idioms may also allow modifiers within the idiomatic construction. It is useful to distinguish here between

43

syntactic and semantic modification. Syntactically, these items may appear as either modifiers of the whole (idiomatic) construction, or as modifiers of an idiom part. Semantic or syntactic modifiers of idiom parts are referred to here as cases of internal modification.

(2)   syntactic modification of whole:

        John unexpectedly kicked the bucket.

(3)   syntactic modification of part:

        They kept close tabs on John.

The case of internal modification illustrated in (2) above is purely syntactic semantically, 'close' modifies the meaning of the idiom as a whole:

(4)   They observed John closely.

In cases such as these, we would like to treat the modifier as a case of compositional translation. The following example demonstrates that syntactic internal modification of this type is relatively unproblematic.

(5)   They kept close tabs on John

        < = > They observed John closely keep [1, tabs[2], on[3]]

        < = > observe [1,3,2-ly]

```
        !{#keep}.[ 1!subj,
(6)                !obj={#tabs}.[ 2!*mod ],
                   !pobj={#on}.[ 3!obj ],
                4!*mod ]
            <=>
        !{#observe}.[ 1!arg1, 3!arg2, 2!*mod, 4!*mod ]
```

        That is: in analysis, given a structure headed by #keep, containing an obj headed by #tabs (containing any number of modifiers), and a p(repositional)obj headed by #on, create a structure headed by #observe. #keep's subject becomes arg1, the object of #on becomes arg2, and any modifiers of tabs become modifiers of #observe (along with modifiers like 'on Tuesday', 'in London', etc). To make this work, it has to be assumed that adverbs and adjectives constitute sub-categories of a single category, so that constructions headed by, e.g., #close are not intrinsically marked as being adjective phrases rather than adverb phrases. The relevant sub-category can be determined by the head of the construction they appear in (verbs will assign features appropriate to the adverb subclass, nouns will assign adjectival features). Without this assumption, since frames of verbs like #observe will presumably not accept adjectival modifiers, the attempt to build the IS structure will fail, and the system will be unable to translate examples such as (2). Generation is essentially the reverse: modifiers of #observe will be divided (non-deterministically) into two sets, and the ERS G will attempt to make one set modifiers of #tabs, and the other set modifiers of #keep. From an IS of the form (7), we will produce all the following sentences.

(7)   'observe [they,John,careful,on Tuesday]'

They kept tabs on John carefully on Tuesday.

They kept careful tabs on John on Tuesday.

?They kept [careful tabs on Tuesday] on John.

(Disregarding alternative word orders). (7c) would be excluded if the ERS entry for tabs indicates that it does not allow pp modifiers.

GKPS (Gazdar, Pullum, Klein and Sag (1985)) discuss cases of true or semantic internal modification. In these examples, the modifier is interpreted as a modifier of an idiom part:

(8)   a theoretical axe to grind

(9)   pull a string or two

The problem with these cases is that the treatment of idioms proposed here leads us to expect that the idiom parts themselves will disappear (and thus obviously not be available for modification) when the idiom is given a unit interpretation, as, for example, in the 'pull leg' < = > 'tease' case discussed above.

There are two options here, and they may be appropriate to different idioms. One option is to treat the idiom as a metaphor or a literal phrase, that is, pass it through the normal compositional route. In many cases, we suspect that literal translations of such idioms work well enough. Obviously, in this case, the modifier too would receive a literal translation in transfer. The second option is to translate the idiom into a literal construction of the same internal form. An example would be:

(10)   an axe to grind < = > a point to make

Any modifiers of 'axe' (theoretical) will receive their expected translation, as modifiers of 'point'.

We can envisage various ways of following this second option: in the translator or in the generator. One possibility is to use an idiom rule with complex left and right hand sides:

(11)   [#grind np[#axe *mod]] < = > [#make np [#point *mod]]

        #theoretical < = > #theoretical

Essentially, what we are doing here is translating 'grind' < = > 'make' and 'axe' < = > 'point' in the mutually defining context of the t-rule. Such a treatment differs from the treatment of the idioms discussed in Section 3 only in that both sides of the relevant rules are complex (it follows that only constructions which observe the headedness condition could be related in this way).

A second possibility involves adding translations using the normal translation rules:

(12)   #axe < = > #point

        #axe < = > #axe

        #grind < = > #make

        #grind < = > #grind

This clearly adds enormously to the ambiguity of lexical translation, so we have to depend on the target generator to perform a filtering function (the translation of 'axe' as 'point' is only acceptable in the context of the gov 'make'). The formal apparatus for this is present in the mechanism by which heads place requirements on what will fill slots in their frames. However, it is rather unclear in

46

advance whether we can sensibly rely on target generators to make the distinctions necessary for this strategy to work.

In these cases, it has been possible to translate the modifier in the normal way (#theoretical < = > #theoretical), but there could also be cases in which the modifier is a semantic modifier of the idiom part, but cannot be used with the translation of that idiom part (as if, e.g., 'theoretical' couldn't go with 'point'). In such cases, the modifier must be treated as an integral part of the idiom along the lines suggested by the treatment of 'give a helping hand' above.

(ii) Challenges to the headedness constraint

The analysis presented in Section 3 is problematic in another respect. The treatment of idioms is dependent on locality: only idioms which satisfy the headedness condition can be generated, and though a wider class of idioms could be recognised, only idioms which occupy a specifiable portion of a tree could be recognised (since the source side of a translation rule has to be able to describe all the parts of the idiom).

A number of counterexamples to the headedness condition are well-known. The examples below show that idiom parts may undergo a variety of potentially non-local syntactic processes. We can divide these into three groups.

(a) A lexically governed process which may remove any idiom part from subject position, thereby producing violations of the headedness condition (raising and some cases of passive):

(13)   The cat is likely to be out of the bag.

John's leg seems to have been pulled.

John's goose is believed to have been cooked.

(e.g. 'The cat' is part of an idiom with 'to be out of the bag', but the former is part of a construction headed by 'likely', which is not part of the idiom). There are two important points. The only restriction on the target of this syntactic operation is that it is a subject, so relatively large numbers of idioms may be subject to raising. Secondly, the displaced subject may be moved any distance by successive application of this process:

(14)   The cat seems to be likely to be out of the bag.

         John's leg seems to be likely to have been pulled.

         Close tabs are believed to have been kept on Kim by the FBI.

So, although raising and sentential passivisation of this sort are lexically governed (and therefore restricted to operating with certain predicates), actually specifying the range of possible structures within which an idiom chunk may be displaced is not an option.

(b) The second challenge to the headedness condition involves idiom parts which
     contain free arguments or modifiers (i.e. which are not themselves part of the
     idiom):

(15)   pull [X's leg]

Although the unbounded movement possibilities are restricted with the majority of idioms, movement of these idiom parts is found as a strategy to avoid the production of left-branch violations. Compare (16)-(19):

(16)   Whose leg do you think John pulled?

(17) $Which bucket did Mary say John kicked?

(18) $The bucket I said Mary kicked.

(19)   *Whose do you think John pulled leg?

(17) and (18) show idioms which do not maintain an idiomatic interpretation under movement, while (16) does. The left-branch violation in (19) shows that displacing just a 'free' element is not possible.

These are unbounded, non-lexically governed processes which may displace a construction headed by an idiom part but containing a non-idiomatic argument or modifier, and apparently counterexemplify the headedness condition.

(c) GKPS point out the existence of a small class of idiomatic expressions where items which are actual parts of the idiom (i.e. not 'free') undergo these unbounded processes quite generally:

(20)   Close tabs, they'll never keep on us.

         Those strings, I don't think even John will pull for you.

         That's the third gift horse she's looked in the mouth this year.

         What do you think is eating John?

Following Wasow, Nunberg and Sag (1982), GKPS (1985) treat the group of idioms which display this property (the 'syntactically versatile idioms') as being essentially compositional. They show that these same idioms have other properties which support this view. They allow semantic internal modification (cf. above), and VP ellipsis, and parts can be quantified. On their analysis the notion of a partial function is exploited, so that principles of semantic interpretation apply to these expressions in the normal manner to assign an interpretation (e.g. the interpretation of 'tabs' is undefined unless it is an argument of the interpretation of 'keep'). In support of this compositional treatment, they suggest that the syntactically versatile idioms all have a metaphorical basis.

These constructions violate locality conditions on idioms in an obvious way, and could not be recognised given the apparatus of Section 1. Recognition would require the displaced idiom part to be re-united with the rest of the idiomatic construction. Otherwise, the idiomatic translation rule cannot be applied, and the construction will receive only a literal translation. In the current framework, the most abstract level of representation indicates the source site for displaced elements by binding the displaced constituent to an empty slot in the frame of the lexical governor. Thus the problematic cases presented above receive a representation at this level which may be indicated schematically as below:

(21)

```
[ is_likely[ the cat_i, be[ t_i, out of the bag ]]]
[whose leg]_i, think[ you, [ pulled [ John, t_i ]]]
[those strings]_i, think[ I, [ pulled[ they, t_i ]]]
```

On a normal view, the relevant antecedent-trace relationship would be 'transparent' for some syntactic features, such as number and case (so antecedent and trace receive identical values for such attributes). But establishing this relationship is not enough to allow the idioms to be recognised in such structures, since e.g., the lexical content of the displaced items will not be indicated on the trace, and this is crucial to the recognition of the idiom.

A number of different solutions may be envisaged, differing in how radical a change they require in the basic machine and/or definitions of the levels of linguistic representation.

Perhaps the smallest change would involve making the lexical content of the antecedent somehow available on the trace (as is done in LFG, for example). We cannot do this directly, since the indication of lexical content (e.g. #leg) is in fact not treated as a feature, and so cannot be transmitted by anaphor rules (in virtue of being transparent between antecedent and anaphor) in the manner of features such as number and person. Thus, we would have to introduce a feature (e.g. 'form') which would carry equivalent information, and which could be transmitted. (We would also have to alter the normal matching mechanism to allow a specifications of #leg in an idiom rule to be satisfied by a trace even though, by definition, the trace does not itself have #leg as its head). Introducing such a 'form' feature would be costly, and somewhat redundant, of course. Moreover, it would also not be possible to deal with examples where not only the lexical content of the head of the displaced item, but also some modifier of the head is crucial (e.g. suppose 'pull X's metaphorical leg' was an idiom, but no other modifier of 'leg' was possible). Clearly, transmitting the lexical identity of the head would not be enough in such cases. We do not know of any such cases, but they are imaginable, and are certainly possible given the rest of the theory (in particular, they are consistent with the headedness condition).

More radical alternatives involve manipulating the structure in such a way that the antecedent is actually represented as part of the idiomatic construction

50

(i.e. 'undoing' the displacement operation). This is attractive for at least the raising cases: (22)a would then receive a representation like b, not c.

(22)   a John seems to admire Mary.

       b seems [admire [John, Mary]]

       c seems [John/i, [admire [pro/i,Mary]]]

There are several ways this could be achieved, most obviously, perhaps, by extending the anaphora specialist so that it could copy structure between antecedent and trace positions. One virtue of this proposal is that it seems to have a reasonably natural generation analogue by which extraction could be performed. However, it may also be worth considering increasing the power of translation rules to perform this function under some conditions.

6   NOTES

1 The work reported here has been carried out in the context of the Eurotra machine translation project (cf. Arnold & des Tombe, 1987), and has been supported by the CEC and the Department of Trade & Industry. We should emphasise, however, that it is not part of the mainstream Eurotra research or development work, and in particular, that the system we describe differs in many critical ways to the 'official' Eurotra software.

The system we describe in Section 2 has been implemented in c-prolog, and several small-medium scale modules have been written for fragments of Dutch and English. It is still experimental, however, and the work we report here is very much 'work in progress'. The design of the system, and the basic ideas about its application to linguistic description and translation are the result of collaborative work with (in no special order) Louis des Tombe, Steven Krauwer, Gertjan van Noord, and Coby Verkuyl (all of the University of Utrecht), Dominique Petitpierre (ISSCO, University of Geneva), and Andrew Betts (Essex). Dominique Petitpierre wrote the great majority of the prolog code which the system uses. Errors and misrepresentations, etc., are all our own fault, of course. An early version of the paper was presented at the Autumn LAGB in Bradford.

2 There should not be a single 'modifier' slot at IS: distinctions between, e.g. time, place, manner and modifiers should be recognised. Nothing hangs on this here.

3 This idea of compositionality amounts to a very strong version of the 'rule-to-rule' hypothesis, and corresponds roughly to that used in Rosetta (Landsbergen (1986), and Schenk (1986)). It is stronger than the normal rule-to-rule hypothesis, which (e.g. in Montague's PTQ) pairs syntactic rules with arbitrary expressions of Intentional Logic (rather than pairing them with formation rules of Intentional Logic). This is not the place for a proper comparison of Rosetta and the system described here, but it may be useful to note four fundamental properties which set this system apart: (i) the use of abstract ISes distinct from the surface grammar of the languages; (ii) the centrality of the idea of 'dependency'; (iii) the emphasis on the internal linguistic coherence of representation languages (Rosetta explicitly seeks to 'tune' source and target grammars, at the expense of internal naturalness, if necessary); (iv) the idea of a relaxed version of compositionality (see below).

4 This example is simplified: (1) 'graag' is in fact a subject oriented adverb (cf. 'willingly'), so that correct translation require reference to the grammatical relation of subject. Thus the appropriate place for the rule is in Dutch analysis (ERS-IS), rather than transfer (Dutch IS will treat 'graag' as a control predicate, like 'like', and transfer will be straightforward); (2) there are complications to do with the way properties of the single Dutch sentence are shared among the main and embedded clauses in English (e.g. tense has to become a property of the main sentence), and about which the English clause contains the 'empty' pronoun (the example has the empty element in the embedded clause, but the informal description would result in it being in the matrix clause). These complications are not problematic, but dealing with them would obscure the main point here.

5 Integers stand for variables, if a variable is bound to an item **a** on one side, then it is understood to be bound to the translation of **a** on the other side. On the source side, '!' can be read as an instruction to remove or extract a piece of

structure, or a feature (or, if its scope is a whole structure, to decompose the structure), and if a variable is given, to bind the structure (feature) to the variable. On the target side, it can be read as an instruction to insert a structure (feature) in a particular slot (or again, simply to build a structure). From left to right, the rule can be read as saying: split a structure built using the s rule into an np and a vp, translate by putting the translation of the np in the subject slot of the translation of the vp. The translation of the vp will be marked as being of category s (if it has no category marking, the t-rule will 'inject' this feature, if it is already marked cat = s, nothing happens. If it has some other category, the rule will fail, as it will fail e.g. if the translation of the subject is of a category that the main verb will not accept in the subject slot). From right to left it can be read as: for any structure marked as cat = s, extract the subject (bind to variable 1) and the category feature (do not bind this to anything i.e. simply discard), and bind everything else to variable 2; use the #s rule to build a structure where the structure bound to 1 (i.e. the translation of the subject) fills the np slot, and everything else goes into the vp slot.

6   This and the previous example are due to Schenk (1986).

7   Pulman suggests, and we agree, that there is an essentially non-linguistic element of inferencing involved in understanding these. We are primarily interested in exploring the extent to which translation can be thought of as a linguistic activity, and the framework is intended to perform translation qua linguistic activity. Such cases are interesting, because they show some of the limitations of the approach. However, it is not really a worry that the framework cannot handle cases where the non-linguistic component is critical. We discuss some examples where there is a somewhat smaller degree of variation, and where we think a 'linguistic' approach should work, in Section 4.

8   Here, '$' means that only a literal interpretation is possible. Intuitions differ about particular cases, but most people, including all published sources, seem to agree that there are cases where V-NP-NP structures are idiomatic, while the corresponding V-NP-PP structures have only literal interpretations.

9   Pesetsky attributes the basic idea to Chomsky (1965), and Marantz (1984) for sentence level idioms.

10 Schenk (1986) takes the need to permit recursive application of this headedness condition to deal with forms such as these to be a problem for Pesetsky's account.

11 There is, of course, sometimes a problem in finding any translation for an idiom. We will concentrate on examples where this problem does not arise.

7   REFERENCES

1   Arnold, DJ & des Tombe, L (1987), 'Theory and Metatheory in Eurotra' in Nirenburg, S. (ed.) Machine Translation: Theoretical and Methodological Issues pp114-135, CUP, Cambridge.

2   Bresnan, J (1982), 'Control & Complementation'in Bresnan (ed.), pp282-390.

3   Bresnan, J (ed.) (1982), The Mental Representation of Grammatical Relations, MIT Press, Cambridge, Mass.

4   Chitra, F and Flavell, R (1981), 'On Idioms: Critical Views and Perspectives', Exeter Linguistic Studies Vol. 5, University of Exeter.

5   Chomsky, N (1965),Aspects of the Theory of Syntax, MIT Press, Cambridge, Mass.

6   Chomsky, N (1980), Rules and Representations, Blackwell, Oxford.

7   Chomsky, N (1981), Lectures on Government and Binding, Foris, Dordrecht.

8   Gazdar, G, Klein, E, Pullum, GK and Sag, I (1985), Generalized Phrase Structure Grammar, Blackwell, Oxford.

9   Jaeggli, O (1981), Topics in Romance Syntax, Foris, Dordrecht.

10 Kaplan, R & Bresnan, J (1982), 'Lexical Functional Grammar: a formal system for grammatical representation' in Bresnan (ed.) pp173-281.

11 Kayne, R (1975), French Syntax: the transformational cycle, MIT Press, Cambridge, Mass.

12 Krauwer, S & Des Tombe, L (1984), 'Transfer in a multilingual MT system'in Proceedings of COLING 1984, Stanford, Ca. pp464-467.

13 Landsbergen, J (1986), 'Montague Grammar and Machine Translation', in Proceedings of the Alvey/ICL workshop on computer applications CCL/UMIST report no. 86/2, pp76-94, UMIST, Manchester.

14 Marantz, AP (1984), On the Nature of Grammatical Relations, MIT Press, Cambridge.

15 Matsumoto,Y, Tanaka, H, Hirakawa, H, Miyoshi, H, Yasukawa, H (1983), 'BUP: a bottom up parser embedded in prolog' in New Generation Computing 1:145-158.

16 Newmeyer, F (1974), 'The regularity of idiom behaviour', Lingua 34: 327-342.

17 Pesetsky, D (1985), 'Morphology and Logical Form', Linguistic Inquiry 16:2, 193-246.

18 Pulman, S (1986), 'The recognition and interpretation of idioms', ms, Cambridge University Computer Lab, Cambridge.

19 Rose, JH (1978), 'Types of Idioms', Linguistics 203, 55-62, Mouton.

20 Schenk, A (1986), 'Idioms in the Rosetta Machine Translation System', Proceedings of COLING 86 Bonn, pp319-324.

21 Wasow,T, Nunberg, G, and Sag, I (1983), 'Idioms: an interim report' in Hattori, S, and Inoue, I (eds) Proceedings of the XIII International Congress of Linguists, Tokyo, CIPL, pp102-15.

22 Wood, MM (1986), 'A Definition of Idiom', IULC, Indiana.

Chapter 4

Japanese for Speakers of English: The UMIST/Sheffield Machine Translation Project

M MCGEE WOOD,
Centre for Computational Linguistics, University of Manchester

1   BACKGROUND

Under the Alvey Directorate's research programme in natural language processing, a machine translation project involving English and Japanese has been carried out at the Centre for Computational Linguistics, UMIST and the Centre for Japanese Studies at the University of Sheffield. The industrial collaborator has been International Computers Limited (ICL), within their Translation and Publishing Services division. The project, entitled 'Read and write Japanese without knowing it', was funded for the two years from October 1984 to October 1986 by IKBS 022 and for a third year from October 1986 to October 1987 by IKBS 037.

Under this unified heading, the project was in fact made up of two distinct parts: the UMIST group have developed an English-to-Japanese prototype, while Sheffield have been working from Japanese into English. The two prototypes, although very different in some aspects of their linguistics and computational approaches, share an important and distinctive design philosophy. Both are interactive, and, unlike present commercially available interactive machine (aided) translation systems, both can be used by a monolingual speaker of English. The means by which each system achieves this will be discussed in the fourth and final sections of this talk.

The following two sections will describe the Sheffield and UMIST systems in more detail. It is appropriate here, however, to express our gratitude for the continuing close involvement and invaluable support we have received from our Monitoring Officer, Prof. Frank Knowles of Aston University.

2   AIDTRANS:
THE SHEFFIELD JAPANESE-TO-ENGLISH SYSTEM

The work at Sheffield has been carried out by Dr. George Jelinek, who has extensive experience both of teaching the Japanese language and the use of computers for natural language processing, assisted by Mary Gillender and Malcolm James of the Centre for Japanese Studies, and by Graham Wilcock on secondment from ICL. The system is implemented in C and runs on a Sharp Unix-based microcomputer.

The Aidtrans Japanese-to-English prototype is an implementation of a comprehensive, highly detailed and sophisticated algorithmic grammar of Japanese developed by Dr. Jelinek as a teaching tool for rapid intensive instruction in technical Japanese (Jelinek 1978). The core of this grammar is its Integrated Dictionary system (IDS). The philosophy of IDS is to incorporate as much as possible of the grammar and the analysis heuristics in the dictionary. This is done in an explicitly language-specific and, as applied to translation, language-pair specific form, allowing great accuracy and precision. The dictionary of the finished prototype contains entries for some 6,000 words.

While committed to the maximum use of lexical resources, Aidtrans also sees translation as a relation over whole texts rather than individual words or even sentences. The purpose of each act of translation is to retain the sense, rather than the concatenation of word-meanings, of a text as it is reformulated in a different language. To achieve this, it is clearly not enough to produce one acceptable translation for each separate sentence of a text and adjoin them. Just as any syntactic parser will produce alternative analyses of an ambiguous sentence from which the one intended must be selected, so Aidtrans produces all possible translations of each part of the input text, from which the one most appropriate for each part in its context must be selected.

Such selection from among possible translation equivalents is familiar from conventional human translation or post-editing. Here, however, much of the selection, or rejection, is carried out by the system itself. A text-type-specific linear predictive model is the basis for determining priorities or preferences among the possibilities. Patterns can be recognised at the general level of syntactic configuration and at the more specific level of individual lexical items and collocations; at present the system recognises well over 200 different types of juxtapositional linkage. In other words, the selectional function in Aidtrans is driven by a generalisation of valency, augmented with priority weightings for the possible valency values.

Aidtrans also incorporates in its English generation an active derivational morphology, so that on occasions when a suitable translation equivalent for a Japanese word is not available one can be coined. For example, in one recently translated text, a Japanese word meaning 'making small' was rendered with the English coinage 'microfication'.

This high degree of detail, incorporation of most information in the IDS dictionary, and exact tailoring of the system to the task of Japanese-to-English translation has as an inevitable complement a restricted potential for adaptation to other applications. As an implementation of a teaching grammar, it has obvious potential as a computerised learning aid for the teaching of Japanese. Further extensions would require greater effort, but might well nevertheless prove cost-effective, and careful investigation of various possibilities is currently under way.

Further development to commercial, marketable standard will take place in collaboration with the Sharp Corporation.

3   NTRAN:
THE UMIST ENGLISH-TO-JAPANESE SYSTEM

The Centre for Computational Linguistics at UMIST forms part of the Department of Language and Linguistics, headed by Professor JC Sager. The director of CCL and Principal Investigator of the Ntran Project until his move to Geneva in January 1987, was Rod Johnson. For the first two years, the project director was Peter Whitelock, with myself, Natsuko Holden (a native speaker of Japanese), and Heather Horsfall, with Brian Chandler (a computer scientist and Japanese speaker) on secondment from ICL. In October 1986 Peter Whitelock moved to the Department of Artificial Intelligence at Edinburgh University, but remained a consultant on the project. I took over as project director, and we were joined by Elaine Pollard, and experienced computational lexicographer.

Ntran is less target-specific in design than Aidtrans. The prototype, implemented in Prolog for the sake of fast and perspicuous development, presently runs on a Sun 3/50 workstation, an ICL PERQ, and a Dec MicroVax II. Through a system of nested menu, it functions on three levels: as a system development system, a grammar development system, and as a translation system proper. Each level offers specific facilities for the writing, testing and debugging of appropriate areas of program code. (For details, see Whitelock et al., 1986).

Although both prototypes give the maximum weight and information content to the lexicon, another point of difference between them is that Ntran is committed to the principle of translation as linguistics (cf Johnson, 1987), and was designed and implemented as an explicit embodiment of contemporary lexicalist linguistic theory. The English analysis grammar is based on Lexical-Functional Grammar (LFG; Bresnan, ed.1982) and Generalised Phrase Structure Grammar (GPSG; Gazdar et al., 1985), the Japanese generation grammar on Categorial Grammar (CG; Steedman; 1985, Whitelock, 1987).

In analysis, words are first looked up in an English morpho-syntactic dictionary which determines grammatical category and morphologically determined features such as tense and number. The entries in this, as in all dictionaries, are compacted by 'feature co-occurrence restrictions', which factor out any feature values which are predictable on the basis of others. These derive largely from the fcrs of Generalised Phrase Structure Grammar (Gazdar et al., 1985), which are in fact classical redundancy rules as in Chomsky (1965), and Chomsky & Halle (1968). In English, for example, any lexical item which has tense must be finite and a verb. In a lexical entry assigning any value to 'tense', the specification of finiteness and verbhood would be redundant, and can be supplied by a generalised rule of the form

fcr (tense = _,[fin = finite, stemtyp = verb]).

Similarly, as any verb has no noun features, but sets (possibly empty) of prepositional complements and adjuncts, and as any '-ing' form is a progressive finite verb, we have rules

```
fcr (cat = verb,[nounfeats = [],

pcomp = set(_),adjunct = set(_)]).

fcr(nfform = ing,[stemtyp = verb, aspect = progress,inf = no]).
```

Using this limited information, the parser builds up all possible 'functional structures' (the 'f-structures' of LFG). These serve as an intermediate representation which abstracts away from surface constituent structure, a particularly valuable level when mediating between a configurational language such as English and a non-configurational one such as Japanese.

A second stage of lookup in the English 'subcat' dictionary, which holds possible valency, or subcategorisation, patterns, eliminates many of these, and provides a semantic interpretation for those which remain. (cf Wood et al, 1987). This 's-structure' forms the basis for transfer, driven by bilingual dictionaries; the only component to hold contrastive information. The resulting Japanese s-structure is the basis for generation of a Japanese f-structure, using syntactic information held in the Japanese dictionaries in the form of the complex categories and combinations rules of a unification categorial grammar. Surface Japanese output is finally carried out by linear precedence rules. The role and form of user interaction will be discussed below.

The modularity of Ntran, in both the levels of system development and the stages in the translation chain, make it readily extensible and adaptable. It could be used by a technical writer for purely monolingual purposes, or as an intelligent style-checker, eliminating ambiguities in an English text. Its grammar development facilities make the addition of further output languages relatively simple; indeed, postgraduate students in CCL have already implemented small French and Dutch grammars within the system. The design philosophy, and a certain amount of the program code, could be run in the opposite direction, from Japanese to English for use by Japanese monolinguals. The system could be used, and further developed, as a teaching aid in both languages and in computational linguistics.

The future of Ntran is, at the time of writing (October 1987), still unclear. Further development of the prototype to full commercial standard is hoped for, possibly with some combination of ICL and government or other industrial support, and we hope to realise some of its potential for expansion and adaptation.

4 TECHNIQUES FOR INTERACTIVE TRANSLATION

As mentioned earlier, both Aidtrans and Ntran are designed for an English monolingual end user. This approach - reflected even in the joint project's Alvey title, 'Read and write Japanese without knowing it' - has led to a number of distinctive design decisions.

In the case of Aidtrans, the intention was, while leaving the final selection of the exact translation to the end user, to produce output of greater accuracy and coherence than is generally found in correct post-editing systems. The strategy of multiple generation produces a set of complete alternative translations, rather than one which must be amended piecemeal by a post-editor, while the text-type-based predictive model and preference-weighted linkages cut down greatly on the range actually offered to the end user, and group those which survive into semantically and stylistically coherent wholes. Thus, while a conventional post-editor needs access to the source text to check the accuracy of raw output and as a guide to its revision, here, enough information is available in the output to form the basis of the end user's final selection.

The facilities for, or demands on, the end-user of Ntran are somewhat more complex: both the complexity of the task and the inner articulation of the system are greater, giving both the need and the opportunity for a variety of interactions (cf. Johnson & Whitelock, 1987). To ensure to an English monolingual technical writer the output of accurate and acceptable Japanese, the conventional strategy would be pre-editing, passing to the machine only text in a restricted sub-language known to be within its translation capacity. Our system could perhaps be said to offer interactive pre-editing interleaved with translation, rather than interactive translation proper, as no contrastive or bilingual information is presented to the end user in the interaction. The restricted input sub-language, however, is simply grammatical English, which if ambiguous must be disambiguated.This should be seen not as a constraint on a technical writer but as a desideratum.

The Ntran prototype currently includes three forms of interactive query: on-line dictionary creation, syntactic disambiguation of English input, and Japanese lexical selection in transfer.

When a word is found in an input text for which no dictionary entry yet exists, the user is offered the option of creating an entry for it immediately. This is done using a tree-structured question procedure, eliciting the category of the English word and its values for the features associated with that category, such as mass/count and animacy for nouns, valency and aspectual type for verbs, gradability for adjectives, and so on. The on-line dictionary building routine, although it incorporates a reasonable range of information about an English word, does not ask for Japanese translation equivalents. Instead, entries created in this way are held in a separate dictionary file, where they are accessible to the analysis component, but also set aside for later completion by a bilingual linguist. Until this is done the English word is simply passed into the Japanese output in its original form or in katakana transcription. (Given a reasonable core dictionary, most new words will be specialised technical terms, for which this will in fact be the correct rendering).

Syntactic ambiguities in the English input are also referred to the user for disambiguation. The set of deep-case names which are used to distinguish adjunct types in semantic structure are used also as what Hudson (1985) has called 'natural meta-language', a formal but familiar and perspicuous terminology, in presenting the alternative analyses of an input sentence. An example query is the following:

UMIST English-Japanese MT System   Version 0.7 Level 31a

Type the number of any true statement or number of any false statement

---

1. between is location of transport	true for parses [5-1]
2. between is location of use	true for parses [4-1]
3. between is location of information	true for parses [1-1]

They can be used to transport information between systems.

parsing 64sec parses: 5 deep: 3

Finally, ambiguities, or alternatives, may arise in the selction of a Japanese translation equivalent for an English word or expression. Interactive systems standardly offer such alternatives directly to the user, who must have some competence in the target language to be able to make the choice. Ntran's Japanese dictionary entries include English glosses, and the user is offered these to choose between, rather than the Japanese head-words.

Clearly, ensuring reliable translation for a monolingual user in either direction requires a system design carefully tuned to the task. When translating into the user's language, the information content of the output text must be sufficiently rich that, in cases of uncertainty, reference to the source text, the traditional recourse of the posteditor, is adequately replaced by reference to the set of coherent possibilities offered in that output. This is exactly the strategy implemented in Aidtrans.

When the user is a speaker of the source language, choices may be needed at a number of stages in the translation chain. Ntran's modularity of design isolates these stages from each other, while our commitment to the implementation of linguistic theory offers formats for the presentation of choices by the system and the input of information by the user which are transparent to both.

5 ACKNOWLEDGEMENTS

I am grateful to sponsors and to past and present colleagues for their material and moral support throughout the project. Colleagues in CCL and at Sheffield , and Prof. Frank Knowles, have kindly allowed me to plunder various technical reports for present purposes. Dr. Jelinek, in particular, supplied the information on which Section 2 is based. Brian Chandler, Natsuko Holden, and Pete Whitelock commented on earlier drafts. Any remaining errors are my own.

6 REFERENCES

1 Bresnan, J ed.1982, The Mental Representation of Grammatical Relations. MIT Press, Cambridge, Mass.

2 Chomsky, N 1965, Aspects of the Theory of Syntax. MIT Press, Cambridge, Mass.

3 Chomsky, N & Morris Halle, 1968, The Sound Pattern of English. Harper & Row, New York.

4 Gazdar, G, Klein, E, Pullum,G & Sag, I 1985, Generalised Phrase Structure Grammar. Basil Blackwell, Oxford.

5 Hudson, RA 1985, 'What is a Grammatical Relation?' Linguistics Association of Great Britain, Salford, Spring 1985.

6 Jelinek, J 1978, Integrated Japanese-English Grammar Dictionary, Sheffield.

7 Johnson, RL 1987, Translation,. In Whitelock, PJ, McGee Wood, M, Somers, HL, Johnson, RL and Bennett, PA eds. Linguistic Theory and Computer Applications. Academic Press, London.

8 Johnson, RL & Whitelock, PJ 1987, 'Machine translation as an expert task'. In Nirenburg, S Machine Translation. Cambridge University Press, Cambridge.

9 Steedman, MJ 1985, 'Dependency and Coordination in the Grammar of Dutch and English'. Language.

10 Whitelock, PJ, McGee Wood, M, Chandler, BJ, Holden, N & Horsfall, HJ 1986, 'Strategies for Interactive Machine Translation'. Proceedings of Coling 86.

11 McGee Wood, M, Pollard, E, Horsfall, HJ, Holden, N, Chandler, BJ & Carroll, JJ 1987, 'Dictionary Organization for Machine Translation'. Proceedings of ACL Europe 87.

Chapter 5

Machine Translation in the Commercial Environment

M MEDHURST,
ESC Ltd

The history of machine translation has had its ups and downs. Soon after the development of the first computer, a mathematician called Warren Weaver realised that the code-breaking techniques developed during the second world war might possibly be applicable to a computer-driven translation system.

In the Cold War years that followed, much research was carried out in America aimed at developing a system which would translate Russian technical and scientific material into English. The first practical system to be invented was Systran in the early sixties. Various research projects continued apace until the devastating, and now infamous, ALPAC report was published by the American Automatic Language Processing Advisory Committee, which completely dismissed the feasibility of ever producing a consistent, high quality, machine translation system. Fortunately they were wrong, but the immediate impact was extremely ferocious: development projects were abandoned, and only a few individuals continued to believe that one day such a system would be produced. Amongst these were the inventor of Logos and a team at the Brigham Young University in Provo, Utah, a group of Mormons for whom the idea of being able to translate their religious material into many languages at greatly increased speed became a kind of vocation - a desire to spread the word of their creed to all corners of the globe. From this group came the base that led to the development of both the Weidner and the ALPS machine translation systems.

The ESC team is a small, dynamic group of translators, linguists, terminologists and computer experts, operating out of Harlow in Essex. We have been in existence since the mid-seventies and were originally founded to satisfy the translation needs of ITT worldwide through a single, centralised, self-supporting, specialist centre. We have NEVER been a funded in-house translations group and have, therefore, always been subject to the cold, hard realities of the commercial world. We were always expected to quote competitively against other suppliers in the general marketplace. As part of the ITT group we were expected to handle ITT technical documentation for any of their many products, and to perform translations from or into any language.

The fields covered at that stage were largely those concerned with telecommunications systems and equipment, radar, fibre–optics, submarine cables and electronic component technology.

At that time all translation work was handled manually, although even at that early stage we were beginning to explore the idea of machine translation, an idea which was then quite revolutionary in the European translations world. Our initial requirement was for a system that would translate from English into French, German and Spanish and vice versa. We therefore soon discovered that, at that time, there were only two major suppliers who could meet our requirements, Weidner and Systran. The Weidner system (which is now known as the WCC system) was finally chosen and duly installed in 1979, when we became the first group outside the North American continent to use a machine translation system on a commercial basis.

Why did we choose the WCC system? At that time it was the only system which offered the language combinations we required and, most importantly, worked in plain, natural language with a direct man-machine interface. The dictionary entry could be performed direct on screen in 'normal' language with direct human intervention, and any new terminology could be entered immediately by the translator without having to wait while computer programmers coded the terms in a way which the software would understand (as was then the case with Systran).

The WCC system also provided a good (for that period) multi-lingual word processing system, a split screen editing facility, and a flexible method of handling the entry of those grammatical properties which are required for accurate translation.

Finally, it also provided both an immediate and a deferred batch translation facility. This meant that we could perform batch translation overnight (when the computer had fewer users and the time was charged at a considerably cheaper rate), thus leaving the system free in the day for the translators to edit the raw translation produced overnight. All these factors helped to make the WCC system more economic and efficient to run on a commercial basis than any other system then available.

However, times, methods and expectations have changed. We now operate with the WCC MICROCAT machine translation system into French, Spanish, German, Italian and Portuguese, and currently from French and Spanish into English, with the promise from WCC to have the German into English fully operational during calendar year 1988. In addition, we also still organise the manual translation of any language combination requested by our clients, some internally and some through our extensive freelance network.

Why did we change? In a nutshell, for reasons of economy and self-sufficiency. The VAX on which our particular Macrocat system ran had become overloaded; we needed to update our word processing facilities and we also needed to be able to use the dictionaries in a more client-specific manner. When, later, I come on to a description of the Microcat system which we currently use, you will understand just how this has helped us develop within our own business area. Don't forget, we have been in the machine translation field since the very early days and we needed to update our system in order to keep abreast of the state of the art, in terms of both hardware and software.

In 1986 ITT sold all its telecommunications interests to Alcatel and this deal involved the ESC. Alcatel then decided to reduce its presence in Great Britain, and while it is redeploying many of the ESC research and development functions in Europe (including many of the personnel), it has decided, in its wisdom, to discontinue one of the best and most experienced machine translations units in the world - and one, furthermore, which is completely economically viable. However, you do not kill an ideal and an ethos as easily as that and the work will continue.

The new ESC is already established as a separate entity and as a wholly owned subsidiary of WCC.

We still handle material for both Alcatel and various other ex- ITT companies, but we now also handle all kinds of material from a wide range of other clients. We still specialise in technical matters and consider our main specialities to be the very widest range of those fields which relate to the worlds of telecommunications, computing, electronic and electrical engineering, industrial control, and instrumentation and robotics.

The Microcat software can run on an IBM PC, XT or AT, and a wide range of compatibles. [These include ITT Xtra, Tandy 1200 and 3000, Leading Edge Models D and M, Zenith ZW158 and ZW241 and Compaq DeskPro Model 20.]

Our current machine translation system, Microcat, operates on an XTRA XL personal computer. The XTRA XL is an AT compatible PC, based on an 80286 processor. It has a 70 megabyte Winchester disk with 640 kilobytes of RAM. It has a monochrome display and has been modified by means of the WCC Enhancement package to give it a full European character set. This package is made up of an EPROM added onto an IBM Monochrome Display and Printer Adapter card which enhances the basic PC character set with the foreign accents and diacritics not normally available in a standard English character set. This modification does not in any way alter the PC; the additional characters are only loaded into memory when using the Microcat software and they do not affect the resolution of any other standard word processing package that you might need to use on the same PC.

In our current configuration the Xtra XL regularly translates well over 6,000 words an hour. This is nearly double the average number of words per hour we used to achieve with our previous Macrocat system which ran on a VAX 11/785, and probably more than four times the amount that we could get through when the VAX multi-user system was busy with programs and work from other departments of the ESC. With the old system we had to do a lot of our translation work overnight in order to obtain the quickest results, and the system was occupied during the day by the translators editing the previous night's raw translation. With Microcat not only can we translate at a much faster rate at any time we please, but we can also download the resultant raw translation onto diskettes or to a network file server for editing on any IBM compatible PC, thus releasing the XL for further translation or dictionary update. Clearly, such an increase in the production of raw translation boosts our throughput and increases the amount of translation work that can be handled in a limited timespan.The current system also ensures that maximum productivity can be achieved at all stages and that expensive equipment is in full-time productive use.

Translation work which is put through the machine translation process is normally fed into the system from IBM compatible diskettes. It is also possible to use magnetic tape, via the VAX link, and we hope soon to be able to read text into the system via an optical scanner and to input it remotely via a modem. Whilst the WCC Microcat has an interface program to convert Word Perfect to the Microcat multilingual word processing package, and whilst other word processing packages, such as Microsoft and Wordstar, have features which allow the user to 'export' files into a DOS ASCII format - a format which can be 'imported' into the WCC system, we also use an Intermedia MMC4000 disk conversion system to assist the smooth input of documents from other types of machine and other formats. It must be admitted that some of these conversions work better than others, the main problem being the loss of formatting characters. This disk conversion system is also used for preparing diskettes containing completed translation for return to clients in a format suitable for their own machines, and for onward transmission to typesetting equipment or desk-top publishing systems.

The Microcat multilingual word processing package resembles Word Perfect in many ways, but also includes various other features as standard: for example, a full European character set. We can perform pre-editing, before translation, to protect words and phrases that should not be translated or to delete characters, such as slashes, that can cause problems or garbling of text during the translation process. Once raw translation has been produced, the translators use the text manipulation capabilities of the multilingual word processing package and the split-screen facility to edit the raw text and produce a high quality final version of the translation. The word processing package includes all the standard high-level facilities of a modern word processing system including word swap and phrase movement, both of which are particularly useful when polishing the stylistic and syntactical aspects of the final text. For the first time we have actually found a system which will translate text in columns without garbling, (provided it is submitted in Word Perfect column format) and will allow you to edit in a column mode. Other formats could, of course, be handled, but only after suitable interfaces have been created.

Before a text is processed by the translation tool itself, the text must be searched to check that all the words in the text appear in one or another of the system dictionaries. The ability to create a whole series of dictionaries within a single language pair is probably the most significant of all the improvements introduced with the Microcat system. This one facility has increased enormously the accuracy of the raw translation produced, and hence the commercial viability of MT, since you can now tell the system in which order to search the dictionaries when performing the translation task.

For general language translation the adjective 'central' and the verb 'exchange' would appear, each with their own meaning, in either the general dictionary or the 'core' dictionary, but when these words appear together as the term 'central exchange' in a telecommunications text they need a completely different composite noun translation. Similarly, 'exchange' as a noun would need yet another translation in a text dealing with finance or banking, and yet another for legal documentation. This ability to specify exactly which translation is required for both single words and multiple word groups in each individual field makes an enormous difference to the quality of the raw translation produced. In fact, the importance of the creation and maintenance of these multiple dictionaries and the grammatical precision and detail used in dictionary update procedures are vital to the viability of machine translation in the commercial environment.

After any unfamiliar or unrecognised terminology has been entered into the system, the original language text can be submitted for translation.

The Microcat translation software processes and translates the text by passing it through five stages of linguistic analysis.

The first stage is known as preprocessing, where translatable text is isolated (i.e. numbers are split off etc.).

The second stage is analysis, which progresses, one sentence at a time, through the text. This produces a parse tree representing the structure of the sentence under consideration. A segmentation process then finds sentence and word boundaries and enables morphological analysis to be used to determine the 'root' or base form of words (i.e. soldering iron would be entered into the machine translation dictionary as solder iron). This morphological analysis process also looks up the 'root' form in the dictionary, retrieves the grammatical information and the translation, handles inflection, contraction, hyphenation, compounding, etc. and, where appropriate, determines the part of speech and grammatical features. In particular, verb morphology analysis reduces compound verbs to a main verb plus any additions.

The homograph analysis procedure removes ambiguities in certain parts of speech, based on the dictionary information available, such as morphology and context (or, if you prefer, syntax). The idiom analysis procedure checks for idiomatic phrases - in 'WCC-speak' an idiom is any sequence of two to eight words (including optional or obligatory variables) for which the word-for-word translation is not appropriate. This stage also includes the parsing proper, and builds a syntactic/semantic structural representation of the entire sentence.

The third stage is the transfer phase. Here the structural transfer works on the output of the parser to produce a representation of the equivalent target language sentence by reordering, inserting, deleting, etc. At this stage you also have a lexical transfer for any alternative translations (especially prepositions) and idiomatic expressions.

In phase four verb morphological synthesis generates corresponding tenses and inserts auxiliaries. The morphological synthesis (or inflection) process then effects any contraction or capitalisation tasks which may be required. This phase also handles the formatting and the output to file with proper spacing.

The fifth and final phase is the post-processing stage which restores the original text format to make up the 'raw' translation file.

Having described at some length how our Microcat machine translation system operates, let us now consider the requirements of the commercial environment with regard to translation. Whether you operate in a single organisation, in-house environment or in the wider commercial bureau environment, many of the requirements are the same. Where translations are concerned there are at least seven major problem areas, all of which can have a considerable impact on your commercial viability.

TIME

Translations are always wanted yesterday, very often they were needed last week and occasionally they were wanted even before the author started creating the original document! If there is any delay in the document production schedule it is always the translation time that gets squeezed, and 'You want it when?' is the commonest cartoon on any translator's wall.

VARIETY

Be it variety of product, variety of subject area, variety of style or variety of size, each creates its own problems. The translation may be a short piece of advertising copy, a brochure, a specification, a system description or a whole shelf-full of maintenance manuals. Each requires a different approach, a different methodology.

SECURITY

Your company information is extremely valuable, especially in a competitive field where products have a short projected life span and everyone is constantly trying to provide something that the competition has not yet managed to supply.

CONSISTENCY

Every client has his own 'variant' on standard terms, as well as his own product, field, or company specific terms. To sell his product he must make it appear different from, and more attractive than, all the other products in the marketplace, and we only get to do the translations if we help him to sell more goods. This means using his terms, and his terms only, at all times.

COMPATIBILITY

The client wants the translation returned in a particular format, for a particular machine or a particular process, and prefers to use a translations service which can provide exactly the format he requires - after all, he is footing the bill!

COST

Value for money is of prime importance. In a commercial environment it is essential to keep costs as low as possible so that prices can be kept within bounds without adversely affecting the final and, in the ultimate analysis, the most crucial major requirement - QUALITY.

The amount of documentation requiring translation seems to grow arithmetically with every year that passes and there is now an acute shortage of really first-class translators, especially in the highly technical 'state-of-the-art' fields in which we specialise.

So, we have seven major areas of concern - **TIME, VARIETY, SECURITY, CONSISTENCY, COMPATIBILITY, COST** and **QUALITY.** Let us examine how each of these can be helped or hindered by the application of machine-assisted translation in the commercial environment.

TIME - by using machine translation to cut out the 'donkey work' we can reduce the time spent on some translation tasks by up to 40%. The amount of time saved depends on many factors, some of which will be covered under VARIETY, CONSISTENCY and QUALITY. Suffice it to say that the amount of time saved is variable, but if the work to be translated by a machine-assisted translation system is carefully chosen, the TIME factor can be substantially reduced.

VARIETY - whilst small jobs, especially those of a descriptive, promotional or sales nature, are not suitable for machine translation, large technical manuals which are available in machine readable format make ideal machine translation texts. The larger the document, the more repetitive the document, the more linguistically controlled the document from a syntactical point of view, the better it will suit a machine translation system.

SECURITY - can be maintained by putting passwords on the files so that only those authorised to handle the material will see it. There are no extra copies that can 'go missing', and once the translation has been safely returned to the client the work can be deleted from the system.

CONSISTENCY - requires the co-operation of the client to establish the specific terminology for the product concerned. However, once this has been established, and correctly entered into the machine translation system, every term will appear

73

with the same translation every time it is required. One of the major advantages of machine translation is the lexical consistency which can be achieved. Even if several editors have to be used for different volumes in order to turn around a whole series of manuals about the same product in a limited time-span, lexical consistency for specific terminology can be assured. We have found, over the years, that this is probably the single most important benefit which can be achieved by using machine translation. The time and cost savings which can result from just this one aspect are potentially very substantial indeed.

COMPATIBILITY - is the area where the developers and producers of machine translation systems and all other types of word processors and PCs need to concentrate their efforts. Now that word processing packages and PC types are proliferating at an alarming rate, it is essential that more effective and cost-efficient methods are found for converting text at both input and output stages.

It is no longer sufficient to supply a print-out of a translation. Clients need to input text from any machine, in any format, via any media and we need to return the finished translation in exactly the same way as it was supplied to us. Optical character reader interfaces need to be simplified and made more flexible. Greater inter-machine and inter-format compatibility is a fundamental requirement. Interfaces to typesetters, laser printers and desk-top publishing systems, with full graphics and foreign language character facilities, must be created. It is no longer sufficient that these interfaces work in English only, they must work for and between any language, any format, any machine. This is the one major area that everyone seems to neglect, especially for foreign language work. Manufacturers must appreciate that if they too are to reap the benefits of cost-effective, speedy, consistent, high quality translation they must make it easier to move from one system to another and forget their desire to be unique.

COST - anything which reduces the time involved in translation will reduce the cost. Be it ease of inter-system transfers, quality and depth of product and field specific dictionaries or laser printers - everything that saves times reduces cost.

QUALITY - the quality of the input is every bit as important as the quality of the ouput when you use a machine translation system. Machines, just like humans, suffer from the 'rubbish in, rubbish out' syndrome. Clear, simple, unfussy language always produces the best translation, be it manual or machine. In the translation of technical material we are aiming at imparting precise, clear and well-defined information of a scientific or technological nature, not competing for the Nobel Prize for literature. Translators are highly skilled professionals and if you want top quality results without prohibitive cost you must use their time more efficiently. By using machine translation with highly developed product, company, or field-specific dictionaries and by allowing time to concentrate on editing and polishing a translated text, a translator's productivity can be greatly increased. The rate of improvement varies from 0% to 60% depending on the syntactical quality and the technical clarity of the original text and on the quality of the dictionaries which are used in the machine translation process.

The creation and maintenance of the MICROCAT multiple dictionary system is the single most important factor in the production of high quality, consistent, accurate raw translation that needs very little final editing. In a highly competitive commercial environment all these factors will improve your cost/time effectiveness ratio. The better and more comprehensive your dictionaries are, the more economically viable your machine translation system will become. One of the main reasons for negative reactions to machine translation in the past is that very few people have ever had the time, the resources or the determination to really develop their machine translation dictionaries to the point where raw translation of a very high standard can be produced.

Microcat is currently supplied with a core dictionary of approximately 13,000 terms per language direction - an enormous improvement on our original Macrocat package which came with a core dictionary of 4,000 terms. Over the years we increased our dictionaries on a weekly basis in order to spread the cost over as many translations as possible, but the real break-through came with the change-over to the Microcat system. We can now have up to thirty separate field, product or company-specific dictionaries and can instruct the translation program to use these dictionaries in any order we specify. This means that we can accommodate a large number of variants for different clients for the same original language terms: for example we can enter 'exchange' as a noun with different translations for any field we care to cover. It also means that we can build specific dictionaries for any purpose and this, more than any improvement in the grammatical analysis or syntactical resolution (although these have been many and most welcomed over the

75

years), has dramatically improved the quality of our raw translations - with all that such time saving can mean in the commercial environment.

One thing all of you experts out there might like to consider, something which would greatly facilitate terminological research, extraction and dictionary building would be some type of glossary tool which would interface easily with machine-assisted translation systems. We have assessed and/or tried out a number of products in this field (amongst them Termex and some of the INK products) and whilst many of them would be very interesting if we were creating terminological databases or if we had not already amassed such vast quantities of terms, none of them can be said to be of real practical value to an organisation such as ours which has been involved in machine-assisted translation and terminological research over such a long period. We need a tool which will interface completely with our system and will generate an original input file which can be fed directly into the dictionary update procedure. What is more, it would need to be able to generate language reversal listings and cross-language and/or multilanguage listings from within material already available in machine readable format.

In conclusion, although you may feel that I am biased, I am confident that machine translation is the only way forward to higher productivity, higher levels of consistency and maintaining current cost-levels in a competitive and cost-orientated marketplace. I am equally sure that we have discovered the way to improve the quality of raw translation and now await, with impatience, for the manufacturers out there in the WP and PC world to solve at least some of our compatibility problems for us.

Chapter 6

Using a Knowledge Base
for
Automatic Text Classification

J A FENN,
Logica Cambridge Ltd

1 INTRODUCTION

An area of natural language processing in which there is growing commercial interest is that of text scanning. This class of applications involves analysing a text for purposes such as routing it to an appropriate department or individual or storing it in such a way as to facilitate later retrieval. Text scanning is of interest to those who deal with large quantities of textual information such as medical case reports, banking telexes, newspaper stories and military or industrial equipment failure reports.

The aim in analysing the texts in these applications is to determine which of a predefined set of semantic categories best describes the contents of each text. For example, a news story may need to be assigned categories to describe its geographic location, such as Middle East or US, and its topic, such as crime, currency or sport, while an equipment failure report may involve selecting an appropriate filler for each field on a standard form, such as part type, symptom and rectifying action taken.

This paper describes an application of text scanning in the medical domain of electromyography. As part of an expert system, the text classification system FACT (Frame-based Analysis and Classification of Text) is being developed to index medical case reports and other texts for later retrieval. A major feature of FACT is that the semantic component is able to take advantage of a large knowledge base developed for use by the expert system, unlike other content scanning systems which have to develop their own purpose-built knowledge bases.

This has meant investigating how well a knowledge representation designed primarily for carrying out a particular expert task matches the kind of knowledge needed to help in understanding natural language.

The next section introduces the electromyography expert system project of which this work is a part and outlines the functionality of the FACT system. Section 3 reviews the kinds of knowledge used in other text scanning applications, particularly those which have reached the stage of commercial exploitation, and compares their knowledge representation formalisms with those available in the electromyography expert system's knowledge base. Section 4 describes the design of FACT, concentrating particularly on the way in which the expert system's knowledge base is incorporated. Section 5 summarises and discusses future directions for the project.

2   A TEXT CLASSIFICATION SYSTEM FOR ELECTROMYOGRAPHERS

The FACT classification system is being developed as part of a project to build the EMG Assistant (Fenn, Foote, Worden and Willison 1986, Andersen, Andreassen and Woldbye, 1986), an expert system for electromyographers. Electromyography (EMG) is a technique for diagnosing neuromuscular disorders by measuring the electrical activity of nerves and muscles. The primary goal of the system is to help in test planning and diagnosis to optimise the use of time during an EMG examination session and improve the quality of the EMG diagnosis.

In developing an expert system, a large proportion of the time is spent collecting and modelling knowledge about the relevant field from a variety of sources. In many cases, a major benefit of the resulting expert system is that it can act as a central repository of domain knowledge for general reference purposes, in addition to carrying out a specific task. As part of the EMG Assistant, a knowledge base browser is being built, which allows physicians to explore, retrieve, annotate and modify the information in the medical knowledge base.

The browser is part of a more general emphasis in the EMG Assistant on providing support for a human EMG examiner rather than creating an autonomous expert system. A result of this approach is that the knowledge base contains additional material over and above that used for inferencing purposes, such as pictures, bibliographic references, case reports and help text to guide electromyographers in performing tests. Some of this extra information, such as help text, is tailor-written by a knowledge engineer and entered, like the knowledge used for inferencing, through an editor, which forces the author to specify where it belongs in the overall structure of the knowledge base.

Some of the other types of texts which are being included in the knowledge base already exist in different information systems, such as a hospital archive of case reports or a bibliographic database. It is to enable these existing texts to be classified automatically against the domain concepts stored in the knowledge base that FACT is being developed. Along with the rest of the updating facilities provided by the browsing system, FACT will allow the knowledge base to grow over a period of time with minimum effort from the laboratory where it is installed, for example by automatically cross-referencing new examination reports as they are entered.

The first prototype of FACT is being developed to analyse and classify the diagnostic comment at the end of an EMG examination report. Figure 1 gives some examples of report comments, which can range from very simple statements to more complex descriptions of EMG test findings with corresponding diagnostic conclusions about nerve and muscle pathology.

1) No abnormality found.

2) Myotonia confirmed. There was no clear evidence of a myopathy in addition.

3) Absent ulnar SAPs, absent or reduced sural SAPs, abnormal ulnar motor study on the right. Borderline lateral popliteal motor conduction and median and radial SAPs. The findings are consistent with a mild generalised neuropathy.

4) There is a mild generalised disturbance of motor nerve conduction and in the lower limbs of sensory conduction. In the left upper limb the radial median digits I and III SNAPs are absent, suggesting a proximal sensory radiculopathy involving the C6 and C7 roots. The C8 component may also be affected, although the median digit IV and ulnar digits SNAPs are still recordable. On the right, there is also a possible ulnar nerve lesion.

Figure 1. Examples of EMG examination report comments

The task for FACT is to analyse a report comment to see which, if any, of the concepts represented in the knowledge base would be appropriate index terms. The browser can then generate the necessary cross references between the report and the knowledge base concepts so that a user browsing through the knowledge base can retrieve case reports relating to a particular concept .

The concepts in the EMG Assistant's knowledge base which are available as index terms include the following sets:

- disorders, a term covering localised nerve lesions as well as diseases

- anatomical structures, primarily nerves and muscles

- pathophysiological states, which describe the states of individual nerves and muscles after they have been affected by a disease, trauma etc. (e.g. demyelinated, reinnervated)

- EMG tests which laboratories can perform

- EMG findings which are produced by comparing test results with what is expected in a healthy patient.

These concepts are represented in the knowledge base as hierarchies of entities, where each entity has a set of attribute-value pairs associated with it. Entities can inherit attributes and attribute values from other entities which lie above it in the hierarchy. Attribute values may represent relations with other entities and through this mechanism the concepts are richly interconnected, for example tests are carried out on anatomical structures and result in findings which indicate that particular pathophysiological states are present, which in turn point to the diagnosis of particular disorders.

For each hierarchy, there is a set of attributes which are the prime key attributes of entities in that hierarchy, which means that the values of those attributes are the defining features of the entity. For example, the prime keys of a finding entity might be its test name, result and anatomical structure, so that the entity representing the concept

reduced motor conduction velocity in the right median nerve

would have the following prime key values:

test name: motor conduction velocity

result: reduced

anatomical structure: right median nerve.

Each entity also contains pointers to additional sources of information about the concept it represents, such as pictures, case reports and bibliographic references. It is this kind of pointer that is set up as a result of FACT's classifications.

In addition to the concept hierarchies, the inferencing systems within the EMG Assistant draw on other kinds of domain knowledge. The problem solving behaviour which physicians follow in carrying out an EMG examination is modelled in rules bound together by a task structure reflecting stages in the reasoning process. In addition, a causal network linking test findings, pathophysiology and neuromuscular disorders has been developed to form the basis of a probabilistic approach to problem solving within the system. Although there is no intention in FACT to index texts with anything more complex than the individual domain concepts, the problem solving knowledge is potentially useful for improving the quality of the indexing by inferring information which is implicit in a text.

The EMG Assistant is being implemented using the KEE (Knowledge Engineering Environment) toolkit and Common Lisp on a Sun 3 workstation.

3   KNOWLEDGE-BASED   TEXT SCANNING

The ability to harness an existing knowledge base for use in a text classification system is potentially a major shortcut in the development process. However, in reviewing other knowledge-based text scanning systems, it can be seen that there are differences in the way that each one stores and uses the information in its knowledge base. This section explores the knowledge representation techniques used in some of the most significant text scanning systems and compares them with those available to FACT in the EMG Assistant's knowledge base.

One of the earliest knowledge formalisms used in natural language processing was Schank's conceptual dependency (Schank 1975). The main feature of conceptual dependency is that it is based on very general semantic primitives representing acts such as ptrans, which is the transfer of the physical location of an object. Each verb is described as a set of these semantic primitives, for example to go is a verb involving a ptrans act. The noun phrases which can occur with each primitive are described in terms of their relation to the primitive, such as whether they are the object, recipient or instrument of the act. Restrictions on the co-occurrence of particular kinds of noun with each primitive are determined by semantic classes such as animate.

With a few semantic primitives capturing the meaning of a wide range of language, conceptual dependency has formed the basis of a large amount of research at Yale on natural language processing. Story understanding has been a major theme, and the FRUMP system (DeJong, 1983) for skimming and summarising news articles is one of the best known systems in this field.

A number of additional formalisms have been developed to cope with knowledge representation at the level of the whole story rather than just sentences and phrases. Representations for the goals of characters appearing in stories and for plans set up to achieve those goals were built as part of the PAM system (Wilensky, 1981), and scripts describing commonly occurring sequences of events were the central theme of SAM (Cullingford, 1981). Both these mechanisms allow inferences to be made to draw out information which is implicit in the text, for example by assuming that stages of a script have in fact been carried out even when not explicitly mentioned in the story.

Commercial exploitation of these techniques is being carried out by Cognitive Systems Inc. in the US, which is currently one of the market leaders in text scanning systems. Products CSI has developed include ATRANS, a system for summarising banking telexes into a standard format, which is being used operationally in two US installations, and ACLASS, a classification and routing package which recognises 60 different types of banking message.

The semantic primitives of conceptual dependency are more general in nature than the domain-specific concepts represented in the EMG Assistant's knowledge base, and so are of limited relevance when trying to optimise the existing knowledge representation rather than starting anew. Some of the additional representations of plans and goals are of more interest, as the EMG Assistant contains a specific model of the steps in the examiner's reasoning process including setting goals and planning for their achievement. In the short term, the kinds of texts that FACT will classify will not need to draw upon knowledge about plans, goals or scripts, as there are no actors or event sequences in the EMG report comments, but this may change when dealing with other text types.

Another major school of development in text understanding is that of case frame representation. Like conceptual dependency, case frame parsing is driven by a set of expectations associated with the main verb of a sentence; for example the verb to go might have cases for the actor, place and time. Unlike conceptual dependency, the same kind of case frame representation is also used for constituents other than verbs, such as a case frame for a time-noun phrase with cases for day, date and hour of day. A further difference is that case frames tend to represent domain-specific concepts rather than general semantic primitives.

Case frame parsing has formed the basis of commercial developments at Carnegie Group, the other major US contender for text scanning applications. One such project is the Tess demonstrator for analysing banking telexes.

Another project based on case frames is MedSORT (Carbonell, Evans, Scott and Thomason 1985), which is of particular interest because of its attempts to draw upon an existing knowledge base, that of the INTERNIST expert system for diagnosing internal diseases (Pople 1982). The goal of the project is to represent the titles of rheumatology bibliographic references in a canonical form for later comparison with retrieval requests mapped into the same canonical form.

Unfortunately, the INTERNIST knowledge base contains atomic concepts as opposed to frame-based hierarchies, so a large amount of effort had to be diverted to redeveloping a thesaurus of the relevant medical concepts rather than exploiting the existing model.

The EMG Assistant's knowledge base is ideally suited to case frame parsing, as it contains frames representing all the major concepts in the EMG domain. Sections 4.2 and 4.3 describe how the EMG entities are treated as case frames in FACT's semantic analyser.

A problem in frame-based processing, particularly in a domain covering a broad range of concepts, is that of selecting one case frame to form the basis of further processing when there are a number of possibilities. Methods for choosing between options have included word experts (Small 1979), which are sets of disambiguation rules associated with words which have more than one sense, and FRUMP's discrimination trees, which disambiguate word senses on the basis of the information in a conceptual dependency description.

One of the earliest text scanning systems to be delivered as a working implementation is based on word experts. The Nomad system (Granger 1983) summarises shipping telexes for the US Navy and is able to cope with ill- formed input such as 'locked on open fired destroyed'. As far as the EMG Assistant is concerned, word experts are tied to the meanings of individual words in the lexicon and would not draw fully on the information in the knowledge base. Also, word experts have been found to suffer from a lack of extensibility with the result that the Nomad system has been rebuilt as VOX (Meyers 1985) using phrasal rather than word-level analysis.

One of the most relevant approaches to frame selection for the EMG Assistant can be found not in a text scanning system but in the MOPTRANS machine translation system (Lytinen 1984), where concepts are represented hierarchically from the most vague to the most specific. Even though a term in the source language may point to a concept at a very general level in the hierarchy, general purpose rules are used to specialise the meaning of the term from its context, so that a more specific term can be used in the target language if appropriate. The EMG Assistant's knowledge base already contains hierarchically organised concepts and so forms a suitable basis for a similar approach to specialisation, as described in Section 4.3.

Another major text understanding project funded by the US Navy is that of summarising equipment failure reports called CASREPS or casualty reports (Grishman and Hirshman 1986). Sets of production rules are used to assign semantic categories to words, to make inferences about the status of components by following a causal chain and to flag particular kinds of information as more important than others (Marsh, Hamburger and Grishman 1984). A model simulating the way the equipment functions is used to improve the quality and the scope of the inferences made (Ksiezyk, Grishman and Sterling 1987).

The CASREP project's use of production rules and a simulation model represents a conscious effort to apply artificial intelligence techniques to the problem of understanding text. There is potential in the EMG Assistant to use knowledge in a similar way, as the system already contains inference rules for the expert tasks of diagnosis and test planning as well as a causal model. It has not yet been established that this kind of knowledge will be needed to understand EMG report comments, although later versions of FACT may need to investigate the way in which the expert system's inferences can help with other kinds of texts.

In conclusion, a number of text scanning and other natural language processing systems make use of knowledge bases organised in a similar way to that of the EMG Assistant. The frames representing EMG entities are similar enough to those used in case frame parsing to form a suitable basis for the semantic component of a text scanning system. The fact that they are organised hierarchically is of further benefit in producing an analysis to an appropriate level of specificity.

4   DESIGN OF THE FACT SYSTEM

Having established that the information in the EMG Assistant's knowledge base is represented in a form that is useful for a text scanning system, a design is needed that will maximise the use that can be made of it. This is the main aim of the first FACT prototype, shown in Figure 2, which is currently under development at Logica and due to be completed in April 1988. This prototype concentrates on the semantic analysis of the texts and intends to integrate an existing parser, grammar and lexicon, such as the deliverables from the Alvey natural language tools project, to meet the system's syntactic processing needs.

This section outlines the way in which the knowledge base is used in preparing the existing lexicon for use by FACT, and describes the design of the semantic processing component, consisting of the semantic grammar, the semantic analyser and the indexer, with emphasis on the way in which the knowledge base is used in the processing.

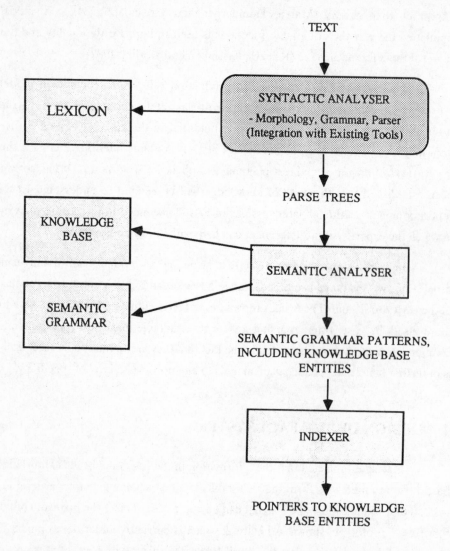

Figure 2. Architecture of the FACT System

4.1 Lexicon

The lexicon contains entries for each word and term that can appear in the texts being analysed. Each entry contains the grammatical information required by the syntactic analyser and, in some cases, semantic information. The semantic information in a lexical entry can be of two kinds: a pointer from a word or term to an entity in the knowledge base, or a semantic category.

In order for the syntactic analyser to generate parse trees which include the information required for semantic processing, any entries in the lexicon which represent concepts in the EMG domain need to contain pointers into the EMG Assistant's knowledge base. These pointers can be generated automatically to a certain extent, as each entity in the knowledge base already has a name and a set of synonyms associated with it for presenting the concept to the user. Where the name of an entity has a corresponding entry in the lexicon, a pointer is created from the lexical entry to the relevant entity. For entity names which are not lexical entries, the system developer must decide whether the name is a term, albeit a specialist one, which warrants inclusion in the lexicon, or whether it is a phrase whose components already appear in the lexicon. In the latter case, the phrase will usually be just one of a number of syntactic variations which express the same concept, so it is inappropriate to make an additional entry in the lexicon. The phrase will be recognised from its constituent parts by the semantic analyser.

In some parts of the knowledge base, there are entities that do not have individual names associated with them because they do not exist explicitly in the knowledge base. Where a class entity has a large number of members, the members may not all be created permanently in the knowledge base; instead the class entity may contain value class specifications, which determine what the members would look like were they to be enumerated. For example, a motor conduction velocity test can be carried out on any accessible segment of motor nerve in the body, in either direction along the nerve, but the representation for this in the knowledge base is as the class of tests shown in Figure 3a rather than as a large number of individual entities. The member entities of this class would look like Figure 3b, but would only be generated as they are required by the expert system. (NB: Figures 3a and 3b are simplified examples of entities.)

```
Entity:   MOTOR CONDUCTION VELOCITY
          Attribute:   MEMBER-OF
                       Valueclass:   ENTITIES
                       Value:        TESTS
          Attribute:   LOCATION
                       Valueclass:   NERVE SEGMENT
                       Value:        Unknown
          Attribute:   DIRECTION
                       Valueclass:   ONE.OF ORTHODROMIC ANTIDROMIC
                       Value:        Unknown
```

Figure 3a. Class entity representing a set of possible entities

```
Entity:   ORTHODROMIC MOTOR CONDUCTION VELOCITY IN THE ULNAR NERVE,
          WRIST TO ELBOW
          Attribute:   MEMBER-OF
                       Valueclass:   ENTITIES
                       Value:        MOTOR CONDUCTION VELOCITY
          Attribute:   LOCATION
                       Valueclass:   NERVE SEGMENT
                       Value:        ULNAR NERVE, WRIST TO ELBOW
          Attribute:   DIRECTION
                       Valueclass:   ONE.OF ORTHODROMIC ANTIDROMIC
                       Value:        ORTHODROMIC
```

Figure 3b. Member entity generated from the class entity in Figure 3a

In these cases, the class entity contains a grammar describing what the names of its members are. This grammar uses the prime keys of the entities and syntactic information such as whether an attribute should appear as an adjective, as in 'ulnar nerve lesion' or as a prepositional phrase, as in 'fibrillations in the APB'. At this stage of complexity, it is not appropriate to generate links between the lexicon and the knowledge base. The names of the member entities are likely to be phrases with alternative surface forms to the one in the grammar, for example 'ulnar nerve lesion' versus 'lesion in the ulnar nerve', which should be handled by the semantic analyser rather than by a lexical entry.

The pointers from the lexical entries to the EMG knowledge base entities form an essential part in the analysis of noun phrases in the texts. The equivalent mechanism for handling verb phrases would be to create pointers from verbs in the lexicon to the relationships between entities in the knowledge base. For example, the verb or verb phrases 'suggest', 'be consistent with', 'indicate', 'be indicative of' and 'identify' are all used to describe the relationship between findings and their associated pathology. However, in FACT the texts are only indexed against the entities in the knowledge base, not against the relationships, so the knowledge about the way the entities are related is only used by the semantic analyser to help identify the entities themselves. For this reason, verbs in the lexicon are assigned semantic categories rather than actual pointers into the knowledge base, although the categories often coincide with the names of relations. If other applications required a more detailed model of the text, then it would be appropriate to use pointers to the knowledge base relations.

While some of an entity's attributes are relationships pointing to other named entities, others contain strings as values, such as the severity attribute of disorders, which can take the values mild, moderate, moderately severe and severe. This kind of attribute is only ever the modifier of a more major concept, so again there is no need for a pointer from the lexical entries to the knowledge base in this application. When the semantic analyser looks for an attribute of this kind in a text, it tries to match the strings exactly.

4.2 Semantic Grammar

The entry point to the semantic grammar is the type of text being analysed, as the long term plan is to extend the coverage of FACT to other kinds of text, such as abstracts or titles of bibliographic references. The grammar for the first prototype is based on an analysis of 45 examination report comments from five EMG examiners at two UK hospitals.

Figure 4 shows an example of the semantic grammar. Each text type consists of a number of possible statement types representing the way in which EMG concepts combine within and between sentences. The order of items within a statement is not significant, although the order of statements within a text type is, and a single statement can match input over a number of sentences. Texts which could be analysed using this grammar would include texts (2) and (3) in Figure 1, using clauses (a) and (b) respectively. For example, in text (2) the sentence 'Myotonia confirmed.' would match the statement *disorder* /exists/,and 'There was no clear evidence of a myopathy in addition.' would match the statement *disorder* .neg./exists/.

89

a) <report comment> = *disorder* /exists/ , *disorder* .neg. /exists/
b) <report comment> = { *finding* } /implies/ *disorder*

KEY:
<xxx>   non-terminal symbol
{ xxx }   element can occur one or more times
xxx   pointer into knowledge base hierarchy
.xxx.   statement modifier
/xxx/   semantic category

Figure 4. Example of semantic grammer

    The terminal symbols of the grammar are of three types: pointers into the knowledge base hierarchies, the semantic categories used in the lexicon, and statement modifiers. The knowledge base hierarchies play the role that case frames would play in other text scanning systems, and a grammar statement with a pointer into a hierarchy indicates that the entities in that hierarchy should be viewed as case frames for matching against the input. A semantic category in a grammar rule means that a verb phrase whose lexical entry is indexed with that category is expected. A statement modifier allows important changes to the meaning of a statement such as negation and uncertainty, to be spotted and recorded, by calling a particular set of rules in the semantic analyser into play.

    In order to improve the coverage of the semantic grammar, references are included to concepts which are outside the scope of the EMG knowledge base but which sometimes occur in texts, such as symptoms, causes of disorders and recommendations for non-EMG tests. These concepts are modelled in an additional section of the knowledge base used only by FACT and enable the semantic processor to recognise that a phrase is in an area where it has no detailed knowledge. For example, in analysing the phrase

    with evidence for overmedication with anticholinesterases

the knowledge that overmedication with a drug is a cause of disorders would allow the semantic analyser to recognise the phrase as a cause without knowing the name of the particular drug anticholinesterases. This wider coverage is important to the robustness of the system.

4.3 Semantic Analyser

The semantic analyser takes a syntactic analysis of the text in the form of parse trees and produces a representation of the text in terms of the semantic grammar and the relevant knowledge base entities, having carried out disambiguation where there is more than one syntactic parse tree for a particular sentence.

For each of the three kinds of terminal symbol in the semantic grammar (pointer into knowledge base hierarchy, semantic category, and statement modifier) there are sets of rules in the semantic analyser which inspect the parse trees to see if the semantic constraints are met.

Upon encountering a pointer into the knowledge base hierarchy in the semantic grammar, the semantic analyser tries to match the information in the parse trees against the most specific possible entity in that hierarchy. For most hierarchies, there will be a lexical item in the parse tree which already points at an entity in the hierarchy, due to the process described in Section 4.1 of precompiling links from lexicon entries to knowledge base entities with the same name. For example, if the grammar is seeking a match for a *disorder* hierarchy pointer, and the noun phrase 'a mild generalised neuropathy' has been parsed, then the lexical item for neuropathy in the parse tree will contain a pointer to the neuropathy entity in the disorders hierarchy. To find the most specific possible entity in the hierarchy below neuropathy, rules are applied which examine the neuropathy noun phrase modifiers in the parse tree for a match with the prime key attributes of each entity. In this example, the location and severity attributes of an entity in the neuropathy hierarchy would need to match the adjectives 'generalised' and 'mild' respectively for the semantic analyser to recognise that it had found an entity representing the 'concept mild generalised neuropathy'.

In some hierarchies, the parse tree will never contain a pointer from a lexical item into the hierarchy, because the names of the entities are composites of other terms and so do not appear as entries in the lexicon. For example, a finding always consists of a test name, test result and anatomical structure. In these cases, the semantic analyser finds the entity E that is pointed to by the head noun in the phrase under consideration. It then searches the expected hierarchy for an entity which has a prime key attribute pointing to E and continues from there to refine

91

further down the hierarchy as above. An example would be in parsing the phrase 'absent ulnar SAPs' as a *finding*, where the lexical item SAP would point to the SAP entity in the tests hierarchy (SAP is an abbreviation for a sensory action potential test). This would cause the prime key attributes of entities in the findings hierarchy to be searched for pointers to the SAP entity. Once all the entities representing SAP findings had been located, the modifiers of the SAP noun phrase would be used to distinguish the single most appropriate entity for the phrase.

As far as possible, the rules for identifying the fillers for prime key attributes from the parse trees are general ones applicable to all the different entity hierarchies. However, there are places where knowledge specific to one particular hierarchy is needed; for example, a plural test in a finding such as 'absent ulnar SAPs' means that the finding applies to both sides of the body and the side of body attribute needs to be filled accordingly. Additional information of this kind is added to the appropriate entities and attributes in the knowledge base by means of an annotation mechanism in the EMG Assistant's knowledge representation language, which allows arbitrary notes about the knowledge to be added without affecting the assumptions that can be made about the knowledge itself. Whenever the semantic analyser is trying to match parse trees against a hierarchy, it checks for specific annotations in the hierarchy as well as using the general matching rules.

Once an entity matching a phrase in a parse tree has been identified, then other alternative parse trees can be ignored, as there will only be one semantic interpretation except in cases of badly written and genuinely ambiguous text. So in the example

> borderline lateral popliteal motor conduction and median and radial SAPs

the semantic analyser would match the sentence against the entities representing the following three findings:

> borderline lateral popliteal motor conduction
>
> borderline median SAPs
>
> borderline radial SAPs

Alternative syntactic parses such as one having 'radial SAPs' as a complete noun phrase would fail because the semantic grammar for report comments does not expect a statement about a test on its own, only in the context of a finding which also demands a result attribute such as borderline. 'Borderline lateral popliteal radial SAPs 'would fail as a component as only one nerve attribute is allowed in a finding. The mechanisms for processing the other kinds of terminal symbols do not draw upon information in the knowledge base, but take the form of additional rules in the semantic analyser. There are sets of rules to match verbs in the parse trees against the semantic categories in the semantic grammar and to check for the statement modifiers such as negation and uncertainty. In addition, there are rules to recognise that intersentential references such as 'The findings' in text (3) of Figure 1 are valid substitutes for instantiated hierarchy entities.

4.4 Indexing

The indexing is carried out as a distinct component, as the requirements may change according to the needs of individual users or due to other factors. In the EMG Assistant for example, if an examination is carried out using the expert system then the findings will appear in a standard format in the case report and do not need to be indexed from the comment at the end, whereas if existing case reports are entered then all aspects need to be included in the indexing.

If there are any parts of the text that have not been understood, then the indexer must make a decision about whether it should index the text or relinquish responsibility to a human. Heuristics are applied to decide how important a particular piece of text might be. For example, encountering an 'also' in a text describing a disorder would lead to a check that another disorder was mentioned previously; if not then the indexer can assume that the piece of text which was not understood is too important to ignore. The fact that the system has a limited knowledge of non-EMG concepts also helps in the decision, as the indexer is able to realise that a phrase lies in an area it does not need to know about in detail.

The indexer either produces a list of entities in the EMG knowledge base against which the text should be indexed or produces a partially built list and refers the text for analysis by a human indexer. If an entity on the list exists only in a valueclass specification of a class entity, then the system creates a new member entity in which to store the cross reference to the text.

5   SUMMARY AND CONCLUSION

This paper has presented an application of text scanning in which texts are analysed for cross-indexing against a knowledge base of EMG concepts. A major feature of the application is that an existing knowledge base developed for use by an expert system is available to the text classification system. A review of other text scanning systems has shown that the frame- based hierarchies of the existing knowledge base form a suitable basis for semantic analysis.

A design for the text classification system has been outlined. It makes use of an existing lexicon, syntactic grammar, morphological analyser and parser, with domain-specific semantic information added to the lexicon. Some of this semantic information can be compiled automatically from entity names in the expert system's knowledge base, although consideration must be given to the fact that some of the names are compound phrases rather than terms which belong in the lexicon, particularly where concepts are represented as classes with valueclass specifications rather than as individual member entities.

The semantic component of the system uses a semantic grammar, with pointers into the hierarchies of EMG entities serving as case frames. The semantic analyser uses general rules and specific annotations to the knowledge in order to compare the parsed input with the prime key attributes of entities. This mechanism is used to find the most specific matching entity in a hierarchy and to disambiguate alternative syntactic parses at the same time. Other rules search the parse tree for input which matches semantic the categories and statement modifiers expected by the grammar. A separate set of indexing rules makes the final assignment of those EMG entities which best describe the content of the text.

In conclusion, the idea of incorporating an existing knowledge base into the design of a text classification system seems a worthwhile way of decreasing the development time. This paper has concentrated on some of the points that need to be addressed in building such a system, although there are others which remain to be investigated.

One of the main unresolved issues is the way in which the expert system's inference rules could be incorporated to improve the quality of indexing or the coverage of texts. The kinds of common sense inference which people make in reading texts (such as the fact that a plural anatomical structure refers to both the left and right sides) are not part of the existing EMG knowledge or inferencing rules but need to be added as part of the semantic component in FACT as in other text scanning systems. Some of the work on the CASREP project has shown that there are places where common sense inferences are not enough and only expert knowledge will enable the text to be interpreted properly, by either a human or a machine (Ksiezyk, Grishman and Sterling 1987). If expert as well as common sense inference proves to be necessary in understanding the EMG texts, then the problem solving knowledge and causal model of the EMG Assistant can be tapped as an available source.

The aim in developing FACT has been to produce a system which will cross- index texts against domain concepts so that a user of the EMG Assistant's knowledge base browser can retrieve texts by following pointers from relevant EMG entities. Although the browser provides an integrated means of viewing all the information in the knowledge base, it would be more powerful to have a separate interface for text retrieval which allowed the user to formulate queries. The knowledge base represents a canonical form of the kind sought after by the MedSORT researchers (Carbonell, Evans, Scott and Thomason 1985) which could be used as an intermediate representation for both texts and user queries. FACT already has to overcome irrelevant syntactic differences in expressing the same concept in order to understand texts, so an obvious extension would be to use the same syntactic and semantic components for analysing queries. In this case it would be appropriate to extend the semantic grammar to include the relationships in the knowledge base as well as the entities and so allow a richer model of the texts and queries to be built.

A report on commercial applications of natural language processing claims that text scanning applications will be worth $110 million in the US and the UK by the year 1995 (Johnson 1985). As most of the current approaches to text scanning depend on a knowledge-based representation of the domain of discourse, if even a small percentage of systems can exploit existing knowledge bases, then a huge amount of resources will be saved. As expert systems are currently a step ahead of natural language systems in terms of commercial take-up, it is likely that other natural language projects will increasingly be able to take advantage of the approach which has been presented in this paper.

6   ACKNOWLEDGEMENTS

This work was supported in part by the ESPRIT programme funded by the Commission for European Communities. Other partners on the project are the Institute for Neurology at the National Hospital for Nervous Diseases in London, Computer Resources International, Nordjysk Udviklingscenter at the University of Aalborg, and Judex Datasystemer in Denmark. The author would particularly like to thank colleagues at Logica for their helpful comments and support.

7   REFERENCES

1   Andersen, SK, Andreassen, S and Woldbye, M (1986),   Knowledge Representations for Diagnosis and Test Planning in the Domain of Electromyography. In B. Du Boulay, D. Hogg and L. Steels (eds) Advances in Artificial Intelligence - II, North Holland, pp461-472.

2   Carbonell, JG, Evans, DA, Scott, DS and Thomason, RH (1985), Final Report on the Automated Classification and Retrieval (MedSORT) Project. Departments of Philosophy and Computer Science, Carnegie Mellon University.

3   Cullingford, R (1981),   SAM.   In RC Schank and CK Riesbeck (eds), Inside Computer Understanding. Lawrence Erlbaum Associates, Hillsdale, NJ.

4   DeJong, G (1983), An Overview of the FRUMP System. In W Lehnert and M Ringle (eds), Strategies for Natural Language Processing. Lawrence Erlbaum Associates, Hillsdale NJ, pp149-176.

5   Fenn, JA, Foote, MH, Worden, RP and Willison, RG (1986),   An Expert Assistant for Electromyography.   Biomedical Measurement Informatics and Control, Vol 1, No 4, pp210-214

6   Granger, RH (1983), The NOMAD System: Expectation-Based Detection and Correction of Errors during Understanding of Syntactically and Semantically Ill-formed Text. Computational Linguistics, Vol 9, No 3-4, pp188-196

7   Grishman, R and Hirshman, L (1986), PROTEUS and PUNDIT: Research in Text Understanding. Site Report, Computational Linguistics, Vol 12, No 2, pp141-145

8   Johnson, T (1985), Natural Language Computing: the Commercial Applications. Ovum, London.

9   Ksiezyk, T, Grishman, R and Sterling, J (1987), An Equipment Model and its Role in the Interpretation of Noun Phrases. In Proceedings of the 10th International Joint Conference on Artificial Intelligence, Milan, pp692-695

10 Lytinen, SL (1984), Frame Selection in Parsing. In Proceedings of the National Conference on Artificial Intelligence, Austin, Texas, pp222-225.

11 Marsh, E, Hamburger, H and Grishman, R (1984), A Production Rule System for Message Summarization. In Proceedings of the National Conference on Artificial Intelligence, Austin, Texas, pp243-246

12 Meyers, A (1985), VOX - An Extensible Natural Language Processor. In Proceedings of 9th International Joint Conference on Artificial Intelligence, Los Angeles, pp821-825

13 Pople, HE (1982), Heuristic Methods for Imposing Structure on Ill- Structured Problems: The Structuring of Medical Diagnostics. In P.Szolovits (ed.) Artificial Intelligence in Medicine. Westview, Colorado, pp119-190

14 Schank, RC (1975), Conceptual Information Processing. North Holland, Amsterdam

15 Small, SL (1979), Word Expert Parsing. In Proceedings of 17th Annual Meeting of the Association for Computational Linguistics, La Jolla, California, pp9-13

16 Wilensky, R (1981), PAM. In RC Schank and CK Riesbeck (eds) Inside Computer Understanding. Lawrence Erlbaum Associates, Hillsdale, NJ.

Chapter 7
Dialogues with the Tin Man: A Natural LanguageGrammar for Expert System Naive Users.

D DIAPER & T SHELTON,
Liverpool Polytechnic

1   INTRODUCTION

The interest currently shown for natural language as an input/output requirement to expert systems appears to be out of all proportion to our current, and perhaps future, technological capabilities. Indeed, the very concept of 'natural language' appears confused and has only become popular within the last decade. It is confused because it assumes that something exists that can be clearly identified as natural language which is apparently independent of native speakers 'or writers' usage. Furthermore, the contrast to natural language, non-natural language presumably, appears to be restricted to communications between people and machines. Thus natural language for communication with expert systems would appear appropriate only if such systems possessed human intelligence, something which is implausible and almost certainly undesirable [1, 3]. One interpretation of all this is that those involved with expert system interface development, in particular, are, as drowning men, clutching at straws. The recent shift in software engineering, even for non-intelligent computers, towards User Centred Design [11, 5] has, amongst other things, exposed the soft under-belly of Human-Computer Interaction (HCI) which has generally lacked both scientifically adequate theoretical underpinnings and methodological rigour in its application to real systems. Such problems become magnified with even marginally intelligent machines, such as first generation expert systems, such that their interface requirements appear, with the current state of HCI, to be insoluble. This has led the proponents of natural language [e.g.14] to suggest that using natural language, whatever it is, will be the panacea that solves expert system interface problems. In this assumption they are dangerously misled. First, it is not at all clear that, even if fully implemented, natural language would solve any of the human-expert system communication problems as recorded history, and our own everyday experience, suggests that people frequently misunderstand each other. Second, it is possible that natural language will be actually disadvantageous both for communicative efficiency, and crucially, for the safety of direct system users [4], those who actually use the system, and for other individuals and groups whose lives may be affected by the system [3]. The detailed arguments for these claims have been reported elsewhere [1,3] though the heart of the matter is the fundamental difference between human cognition and that of machines. The problem is that natural language has evolved to cope, albeit poorly, with the requirement to communicate thoughts between people. To achieve this with any degree of success, each participant obviously possesses a complex model of the other participant's beliefs.

That is, a speaker must not only know what they intend to say but must phrase their utterances so that these are compatible with the speaker's beliefs about the listener. Similarly, the listener needs to understand an utterance within its proper context, and this requires a model or set of beliefs about the speaker. In fact, these belief assumptions become integrated into the evolving language, which, for example, is part of the feminists' objection to the masculine domination of Western languages. The problem of communicating with the non-human, alien intelligence of the machine [1] is thus not obviously solved by such people orientated languages because the beliefs that people may reasonably correctly hold about other people are inappropriate and potentially dangerously incorrect when applied to intelligent machines. Furthermore, there is the quite erroneous assumption, mentioned above, that natural language exists almost in the same way that physical objects can be said to exist. This is the classic dichotomy between the linguist, who studies language, and the psycholinguist, who studies the psychology and use of language. Taking the psycholinguistic perspective, it is clear that there is no real world entity that is natural language that has any existence independently of its users. What people appear to possess and use is a large number of sub-languages [6], a subset of which each individual speaker possesses such that in a dialogue one sub-language is selected depending on the nature of the speakers beliefs about the nature of the dialogue topic, the participants, any non-participative audience and any relevant historical, current or future context. Hence, given the people orientated, evolutionary nature of languages , it is unlikely that any available human sub-language is optimal for human-expert system communication.

The view that one of the major difficulties with using computers is that '... managers of some company may know their company's problems, but they do not know 'computer talk'...' [13] is almost certainly implausible unless one erroneously equates language and thought, a rather ancient fallacy in psychology. Such users' problems are more realistically related to their lack of comprehension of the machines' capabilities and limitations, which may be reflected in their lack of ability at 'computer talk', but the latter is almost certainly symptomatic, rather than causative. The over-optimistic expectations, often unfortunately encouraged by computer salesmen, and the subsequent and often expensive disappointment after delivery and installation of a new computer system, clearly demonstrate the real problem of matching users' understanding of a system to their desires and requirements (**nb:** all this, of course, assumes that users know what they want, a rather dubious assumption [9, 10, 5]).

Thus it seems that the only remaining advantage of using a human-human evolved sub-language is that it does not need to be learnt [14]. However, this too, is probably a spurious benefit given that any learning time is more likely to be determined by the acquisition of the appropriate concepts about the system and its limitations, rather than the learning of any special language. Furthermore, in comparison to a sub-language specially designed for human-expert system communication, the use of human-human evolved sub-languages may actually hinder the acquisition of the appropriate system concepts by, for example, encouraging the natural anthropomorphism of users, which is then likely to encourage beliefs that the expert system is more nearly human than is really the case [1, 3]. Current expert systems, and all those proposed outside of science fiction, are, of necessity, highly restricted to a narrow domain of expertise. In contrast, people possess an incredible width, and a varying depth, of expertise in many domains such that they exhibit what is popularly called 'common sense'. It is highly likely that users will be encouraged to erroneously assume a similar breadth of knowledge in an expert system that appears to converse in natural language. It is quite possible that natural language will occassionally mislead even those who are experts in the expert system field into believing that they are building systems that are more powerful than is actually the case.

One possible solution to part of the human-expert system interface problem is a naturalistic sub-language specifically designed for the purpose [2, 3]. Importantly, the assumption that a domain independent sub-language can be designed that will facilitate safe communication between people and expert systems will need rigorous testing in the future. At present there does not appear to be any empirical evidence from psychology that people use a specialised subset of natural sub-languages when dealing with experts in differing domains. However, the idea that there are people who are skilled at talking to human experts independently of the domain of expertise is superficially plausible and deserves further investigation though there can be no doubt there will always remain some aspects of human-expert system dialogue that will be domain dependent. This domain dependence, however, is only likely to be a problem when the user is not a domain expert. In those applications where future expert systems will be used by untrained, system naive people (for example, an automated sales assistant used by the general public), then it is likely that the users will possess some domain expertise (e.g. general expertise about shopping [8] even if not about the particular products).

The immediate problem, however, remains: how to formally specify either such a sub-language itself or the procedures and investigations that are needed to otherwise provide a suitable specification. It is this latter option that is partially explored in this paper because, at present, there is an insufficient theoretical basis in any of the relevant disciplines of psychology, psycholinguistics, linguistics etc. capable of providing the former type of solution. This chapter will now briefly summarise the research approach adopted and the techniques employed to gather data and to analyse it, in the case of this chapter, into a syntax that specifies the language actually required between naive users and an intelligent advisory system, albeit a simulated one. The analysis is offered as a demonstration of the central 'Wizard of Oz' methodology and its suitability and usefulness for this type of investigation.

2   THE 'WIZARD OF OZ' METHODOLOGY

The 'Wizard of Oz' simulation methodology used to collect dialogues between a user and a simulated, advisory expert system has been described previously [2, 15]. The method uses two subjects, a system subject and a user subject, who are unknown to each other and isolated in separate rooms.   An intelligent system possessing a full natural language processing capability is simulated by the system subject. The purpose of the simulation is to discover how little natural language is actually used, particularly by the user subjects, when there are no system imposed constraints, other than that the dialogue between the subjects is conducted via a standard QWERTY keyboard and screen. Whatever the success of current research in speech input/output technology, it has been argued that there will still remain many applications where keyboard and screen is preferred to speech input/output [3]. The system subject also provides the intelligence so that a paper database appears to function as if it were an expert system.

The user subjects are expert system naive people. They are informed that they have inherited a sum of money and a condition of the inheritance is that they must spend this sum with a fictitious computer company (D3 Computers) and that the equipment purchased must be for their personal use. They are told that their terminal is connected to a powerful, intelligent research computer and that they can type in whatever they may wish and the machine will do its best to understand them and help them select hardware and software suitable for their requirements. They are asked to be a little patient as, though the machine is quite intelligent, it is a little slow (in fact, in general subjects do not complain about the response speed and, to the authors, it appears to be no worse than using a large institutional mainframe during 'busy' periods of the day.). The user subject's screen is initially blank and the input the user types is echoed in the normal way, but starts from the bottom of the screen and then conventionally scrolls upwards. Subjects are given no advice as to what they should type, requests for help to the experimenter are politely refused, and they are not even told that it is up to them whether they even use the return key. User subject input is in lower case, whereas that from the system subject is in upper

102

case, and all system subject inputs force new lines both before and after their appearance on the user subject's screen.

User subjects are extensively debriefed immediately after their session and considerable effort is made to get user subjects to admit to any suspicion that they were not communicating with a machine. All the data reported in this chapter is from subjects who could not be forced to admit to any such suspicion. Indeed, subjects usually express considerable surprise when finally informed of the simulated nature of the system, and in one or two cases, some distress, particularly in the case of an M.Sc. student on a computer science conversion course, who had been trying to work out how the system operated and had spent some time during debriefing describing the sort of algorithm he believed the system used. The system subject is trained on the contents of a paper database about D3 Computer's products and on the procedures necessary to run the system, but not on how to conduct dialogues. Training takes about two weeks, with the first week devoted to learning the structure and contents of the database. In the second week the system subject uses the system with an experimenter replacing the user subject. However, natural language dialogues are not conducted during these training sessions so as to minimise stylistic bias caused by the experimenter's beliefs about how user subjects will behave. During the second week the system subject is tested on increasingly more complicated combinations of hardware and software that can be configured from the items in the database. A paper data-base is used simply because once learnt, the system subject is much faster to access information either from his memory or from a single large sheet of mnemonic tables than would be the case if a computer database were used. The database is quite large in that there are in excess of 50 separate items of microcomputer hardware and software, and there are considerable restrictions on which items can be combined. However, the database is systematically structured and the structuring and the various tabular forms of it are all fully explained to the system subject during the first week of training. The database was designed as a compromise between two antagonistic considerations: it had to be small enough to be relatively easily learnt, yet large enough to engender a rich dialogue between user and system subjects and, in particular, to prevent the selection of one of a small range of possible options based only on the amount of money the user subject had to spend.

As can be seen in the 'General Results' section (Table 1), the dialogues lasted an average of one hour each. The system subjects were allowed to close the dialogue once the user subject was within a 10 per cent overspend of the monies they had available by offering up to a 10 per cent discount for a complete system of hardware and software. Perhaps only slightly surprisingly given the comments made above about the potential anthropomorphism natural language might encourage in users, a number of the user subjects attempted to negotiate a discount near the end of the session on their own initiative, before the system subject could offer one. While it is unknown from these studies whether subjects would have similarly assumed with a more traditionally configured interface (i.e. a non-natural language one) that the system would have the authority to negotiate discounts, it is not an unreasonable suspicion that they would not have attempted such negotiations unprompted by the system.

The system subject has a screen with three windows: the lowest, largest window contains the last 25 lines of dialogue between the two subjects and, apart from being a few lines shorter, is identical with the user subject's screen. Every character that the user subject types is displayed immediately in this window. An upper window is used for two purposes: (i) the system subject constructs messages in this window which are only sent to the user subject (and displayed on the system subject's lower window) once the return key is pressed; and (ii) it can be used to provide a menu of options for running the system's small on-line database. In the original pilot study [2, 15] not all the user subjects were completely convinced that they were dealing with a real system, and one reason for this was that contrary to their expectations, the system was very slow at producing what they quite rightly believed machines should be good at - repeated lists. Thus a small database was built into the software that ran the dialogue so that as the user subject decided to make purchases these decisions were immediately entered and the total spent calculated. This information was displayed to the system subject on a narrow (six character) window running down the right-hand length of the screen. When requested, the system subject could send a fuller version of this information to the user subject. This version showed each piece of selected equipment's identifier code (often used by both subjects after being introduced by the system subject), its price, and a brief description (see: Figure 1). The system subject could enter the database menu at any time, but each time this was done the software automatically sent a 'PLEASE WAIT' message to the user.

Computer:	C1	£500	256K
Backing Store:	FD1	£120	100K.1 driv.1 dens.1 side
Monitors:	MC2	£200	mono. med.res.
Printers:	DM2	£150	mat.120 cps. 4 char.set
Softwares:	WP2	£100	word processor two
	GR3	£100	graphics three
	P3	£50	programming
Total cost:		£1220	

Figure 1. Example of the canned text list of choices that could be sent to a user subject on request

The text was displayed on high resolution monochrome monitors (white on grey) with 80 characters across the screen and 32 lines down. The software, written in C, ran on a Torch Unicorn system under UNIX with 20 Mbytes of hard disc available. Keyboards were BBC B microcomputers and their own hardware provided the screen drivers which ran in BBC Mode 3. The advantage of UNIX for this type of research is that it provides a multi-user, multi-tasking environment, which is an essential requirement. Data capture consisted of every character that the user typed along with the time, to the nearest second, of typing and every block of text sent by the system subject along with the time it was sent (i.e. when the system subject's return key was pressed).

3   SUBJECTS

The data reported in this chapter was collected over two summers (1986 and 1987) using two different system subjects. Complete dialogues (there were a couple of unexplained system crashes in 1986) from seven user subjects were obtained for each system subject. The 1987 system subject used a typist who passively typed what he was told by the system subject and played a minimal role in the interaction. User subjects in both years were respondents to advertisements placed in University College London and Liverpool Polytechnic respectively, and thus most, but by no means all, of the subjects were students.

4 GENERAL RESULTS

Table 1 shows the general results for both the 1986 and 1987 tests. These results are not combined as they illustrate the consistency of the findings when both different system, as well as user, subjects are used. The overall difference between the two sets of results is almost entirely caused by the 1986 system subject typing more than twice as many lines as the 1987 system subject. However, this difference in style appears to make little difference to the overall pattern of results from either subject and little difference to the subsequently described syntactic analyses.

TABLE 1.General descriptive statistics about the dialogues

	1986	1987
USER and SYSTEM SUBJECT		
Mean No. of lines of dialogue per subject	198	116
Mean No. of words per line of dialogue per subject	5.3	5.0
Mean No. of alternations per dialogue per subject	133	107
Mean time (minutes) per dialogue per subject	62	62
SYSTEM SUBJECT		
Mean No. of lines of dialogue per subject	130	61
Mean No. of words per line of dialogue per subject	5.5	4.7
USER SUBJECT		
Mean No. of lines of dialogue per subject	68	55
Mean No. of words per line of dialogue per subject	4.8	5.3
Total No. of different words used by user subjects	468	580

These results are also very similar to those of the pilot study [2, 15] in that although the pilot study interactions were somewhat briefer (mean 40 minutes) the number of lines of dialogue (mean 140) falls between the results of these two later studies. Importantly, the total number of different words (not lexical items and including all proper nouns and numeric inputs) used by all five user subjects in the pilot study (299) is, while slightly smaller, similar to that found in the results described above. This result is important as it supports the claim that only an extremely limited vocabulary is required for interacting with an expert system within a single domain using natural language. While not directly relevant to this chapter, the other linguistic measures reported from the pilot study are similarly replicated in more detailed analyses of these results.

It has been a policy of the whole research programme to concentrate on the analysis of the user subjects' inputs as it may be argued that it is machine comprehension of natural language input which is the major computational difficulty in the area of natural language, as opposed to the problems of machine production (principally because of the ability of the people to understand even poorly formulated naturalistic language). Thus the next two sections will describe the method and then the results of analysing the syntax employed by the users in the simulations.

5   SYNTACTICAL ANALYSIS METHOD

In essence there are two alternative approaches to the analysis of natural language syntax. On the one hand there is the approach of discourse analysis which is principally theoretically driven and, on the other, there is the empirically driven approach of conversation theory [7]. It is this latter approach that has been strongly adopted in the analysis of the syntax used by the user subjects in the simulations. Every input from the 14 user subjects (7 from each year) that was greater than a single word has been subjected to analysis, with the exception of proper nouns such as the user subjects' names and addresses (usually in response to questions from the system subject for this information) which would need to be recognised by their context as not requiring parsing.

The first stage of this analysis was a very traditional parse [12] where each word was assigned as a part of speech (i.e. verb, noun, pronoun, adjective, adverb, auxiliary, preposition, conjunction). This data was represented as an ordered string of parts of speech. The next stage was to represent these strings in a phrase form. This was done on an iterative, trial and error basis, with the goal being to represent as many of the user subjects' inputs as possible in the minimum number of phrase structure orders. The strategy employed was to adjust the definition of a phrase so as to minimise the number of required phrase patterns.

A second and important bias adopted to make such a complex strategy possible was to work strictly in sequential order from left to right on the user subjects' inputs. Four basic phrase types were finally identified and these always occurred in the same order: (i) Adverbial phrase; (ii) Auxiliary Verb phrase; (iii) Noun phrase; (iv) Verb Phrase. An adverbial phrase may consist of a single adverb (e.g. HOW) or a multiple word adverb (e.g. NOT REALLY). An auxiliary verb phrase may consist of one of the 3 primary verbs (BE, DO or HAVE) or one of the 13 modal auxiliary verbs (e.g. CAN, MAY, MUST, NEED, etc.) [12] as well as the qualifying adverbs associated with the verb (e.g. why WON'T; what ELSE DO). A noun phrase consists of one or more nouns with their qualifying adjectives and combined by either a conjunction (e.g. DB2 AND DB3) or a preposition (e.g. EDUCATIONAL PACKAGES FOR MY PERSONAL USE).

Verb phrases were found to have a complex structure and their definition is linked to the left to right analysis strategy causing the empirical result that all user subject inputs terminate with a verb phrase except, of course, when the subjects' input, in response to a question, is just a noun phrase (e.g. ADVENTURE GAMES). Basically, verb phrases have been analysed in a manner very similar to that of the whole user subjects' inputs. The verb, which is the first non-auxiliary verb in the input, is pivotal to the verb phrase and critically divides the phrase into two sections. Prior to the verb there are two possible options: (i) an auxiliary verb; and/or (ii) what we have labelled 'Cell 1' and which may contain either a noun, adverb, preposition or a pronoun. The vast majority of user subjects' inputs possess only a single verb and this paper will concentrate on these single verb cases as, while there is no evidence from this research to suggest that multiple verb inputs are different in structure, they are sufficiently infrequent to make the full analysis of their patterns suspect. Where the verb is not the final word in such a single verb input there is a pattern of possible word types, all of which are optional, but which conform to a single order if present. This

108

post-verbial sequential pattern was found to be repeated up to three times. The order of the pattern is: adverb, conjunction, preposition, adjective(s), noun, pronoun (**NB:** there may be more than one adjective in each repetition of the post-verbial pattern).

The complete syntax is describe in Figure 2. It must be stressed that this syntax is the result of the left to right sequential analysis of the user subject's inputs and is strongly driven by the data, rather than by any theoretical model of grammar. The next section will briefly describe how well this syntactic model is able to describe the data.

Figure 2 This figure shows the basic syntactic structure of the user subjects' inputs. The four main phrases are listed in upper case and the indented lower case examples are listed as alternative structures. Options within structures are in round brackets () and repetitions are indicated by curly brackets {}, with a parameter indicating the number of possible repetitions before the bracket.

ADVERBIAL PHRASE

    Adverb

    Adverb Adverb

AUXILIARY PHRASE

    Verb

    (Adverb) Auxiliary (Adverb)

NOUN PHRASE

    Pronoun

    Adjective (Noun)

    Adjective (Noun) Preposition Adjective (Noun)

VERB PHRASE

(Auxiliary) (Cell 1) Verb (post-verbial phrase)

Cell 1 may contain either:

a noun; an adverb; a preposition; or a pronoun.

The post-verbial phrase has the structure:

X{(Adverb)} (Conjunction) (Preposition)

Y{(Adjective)} (Noun) (Pronoun)}

6 SYNTACTICAL ANALYSIS RESULTS

There were 349 user subjects' inputs subjected to analysis in the 1986 study and 316 in the 1987 study. In both sets of data, more than 90 per cent of the inputs could be classified at the level of the four, left to right, main phrase types into five basic patterns by the omission of some of these phrase types (see Table 2).

Phrase String	1986	1987
Adverbial Phrase | Noun Phrase | Verb Phrase	12%	7%
Auxiliary Verb Phrase | Noun Phrase | Verb Phrase	12%	14%
Noun Phrase | Verb Phrase	41%	44%
Noun Phrase	8%	10%
Verb Phrase	19%	16%
Total Percentage of all patterns analysed	92%	91%

Table 2. Summary of the patterns of main phrase type found in both the 1986 and 1987 studies and the percentage of the total number of user subjects' inputs accounted for by each pattern.

110

The individual data for these four main phrase types will be briefly presented before the next section turns to the consequences and utility of investigating natural language grammars in this fashion. In the 1986 study there were 42 adverbial phrases, of which all but three were composed of only a single adverb (93 per cent). There were only 22 in the 1987 study and again all but three were single adverbs (86 per cent). There were 42 auxiliary verb phrases in the 1986 study, of which 37 were composed of a single auxiliary verb (88 per cent) and the remaining six composed of an auxiliary verb with either an adverb before it (two cases), after it (two cases), or before and after it (one case). Similarly in the 1987 study there were 44 auxiliary verb phrases, of which 35 were composed of single auxiliary verbs (80 per cent), with all the exceptions being an adverb before the auxiliary verb.

In the 1986 study there were 255 noun phrases analysed and in the 1987 study there were 238. The most common form of the noun phrase consists of a single pronoun and accounted for 170 (67 per cent) and 173 (73 per cent) instances of noun phrases in the 1986 and 1987 studies respectively. The majority of the remaining instances can be categorised as an adjective followed by an optional noun. There were 64 instances of this in the 1986 study (25 per cent) and 48 in the 1987 one (20 per cent). These two noun phrase types thus account for 92 per cent and 93 per cent of all the noun phrase types.

As mentioned above, the verb phrases were structurally more complex than the rest and will be described in two stages: (i) the main verb and its precedents; and (ii) the post-verbial phrase. Table 3 summarises the main findings of the pattern associated with the verb and the two optional words that may precede it. While the use of Cell 1 is slightly messy, the pattern is relatively clear with respect to the left to right sequence. There was a total of 292 verb phrases subjected to analysis from the 1986 study and 255 in the 1987 study.

Auxiliary Verb	Cell 1	Verb	1986	1987
+	Noun	+	3%	4%
	Noun	+	< 1%	1%
+	Adverb	+	3%	8%
	Adverb	+	6%	5%
+	Preposition	+	4%	1%
	Preposition	+	1%	1%
+	Pronoun	+	10%	13%
+		+	15%	13%
		+	55%	51%

Total percentage of all patterns analysed   98%   97%

Table 3. Table showing the distribution in sequential, left to right order of the pre-verbial pattern found in both the 1986 and 1987 studies. A ' + ' indicates that a word type was present and a '-' that it was absent.

In the 1986 study, 50 verb phrases terminated with the main verb (17 per cent) and 46 (18 per cent) in the 1987 study. These user subjects' inputs thus had no post-verbial phrase. In the 1986 study 203 verb phrases (70 per cent) contained a single verb and in the 1987 study there were 155 single verb phrases (61 per cent). Thus in the 1986 study 13 per cent of the verb phrases contained multiple verbs and 21 per cent contained multiple verbs in the 1987 study. The analysis of these user subject inputs is not reported in this paper but, other than a considerable increase in analytical complexity, these multi-verb verb phrases do not appear to differ in their general syntactical pattern. Of the single verb phrases that have a post-verbial phrase it was found that there is a consistent sequential pattern to this phrase and that this pattern may be repeated up to three times (three repetitions accounts for 96 per cent and 94 per cent of all post-verbial phrase patterns for single verbs). The basic pattern is described in the previous analysis section. All of the elements of the pattern may be considered optional, though the actual number of possible patterns is relatively small and decreases as the repetition parameter X increases from 1 to 3: 15, 12 and 7 different patterns of options in the 1986 study and similarly 13, 12 and 7 in the 1987 study.

7 DISCUSSION

The earlier claims made on the strength of the pilot study data, [2] that when full natural language is available to expert system naive users they use only a very small subset of the language, are strongly supported by the additional data reported from the two replications of the original simulation pilot study.

First, and most obviously, the very small vocabulary size reported by Diaper [2] has been replicated and is so small that it is well within the storage limitations of all but the most modest home microcomputers. Even if the users' input vocabulary estimates from these simulations were in error by an order of magnitude, then the vocabulary would still be minute with respect to its potential size. It must be noted that all the vocabulary estimates are for words (and numbers) and not lexical items. So, for example, the plural form of a word is counted as different from its singular form. Thus any front-end to a machine language processing system that could deal with simple plurals and conjugate regular verbs would reduce the vocabulary storage requirements still further. Second, the very simple syntactic structure of the user inputs suggests that many of the difficult, and currently computationally impossible, aspects of automatic parsing may not be required for machines operating in a limited domain, a restriction that applies to all current expert systems. It therefore follows that if one wished to implement what would appear to be a full natural language processing user input interface to an expert system, then the research reported in this paper suggests that as far as the syntactical analysis of such users' inputs is concerned, most of what users will enter will be parsable by a machine using only currently available technology.

How could such a system work? One very simple method would be for the machine to first attempt to classify all the words as parts of speech using a stored look-up table. Even if the machine only managed to identify 50 per cent of the nouns, prepositions, conjunctions, adjectives etc., this would reduce enormously the likely classification of any other word on a simple probability basis. Furthermore, even within the general data presented in this paper, there are obvious rules that could operate within a typical, rule based expert system environment that could provide a considerable degree of predictive power about

113

words that could not be immediately classified (perhaps because they may, in different examples, be classified differently). For example, most adverbial phrases and auxiliary phrases in fact consist of a single word which should not be too difficult to classify. Adverbs and Auxiliary verbs at the beginning of a users' input are, not surprisingly, mutually exclusive but, more interestingly, if they are present they are always followed by both a noun phrase and a verb phrase, whereas if they are not present, then the input can consist of either a noun phrase or a verb phrase or both.

An alternative, and in the authors' opinion preferable, application of this research might be for the design of a user language which was naturalistic and hence easy to learn. The advantage of this approach is that the number of instances where the system will fail to parse users' inputs will be minimised. Furthermore, the users, not believing that the machine is processing natural language, will be less tempted to use unnecessary, syntactically complex inputs.

It is an open, yet empirically testable question how restricted such a new language could be and still satisfy users' requirements by providing them with a language of sufficient power that their performance was indistinguishable from those users who have available to them, via the Wizard of Oz technique, full natural language.

It is the authors' belief that a well designed, naturalistic language specifically tailored for human-expert system dialogues should be capable of providing safer and more efficient interactions between users and expert system than any sub-language variant of human-human natural language. Such a tailored language, of course, will need to incorporate more than just the syntactical aspects, described in this chapter, if it is to realise its full potential. However, the results of the two reported simulation studies can be used by future language designers as a basis on which to construct such novel human-expert system languages and they would start with the knowledge that the grammar of such languages was both psychologically compatible with users' existing natural language knowledge and also computationally feasible.

This paper has sought only to demonstrate that the structure of users' inputs is generally highly constrained and that the range of patterns of syntactic word class are very restricted. Further work on the data, particularly on the

114

post-verbial phrase is still in progress. In particular, the possibilities of automated rule induction from the data is being investigated.

8   ACKNOWLEDGEMENT

This research was supported by a grant under the British Government's Alvey Programme (Project MMI/098 - The Human-Expert System Interface).

9   REFERENCES

1   Diaper, D (1984), An Approach to IKBS Development Based on a Review of 'Conceptual Structures: Information Processing in Mind and Machine' by JF Sowa. Behaviour and Information Technology, 3, 3, 249-255.

2   Diaper, D (1986a), Identifying the Knowledge Requirements of an Expert System's Natural Language Processing Interface. In M Harrison and A Monk (eds). People and Computers: Designing for Usability. Cambridge University Press, UK.

3   Diaper, D (1986b), Will Expert Systems be Safe? In the Proceedings of the Second International Expert System Conference. Learned Information, Oxford, UK.

4   Diaper, D (1987a), A People Orientated Method for Expert System Specification. In T Addis, J Boose and B Gaines (eds) Proceedings of the First European Workshop on Knowledge Acquisition for Knowledge-Based Systems. Reading University.

5   Diaper, D (1987b), Designing Systems for People: Beyond User Centred Design. In Software Engineering - Proceedings of the SHARE European Association Anniversary Meeting 1987. 283-302.

6   Grishman, R and Kittredge, R (eds) (1986), Analyzing Language in Restricted Domains: Sublanguage Description and Processing. Lawrence Erlbaum, Hillsdale, NJ.

7   Levinson, S (1983), Pragmatics. Cambridge University Press, UK.

8   Long, J (1987), Information Technology and Home-Based Services: Improving the Usability of Teleshopping.   In Blacker, F and Osborne, D (eds). Information Technology and People. The British Psychological Society, UK.

9   Norman, D (1984a), Four Stages of User Activity. In Shackel, B (ed.). Interact'84 First IFIP Conference on 'Human-Computer Interaction'. Elsevier, Holland.

10 Norman, D (1984b), Stages and Levels of Human-Machine Dialogue. International Journal of Man Machine Studies,21, 365-375

11 Norman, D and Draper, S (1987), User Centred System Design. Lawrence Erlbaum, Hillsdale, NJ.

12 Onions, C (1971), Modern English Syntax. Routledge and Kegan Paul, UK.

13 Reichman, R (1985), Getting Computers to Talk Like You and Me: Discourse Context, Focus, and Semantics (An ATN Model). MIT, Cambridge Mass.

14 Sparck Jones, K (1985), Natural Language Interfaces for Expert Systems. In Bramer, M (ed) Research and Developments in Expert Systems. Cambridge University Press, UK.

15 Warren, C (1985), The Wizard of Oz Technique: A Comparison between Natural and Command Languages for Communicating with Expert Systems. Unpublished Master of Science(Ergonomics) Dissertation, University of London.

Chapter 8
VODIS - A Voice Operated Database Enquiry System

J PECKHAM,
Logica Cambridge Ltd

1   INTRODUCTION

With the development of appropriate capabilities in speech input and output technology the telephone is potentially a ubiquitous computer terminal. Although the application of stored voice response and text to speech synthesis coupled with touch tone input is slowly gaining acceptance, this combination is ultimately limited by the range of inputs available on the push button 'phone. In addition, it will be some years before the rotary dial phone is completely replaced, particularly in the domestic market (at least in the UK), thus limiting the potential penetration of this type of terminal for applications such as information retrieval. There are therefore many attractions in the integration of speech recognition into automated information services. For the occasional non-professional user the technology would be required to perform adequately with no specific user enrolment although some 'on the fly' speaker adaption may be possible. For a more regular user some initial enrolment may be acceptable.

In making progress in the development of voice operated information systems there are, however, other significant issues to be addressed apart from making the technology perform adequately over the PSTN with or without enrolment. These issues relate to the flexibility of the user interface and its ability to cope with untrained users.

The speech input applications which currently are the most successful, such as parts inspection, are largely well constrained and have a co-operative and trained user base. Input is mostly menu driven and restricted to a small vocabulary with severe grammatical constraints, sometimes a single word response.   Incorrect recognition in these cases requires both detection and correction by the user.

As part of the UK Government's Alvey research programme, Logica collaborated with British Telecom and Cambridge University to develop a more conversational speech interface with intelligent dialogue control. The primary aim of the project was to investigate the feasibility of voice-based, man-machine interaction with untrained users, by producing a prototype Voice Operated Database Inquiry System (VODIS) for use by members of the public over the telephone. A frame representation language called UFL, developed by Dr SJ Young (Cambridge University) under sponsorship from BT prior to the Alvey project, forms the basis of an intelligent dialogue management system (Ref. 1). This together with Logos, one of the worlds first continuous speech recognition systems developed by Logica in 1981 (Ref. 2), and a text-to-speech synthesis system developed by BT provided the starting point for the project in early 1985. Research effort was primarily directed towards the improvement, extension and integration of these components to achieve robust dialogue between user and machine. The project developed essentially two systems, one a real time prototype for field trials, the other a computer simulation which exploited more powerful linguistic processing. Some of the major goals within the project were the following:

- dialogue design and human factors trials

- development of speech recognition for telephone use and speaker independence

- linguistic processing making use of word lattices

- improvements in naturalness of text-to-speech synthesis, both intonation and quality

An initial speaker-independent prototype (optimised for males speakers only) has been produced and underwent trials early in 1988 demonstrating considerable success for male users in simple train timetable enquiries. The project will be completed in November 1988 at a total cost of around £2.3m.

2   SYSTEM ARCHITECTURE

A block diagram of the VODIS architecture is shown in figure 1.

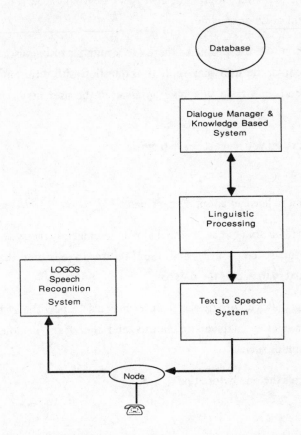

Figure 1. Vodis Architecture

In general the system initiates the dialogue by announcing itself and asking a question. The application that has been chosen for the project is train timetable enquiries.   A finite state network defining the expected word sequences as responses from the user is then generated and loaded into Logos to reduce the pattern matching search space. Stored patterns may be of whole words or parts of words and the recognition output is the best interpretation of the input in terms of the allowable concatenation of sound patterns. This output is then analysed by a parser and converted into an abstract representation which is passed to the dialogue controller.

In practice the output from the recogniser may contain errors in the form of unrecognised words in the sentence or words which the user did not in fact speak. Although these problems may be diminished as the algorithms for speech signal interpretation are improved, there will always be unavoidable errors due to such factors as transient noise on the line.

In addition to these problems there are a number of linguistic issues to be handled, for example, the user may reply to a question with different information than that requested. In a train timetable application the user may respond to the question

'Where do you want to leave from?'

with a reply such as

'I want to leave at about nine o'clock.'

In order to be able to handle the dialogue intelligently the system should be able to switch focus temporarily and then return to eliciting the remaining information necessary to access the database.

As the dialogue progresses the user may also expect the system to know what information had been given previously and therefore be able to resolve superficial ambiguities such as

'When's the one before that?'

and

'When does it arrive?'

In the context of human-to-human dialogue these issues of course appear trivial but in the case of a machine based system are fundamental in achieving an interface that is efficient and suitable for an untrained and possibly non-technical user, avoiding constant correction and repetition.

3   DIALOGUE MANAGEMENT

In order to achieve an acceptable level of interaction with the user, given the potential errors, ambiguities and focus switching that may arise, a powerful dialogue manager is required capable of flexibility and response in an intelligent manner. In principle a sequential state machine could be designed to construct the simple data structure (shown in Figure 2) required to access a database. However the range of possible user replies coupled with the uncertainty caused by recognition errors, leads to a combinatorial explosion in the number of states required. The dialogue management component in VODIS has been implemented with a different approach using a frame based language called UFL and a data driven control strategy. Frames have been used for dialogue control in text based systems, but little use has so far been made of them for speech, where the problems are somewhat different in that the input may contain significant errors.

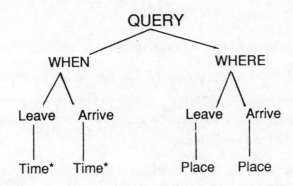

Figure 2. A data structure for a train timetable query.

A frame is a data structure consisting of a number of named slots which hold the data values of the frame as well as procedures which may be executed on certain conditions, such as instantiation of a slot or frame. Frames are linked together by a special slot called the 'ako' (meaning 'a kind of') which thus allows frames to inherit slots from a higher frame.

In building a dialogue, a set of frames is defined which represent the structure of the data to be acquired from the user. To illustrate the concept a simple set of frames is shown in Figure 3.

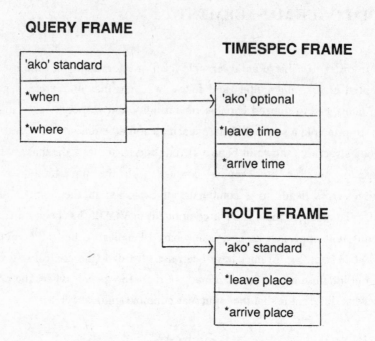

QUERY FRAME

'ako' standard
*when
*where

TIMESPEC FRAME

'ako' optional
*leave time
*arrive time

ROUTE FRAME

'ako' standard
*leave place
*arrive place

Figure 3. A simple set of frames representing data to be acquired from the user.

The goal of the system is to instantiate the top level query frame. This is accomplished when all of the starred slots have been filled in the case of a 'standard' frame, or one of the slots in an 'option' frame. The 'when' and 'where' slots are linked to a 'timespec' and 'route' frame.

A special procedure is included in a frame to provide a mechanism for generating questions to the user and this procedure if present, is executed before attempting to fill the slots. This provides considerable flexibility in the dialogue design, allowing selection of the points in the hierarchy at which questions may be asked. In general, the top levels would generate more general questions than the lower, allowing more flexibility in the user's reply. However in difficult circumstances more specific questions, perhaps only requiring a one word answer, can help overall dialogue recovery.

The frame approach avoids a rigid question and answer sequence by allowing the user to switch the focus of the dialogue. This is accomplished by activating a frame when it is referenced and attempting to instantiate the most recently activated frame first. If a user's response references a frame other than the one currently active, then the focus of the dialogue shifts to that frame until it is completed before returning to the original frame. To illustrate how this works, suppose that in the course of instantiating the 'route' frame the system asked the question

'where do you want to leave from?'

and the reply was

'I want to leave from Cambridge about 9 o'clock.'

The 'where.leave' slot would be filled with 'Cambridge' and the focus would shift to the 'timespec' frame. If the actual time had not been recognised the 'when.leave' slot would be filled with a null value, activating the frame but showing it not yet completed. This would then result in a question to the user such as

'About what time do you want to leave?'

On completion of this frame the system would return to instantiation of the 'route' frame, thus shifting the focus of the conversation again.

Another important aspect of the dialogue management is the detection of and recovery from errors (apart from non-recognition of a word). The current system handles errors in two ways by

- consistency checking
- confirmatory dialogue (explicit or implicit)

Consistency checking is carried out when a frame has been instantiated and includes checking, for example, that departure and destination station are different.

Confimatory dialogue also takes place when a frame has been completed and can be either explicit or implicit. For example, if the user had requested times for travel to London the system might reply with

' to London?'

in rising intonation. Implicit confirmation occurs when previous user input (as below) is contained within a reply, for example

' what time do you want to arrive in London?'

If the user responds with a time then the destination is confirmed, otherwise the user may reply

' I want to go to Cambridge not London'

The inheritance mechanism is particularly useful in this context, allowing a general confirmation strategy to be defined as a frame which is then inherited by more specific frames dealing with specific types of information such as times or places.

4   LINGUISTIC PROCESSING

The Linguistic Processing module provides the interface between the frame based dialogue manager and the speech recogniser. In the current implementation there are two major components, a semantic parser and a syntax generator.

The semantic parser processes the word string from the recogniser to produce an abstract semantic structure suitable for use by the dialogue manager. The advantage of this approach is that partially recognised responses (where a particular word fails to match well enough) as well as those containing errors can usually be processed and transferred to the dialogue manager for interpretation.

A syntax generator is used to compile appropriate finite state networks 'on the fly' whenever a response is expected from the user. These rules are derived from a central dictionary and grammar and are determined by all the expected responses to a particular question. When recognition is performing well the range of allowable responses is much larger than when recognition performance is poor and in the limit may be constrained to yes/no replies to very specific questions.

The model II simulation (Ref. 3) is substantially different from the trials model in that it makes use of word lattices with word scores derived from the acoustic pattern matching stage in Logos.

5 SPEECH RECOGNITION

The speech recognition system is based on Logos, developed by Logica for the UK Government's Joint Speech Research Unit in 1981. Aimed primarily at the research market, a number of systems have been sold since then both in the UK and Europe, for applications research. The technology is also available for licence and agreements have been signed with Racal Acoustics and Smiths Industries (Aerospace Group).

Logos uses a parallel processing architecture combined with special purpose pipelined processing to allow the simultaneous matching of several hundred words in real time (see Figure 1). The basic techniques used in Logos include a spectral feature representation of words or subword segments with a one-pass dynamic programming algorithm employing partial traceback to determine the most likely word sequence. The word sequences are constrained by a finite state network which includes silences to allow pauses at appropriate points in a sentence and 'wildcards' to represent poor matches or non-vocabulary items. The algorithms and architecture will also allow a vocabulary to be defined by a set of sub-word patterns such as diphones and the hardware was designed to allow stochastic models to be run. Current research is directed towards improvement of the word models utilised in speaker dependent recognition (fluent speech including co-articulation) as well as speaker independent matching techniques.

Logos contains a number of processing stages designed to deal with factors such as background noise and to improve the spectral feature representation used in the word patterns, particularly emphasising regions of spectral change. Further work is currently in progress within the VODIS project to accomodate the inherent variability in speech signal quality received over the PSTN. A major consideration is the differences in 'loudness' between calls, which may originate from the line itself or the positioning of the telephone handset with respect to the user's mouth. The perceived difference in 'loudness' may include spectral tilt as well as overall level variations.

The second phase of research concerning the Linguistic Processing module will make use of a much closer link with the acoustic pattern processing stages within Logos. This link has been accomplished with a high speed parallel interface (IEEE 488 or DEC DR11-W) and supporting software and protocols allowing a host to read and write to all areas of data memory in Logos. Most of the pattern matching is carried out in software running on either the Front End Processor (spectrum processing), 12 parallel processors and a Control Processor. This arrangement means that the host can use Logos as a powerful pattern processor engine able to access alternative matches and scores, modifying data and even initiating reprocessing with modified data or parameters if required.

While the largely software-oriented approach of Logos makes it particularly suitable for applications research such as illustrated by VODIS, studies carried out by Logica have demonstrated that the algorithms can be transferred to 2-3 VLSI circuits whilst still retaining the overall processing capacity.

6   MESSAGE GENERATION

All output to the user is delivered by a text-to-speech synthesis system called BTalk based on work carried out at the Joint Speech Research Unit and further developed by British Telecom. Text-to-speech synthesis has the advantage of providing more freedom in the specification of output messages than digitally stored responses but suffers from limitations in quality and prosody. The aim of research in this area within VODIS is to improve both the voice quality and the prosody, particularly intonation. Better intonation contours at the phrase level and above will be derived from deep structure knowledge of the dialogue itself (Ref. 4).

7   HUMAN FACTORS RESEARCH AND TRIALS

All of the basic technology development in the VODIS project was supported by a number of human factors studies on the nature of dialogue in inquiry situations, with the results being fed into the system dialogue strategy and design. The studies carried out to date include the capture and analysis of two types of conversation:

1 Unconstrained human-human conversations in natural enquiry situations.

2 Constrained enquiries where the enquirer was provided with a query scenario.

From these studies a dialogue model was derived and tested using a simulated query system and further refinements implemented. Analysis of the naturally occurring conversations has also provided valuable ground rules for confirmation and correction in the VODIS dialogue. An example VODIS dialogue is shown in Figure 4, whilst Figure 5 for comparison is a transcript of a simple, but naturally occurring enquiry. The dialogue in Figure 4 illustrates some of the strategies discussed previously for handling errors, ambiguities and confirmation.

Other issues being addressed relate to the attitudes of general public users to a machine based interaction. One set of studies for example indicated a tendency for users on simulated machine interaction (using degraded natural speech) to adopt a more formal and constrained conversation. This has some interesting implications for the quality of the speech output to be chosen in that a machine-like quality provides a continuous reminder that the interaction is machine based, thus potentially reducing the complexity of the user input to be handled by the system.

Human factors trials of the first VODIS model were completed early in 1988 and demonstrated 100 per cent successful completion of transactions for male users in a single train journey enquiry. Female users (for whom the system was not optimised in terms of speaker independence) fared much less well, as did also both male and female for more complex multiple journey enquiries. To facilitate analysis of the trials the VODIS architecture includes transaction and performance monitoring capabilities.

8 FUTURE WORK

Following on from the VODIS system, Logica has developed a new architecture based on the use of Hidden Markov Models (HMMs) of acoustic/phonetic units for the generation of phonetic and word lattices. A maximum likelihood error correcting parser has also been developed which interfaces with a Prolog version of the Dialogue Manager.

These techniques and others will be developed further within an ESPRIT project called SUNDIAL led by Logica and involving several partners from France, Germany and Italy. The goal of the project is to develop speech understanding to support oral dialogues over the telephone for applications such as computer based information services.

9 ACKNOWLEDGEMENTS

The author would like to thank British Telecom and Cambridge University Engineering Department for their assistance in preparing this paper, in particular Dr Steven Young of Cambridge University for material supplied on UFL.

10 REFERENCES

1 Proctor, CE and Young, SJ 'Dialogue Control in Speech Interfaces', Presented at NATA ASI, Corsica, 1987 and forthcoming.

2 Peckham, JB et al., 'A real time hardware continuous speech recognition system', Proc ICASSP 1982.

3 Young, SJ et al., 'Speech Recognition in VODIS II', Proc ICASSP, 1988.

4 Youd, NJ and Fallside, F 'Generating words and prosody for use in speech synthesis', Proc. European Conference on Speech Technology, Sept. 1987.

Chapter 9
Speech Language Translation

M G STEER and F W M STENTIFORD,
British Telecom Research Laboratories

1   INTRODUCTION

To be able to lift up a telephone handset, dial abroad via a language translation system and freely converse with a foreigner whilst both parties are speaking in their mother tongue is perhaps the ultimate goal in automatic speech translation. This was suggested as a possible telephone service of the future by NEC at Telecom '83 [1].

By converging the technologies of speech recognition, speech synthesis and machine translation the possibility of automatic speech translation could become a reality [2]. Indeed, much can be be done today using commercially available speech recognisers and synthesisers together with innovative software [3].

This paper describes the research behind and the implementation of a prototype speech driven language translation system developed at British Telecom Research Laboratories (BTRL), Martlesham Heath, UK.

2   REQUIREMENTS OF A SPEECH TRANSLATION SYSTEM

An automatic speech translation system must clearly meet the following criteria :

- The system must operate without the intervention of a human translator.

- It must translate quickly, avoiding any lengthy delays, so that a telephone dialogue can be established.

- The user must have confidence that he or she has been correctly recognised.

- The accuracy of translation must be guaranteed.

In addition, simultaneous translation into several languages would be an advantage.

Unfortunately, existing text language translation packages are unable to meet these criteria and fall short of the requirements in the following ways:

- Most packages have been designed as aids for professional translators, producing an output which has to be post-edited before being presentable in the target language.

- Most packages are either interactive or operate in a slow batch processing mode, neither of which is suitable for speech operation over the public switched telephone network.

- Translation packages tend to be unreliable, as idioms and other exceptions can easily cause erroneous output. The user has no guarantee that the output is correctly translated.

- Existing systems are CPU intensive. It would be an uneconomical proposition to offer an automated service requiring one computer system per translation direction.

In contrast, the advantages of a phrasebook oriented translation system are fivefold:-

- The actual translation can be carried out in advance, thus only a fast look-up operation is required at run time.

- The user can have recognition confirmation by having the system echo the source phrasebook text back to him or her before proceeding with translation.

- The phrasebook would contain accurate translations thus giving an acceptable output in the target language.

- A multiple phrasebook could give simultaneous output into several languages.

- Phrasebooks can be compiled by skilled linguists who need not have any knowledge of computing.

Disadvantages of a phrasebook include:-

- The system is unable to handle expressions which are not adequately represented in the phrasebook.

- Certain variables, such as dates, require careful handling to implement a phrasebook which has enough flexibility to be of practical use.

- A phrasebook needs to be tailored to a particular domain of discourse such as holiday booking or car-hire.

3 TECHNIQUES USED FOR IMPLEMENTING A SPEECH DRIVEN PHRASEBOOK

A simplified diagram of a speech translation system is shown in Fig 1.

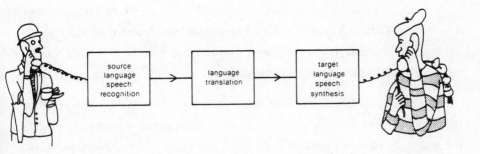

Figure 1. Speech translation system

It can be seen that the key components required are:

(i)   Speech recognition for input

(ii) Language translation process

(iii) Speech synthesis for output

The speech input and output devices could either be duplicated or reconfigurable to allow for bi-directional conversations.

131

It should be noted that the technologies behind these three components are still being researched both within British Telecom and at numerous companies, universities and other research institutes around the world. However, commercially available products do exist for speech recognition and speech synthesis.

Text-to-speech synthesis systems have a long way to go before they sound perfectly natural, but their output is considered adequate for the time being in a speech translation system if the users of that system are suitably motivated.

Furthermore, speech recognisers are prone to errors, particularly in a demanding application such as speech translation. No recogniser exists which is capable of handling a suitably large vocabulary at a level of accuracy which would retain the original grammatical structure of a phrase for subsequent processing. In addition, the very nature of spoken language itself is often informal and non-grammatical. These facts indicate that parsing techniques, which would reject an input if it differed from the grammar by even one word, would be inappropriate in this application.

A speech recogniser can, however, be used in a word spotting mode, searching for a carefully selected set of keywords which effectively extract necessary information. The number of words to be recognised will certainly be much less than the number of words in a set of phrases, and in fact only the keywords which will successfully distinguish between all the different phrases need be recognised.

The performance of the translation system as a whole, therefore, rests on the ability of those keywords to correctly distinguish between phrases. The greater the separation of phrases achieved, the greater the tolerance to recognition errors.

A possible translating telephone arrangement using these techniques is shown in Fig 2.

4   KEYWORD SELECTION CRITERION

For a given phrasebook there will be N uniquely identifiable words. Software running on a mini-computer selects a subset of M keywords (from total, N) where M is the number of words which can be handled by the recogniser. These M keywords are chosen to optimally separate the given phrases.

In theory, a phrasebook could be accessed using a minimum number of keywords if each keyword is present in orthogonally different binary partitions of the set of phrases. In practice, the phrases are predefined and hence this optimum cannot be reached, but it does indicate a useful criterion for keyword selection.

The ability of any candidate keyword to separate phrases is dependent on the set of keywords already selected, therefore an iterative search procedure is required. Research into feature extraction for pattern recognition has shown that it is a prime requirement that such features act independently of each other to achieve optimum results. This, together with a formal definition of a search criterion is given in reference 4.

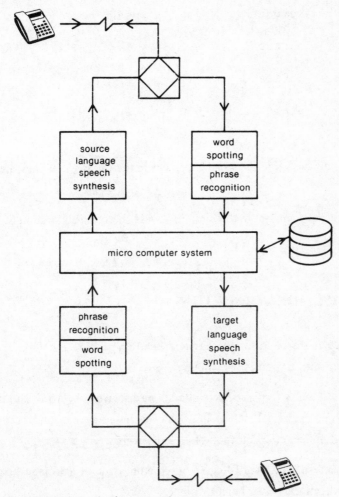

Figure 2. The translating telephone

A simplified example of an orthogonal set of keywords is shown using the three phrases below.

1   Whom do you want to speak to?

2   I cannot hear you.

3   May I speak to Mr Smith please?

Three keywords, 'you', 'speak', and 'I' could be selected to give the following phrase reference matrix.

keyword	'you'	'speak'	'I'
phrase 1	1	1	0
phrase 2	1	0	1
phrase 3	0	1	1

Where a '1' indicates that the word is present in the phrase, a '0' indicates that it is nc*.

It can be seen that in this simplified case there is a separation of 2 between any two phrases.

5   PHRASE IDENTIFICATION

Once a set of keywords has been chosen, a phrase reference matrix is generated and stored within the computer.

To use the system a speaker utters a phrase, word by word, and the speech recogniser 'spots' keywords. A response pattern similar to one row of the reference matrix is built up from the detection of these keywords.

On uttering the word 'enter' or its equivalent in a foreign language the phrase identification process begins.

The response pattern is compared to the reference pattern for each phrase in the phrasebook (i.e. each row of the reference matrix). If an exact match is found the corresponding phrase is echoed back to the user for confirmation. If no exact match is found the phrase whose reference pattern has the closest match of keyword presences is chosen as the most likely phrase and is echoed back to the user for confirmation.

6   RESULTS

As mentioned previously, the performance of this translation system is dependent on the separation of phrases achieved with the chosen set of keywords.

A set of several hundred business letter phrases has been analysed and it has been found that using just 100 keywords virtually all the phrases differed from each other by three keywords or more. This gives the translation system as a whole a high immunity to speech recognition errors.

In practice it has been found that up to half of the words in any given phrase can be mis-recognised before the wrong phrase is selected.

It has also been found that the keywords chosen closely resemble the words obtained from a frequency of occurrence list for that particular phrasebook.

An example of the ten most useful keywords in English, French, German and Spanish for a hotel booking phrasebook is as follows:

	ENGLISH	FRENCH	GERMAN	SPANISH
1	the	chambre	sie	el
2	a	vous	ein	habitacion
3	I	de	ich	de
4	you	est	zimmer	una
5	to	je	fur	hotel
6	room	pour	hotel	tiene
7	is	une	wir	para
8	hotel	a	das	la
9	for	la	ist	por
10	of	il	bitte	lo

7   PHRASE VARIATION

In order to implement a practical system based on a phrasebook careful attention must be paid to the handling of certain variables. These include dates, times, prices, persons' names and other proper nouns. For example:

- I would like to book a room for the night of 8th December 1987.

- I expect to arrive about 7pm.

- A single room with bath will cost £55.

- My name is Mr Steer.

- This is the Royal hotel.

Obviously in the above examples the dates, times and prices require translation before synthesis in the target language; the proper nouns do not. It would be incorrect, for example, to translate 'Mr White' as 'Monsieur Blanc' in French rather than 'Monsieur White'.

These parameters are handled by simultaneously recognising and storing each individual word in the spoken phrase. Then, assuming that the correct phrase has been selected by the system, two processes may take place:

(i) Proper nouns can simply be coded and transmitted to the receiving end for embedding in the foreign speech output.

(ii) Other parameters requiring translation can be handled by a second recognition pass. Having already chosen the phrase the location of a parameter is known, or can be deduced. New speech templates corresponding to that parameter can be loaded into the recogniser and the appropriate stored words replayed for recognition.

This two-pass process effectively increases the recognisable vocabulary of the system without degrading its recognition performance.

Additionally, these sub-vocabularies may be easily increased to include any other type of parameter appropriate to a particular phrasebook.

8 PROTOTYPE SYSTEM HARDWARE AND SOFTWARE

The prototype is based on two BT Merlin personal computers (PCs) linked via a simple datalink. Each PC contains commercially available speech recognition and speech synthesis hardware, and will handle one language at any one time. The serial datalink between the two computers could equally be a connection over the public switched telephone network with a data modem connected at each end.

One PC is initialised to recognise and synthesise one language, the other computer a different language. At present these languages may be any pair of English, French, German or Spanish. Shortly Italian and Swedish will be added.

Assume for example that English and French have been selected: To use the system an Englishman enters a phrase into his computer, uttering each word clearly and in an isolated word fashion. The phrase is terminated by saying 'enter'. The computer then selects a phrase, processes any parameters, and echoes the chosen phrase to the user via the screen and speech synthesiser with a 'Do you mean ...'. If the phrase has been correctly identified, or is similar in meaning to the original spoken phrase the user can accept it by replying 'yes'. If the phrase did not convey the user's intended meaning it may then be rejected and another attempt made.

If the reply was in the affirmative the relevant phrase information is transmitted to the receiving end. At this end the corresponding French phrase is selected, any parameters inserted and the complete phrase is displayed on the screen and synthesised. The French recipient then has the option of re-hearing the synthesised output if required.

The process is repeated in the opposite direction and a dialogue can take place.

It should be noted that although the system is phrasebook oriented it is extremely robust to errors. These may occur from the speech recogniser itself, but equally may originate from the user. The system does not require the user to know the exact contents of the phrasebook. Provided the spoken phrase is close enough to one of the stored phrases then usually a phrase containing the intended meaning will be chosen. An example of this could be:

Spoken phrase (keywords in capitals)

- PLEASE WOULD YOU reserve me A single ROOM WITH bath.

Chosen phrase from phrasebook

- I WOULD like TO book A single ROOM WITH bath PLEASE.

Although the spoken phrase differs from the stored phrase by two keywords (TO, YOU), a minimum phrase separation of three keywords ensures that this stored phrase with the intended meaning is selected.

9 APPLICATIONS

The possible applications for such a system are only beginning to be realised but they include:

- Holiday booking

- International carhire

- Messaging between international telephone operators or linesmen

- Air traffic control

- Inter-business communications

- Channel tunnel messaging

- Immigration offices

In fact, any area where simple message communication is required and a suitable phrasebook can be tailored to suit could become a possible application.

10 FUTURE DEVELOPMENTS

At present the speech input uses isolated word speaker dependent technology. That is, the user must train the recogniser to his voice before using the system, and when speaking to the recogniser must pause between each word. Although connected word recognisers are available commercially they tend to yield a higher error rate in this word spotting application and do not provide other useful information such as the number of words spoken.

Further developments in this area will lead towards better speech recognisers capable of accepting fluent input and perhaps not requiring an exhaustive training sequence before use.

There is also research into developing better, more natural sounding speech synthesisers, the ultimate goal here being to match the speech output to the voice of the originator or any other speaker for that matter!

11 CONCLUSIONS

A speech driven language translation system has been developed which allows translation of spoken phrases between a number of European languages. The system is phrasebook based, overcoming many of the pitfalls associated with some text based machine translation systems. Certain flexibility in use has been catered for by the special handling of phrase parameters such as dates, times and persons' names.

The system has been designed to make full use of existing technology whilst having an in-built robustness to errors from both the speech recogniser and the user.

There are a number of suitable applications for this system and a potential for many more.

12   ACKNOWLEDGEMENT

Acknowledgement is made to the Director of Research of British Telecom for permission to publish this paper.

13 REFERENCES

1   Uenohara, M, 'Speech Products and their Applications in Japan', Speech Tech. '85, April 1985.

2   Fujisaki, H, International Symposium on Prospects and Problems of Interpreting Telephony, Tokyo, 12th April, 1986.

3   Steer, M G, 'A   Speech Driven Language Translation System', European Conference on Speech Technology, Edinburgh, 2nd to 4th September 1987.

4   Steniford, FWM, 'Automatic Feature Design for Optical Character Recognition using an Evolutionary Search   Procedure', IEEE Transactions on Pattern Analysis and Machine Intelligence, Vol. PAMI-7, No. 3, May 1985.

Chapter 10
Speech Simulation
Studies - Performance and Dialogue

A F NEWELL,
Microcomputer Centre, University of Dundee

1   INTRODUCTION

A popular application for Natural Language Understanding Systems is in conjunction with speech recognition machine technology. Speech is claimed to be the 'natural' method by which human beings communicate, and therefore a particularly appropriate mechanism for inputting data into machines. The links between speech input systems and natural language systems are seen to be very close and in both directions. That is:

i) Natural language structures are thought to be more appropriate to spoken input than written input, and

ii) It is claimed that speech input systems would benefit from being able to understand natural language structures rather than being limited by artificial syntactical constraints.

Authors such as Underwood, Newell and Shneiderman, however, have questioned the assumptions which are made about both speech and natural language. Underwood (1984) comments that

'..(the) facile argument..that, as speech is man's most natural form of communication, spoken communication with computers must be worth doing..is no longer sufficient'.

Underwood has expanded his views with particular reference to the use of speech to interact with Intelligent Knowledge Based Systems, in Underwood (1983). Newell (1984) in a paper entitled 'Speech: the Natural Method of Man-Machine Communication?' discusses the various ways in which speech is used in human-human communication and contrasts this with the requirements for human-computer interaction. Shneiderman (1987) comments that: 'So much research has been invested in natural language interaction systems that undoubtedly some successes will emerge, but widespread use may not develop because the alternatives may be more appealing'.

Shneiderman goes on to make a more general point, which applies to much research activity in the area of human-computer interaction, that is that: 'more rapid progress can be made if carefully controlled experimental tests are used to discover the designs, users and tasks for which N.L.I. is most beneficial'.

2   EMPIRICAL STUDIES

Unfortunately there is a dearth of empirical data on the acceptability of speech and natural language systems. To a large extent this is because of the state of the technology. Neither speech recognition nor natural language processing systems are currently good enough for human beings to have spoken 'conversations' with machines which can in any way be described as 'natural'. Indeed this is often given as the reason for the poor market penetration of speech technology to date. It thus not immediately obvious that current technology is appropriate for experimental tests on speech driven natural language systems.

There is, however, one technique which has not been very popular in this field to date, but does have great promise in investigations of the potential usability of such systems. The technique is that of simulation. In the case of investigations into natural language and speech input systems, an appropriate simulation technique is that described as 'Wizard-of-Oz' (Baum, 1974) or PNAMBIC ('Pay No Attention to the Man Behind the Curtain' (Bernstein, 1987)) simulations. In these cases, a human being performs those tasks for which current technology is inadequate, the human operator being able to out-perform machines both as speech recognition devices, and natural language processors, by a substantial margin.

One of the only major studies of this type within a speech recognition environment was the series of experiments reported by Gould in 1983. Gould simulated a 'listening typewriter' by a concealed operator who typed the words spoken onto a QWERTY keyboard and these were subsequently displayed to the subject in the experiment. Although the experiments provided a wealth of data, there have been no reports of them being replicated. Johnson (1987) used a different and ingenious technique for examining the acceptability of listening typewriters. He used a form of PNAMBIC simulation but, instead of the experiment being performed interactively, Johnson produced a video which showed an executive apparently using a listening typewriter. This video was shown to potential users of such technology and they were asked for their views. One of the more disturbing findings of this study was that, although the participants were initially very impressed, the perceived value of the system fell dramatically after they had discussed the video in groups. Sub-groups also concluded that the system would be more appropriate to other sub-groups than to themselves! (The sub-groups were executives, secretaries, and technologists).

The author has also begun an investigation into the usability of listening typewriters for creative writing tasks using the PNAMBIC model, but his experiments are of the interactive type (Newell et al,1987).

3   PILOT EXPERIMENTS INTO A NATURAL LANGUAGE SPEECH INTERFACE

An initial attempt to ask the question whether speech is a 'natural' method of controlling a word processor was combined with an investigation of the appropriateness of a natural language command structure for the dialogue. There is little attempt in the literature to define 'natural' as in the phrase 'speech is the natural method of man-machine interaction' and Newell (1984) has discussed this essentially non-trivial question. For the purposes of our first experiment, however, we assumed that if an interface was 'natural' it would be very easy to use and require no training on the part of the user. Although this hypothesis is open to question the results from the experiment proved to be of significant interest.

We performed two pilot experiments using a PNAMBIC simulation of a listening typewriter. In both cases the subjects were told that we were simulating a listening typewriter, but were given no other instructions as to how it operated. The 'person behind the curtain' used a standard word processing package (LEX) and was asked to attempt to obey the instructions given verbally by the subjects. Thus she could be considered to be acting as a speech recognition machine as well as a highly sophisticated natural language processor.

A total of 14 University students and research workers were used as subjects. They were asked to speak into the microphone and the words they dictated would appear on the screen. Any commands they gave would be acted upon but they were given no advice or training on what commands should be used or how such commands should be phrased.

We initially asked four subjects to perform a copy dictation task. The subjects were asked to copy-dictate a number of business letters, an example of which is shown in Figure 1A. Our subjects found significant difficulties in copy-dictating these letters. There were major problems both in trying to format the letters, and in correcting errors using the voice alone in a unstructured way. Figure 1B shows an example of a complete transcript of the dictation which shows some of the difficulties found by one of our subjects.

It may be argued that the problems in this experiment were caused by the task being a copy-dictation which was not appropriate for a listening typewriter. We thus moved on to a creative writing task for the remaining ten subjects. They were asked to dictate a number of passages based on certain task descriptions (e.g. a job application, a film or book review). In this experiment the subjects were not required to produce particular formats, but again they found considerable difficulties in operating the system, despite the fact that the 'natural language interpreter' was a highly trained secretary. An example transcript of the creative writing task is shown in Figure 2 as an illustration of some of the difficulties which were found.

It should be noted that, not only did our untrained subjects find significant difficulties in operating via an unstructured natural language interface, but also they were very inefficient. Of the words which they spoke, the percentage which actually appeared on the final document varied between 32 percent and 73 percent; about 60 percent of these non-textual words being concerned with formatting and punctuation.

All the subjects in these experiments found the unconstrained command structure very difficult to deal with, and, if anything, allowing a completely 'natural language' structure was a hindrance rather than a help. It is also significant that, even though subjects were using a very high performance speech recognition system together with a very sophisticated 'dialogue processor', which could understand natural language and filter out unwanted input, they were not impressed with the system, and when asked showed no great urge to want to use such a system in the future.

The results of these experiments did not offer much support for the contention that a natural language speech input system was necessarily an appropriate way of producing written text. There was a caveat to the experiment, however, which was that all the subjects were fully aware that they were using a simulation and talking to a person and not a machine. This was underlined by the 'simulation' being able to disambiguate badly structured commands, ignore irrelevant comments, etc. There was, therefore, a possibility that subjects were applying certain social conventions of politeness etc., which perhaps would not be appropriate for, or used when, talking to an actual machine.

In addition it should be pointed out that the use of a QWERTY keyboard to provide a transcript significantly slows down the rate at which it is possible to dictate to the simulation. A QWERTY keyboard can be operated at approximately 60 words per minute, which compares with 120 w.p.m. for commercial dictation, and over 180 w.p.m. for unconstrained speaking.

4 A FULL SPEED SIMULATION OF A LISTENING TYPEWRITER

In our next experiment we simulated a speech recognition machine by using a commercially available speech transcription system which could be operated at full dictation speed. The system is based on computer transcription of Palantype machine shorthand and is described in Downton & Brooks (1984) and Dye, Newell & Arnott (1984). Palantype machine shorthand is a phonetic and syllabic coding system for speech using a specially designed keyboard on which trained operators can encode speech at speeds in excess of 180 w.p.m. The computer system transcribes this coded input into orthography in real time and is commercially available both as a speech transcription system for the deaf and for verbatim reporting in such locations as the Law Courts.

For our first experiment we connected the output from the machine shorthand transcription system to a SUN workstation running a word processing

145

package and a dialogue processor which 'captured' spoken commands, such as punctuation etc. and performed the appropriate functions on the text. A diagram of the experimental system is shown in Figure 3. For this experiment we used the very restricted command set described by Gould (1983). This allowed punctuation, capitalisation and spelling, but only had those editing facilities which one would find in a dictating machine, i.e. only the word or words which had just been dictated could be deleted. The command set was highly structured and did not have any 'natural language' characteristics. Nevertheless this enabled us to perform a partial replication of Gould's experiment and also to investigate the effects of using a full-speed transcription system for this type of simulation.

5   OVERT AND COVERT SIMULATIONS

The major effect we wished to investigate in the experiment was the effect of awareness of the human operator on performance. We thus divided a new set of twenty undergraduate and research worker subjects into two groups. One group were told that they were to be using a simulation, and were introduced to the machine shorthand operator before the experiment began - an OVERT simulation. The other group were simply told that we were conducting experiments in machine recognition of speech, and we were careful to conceal the machine shorthand operator from this group - a COVERT simulation.

An important proviso to the comparison between the overt and covert groups was the extent to which the covert group were 'fooled' by the simulation. It was pleasing to note that the subjects in the covert group all expressed surprise on being told that the experiment was based on a simulation. (Indeed, one subject was substantially embarrassed on finding that a (female) operator had encoded the profanities which he had used when he was having difficulties and which had been faithfully reproduced on the screen!). It thus seems reasonable to make comparison of the results from the overt and covert groups of subjects.

An indication of what it was like to use this system is given in Figure 4. This shows a letter which one of our subjects created, together with a full verbatim transcription of what was said in order to create the text. The transcript shows a number of characteristics of this simulation:

i) Editing: Gould specified 'nuts' as the word to indicate deletion of the previous word, and 'nuts N', where 1 , deleted N previous words.

ii) The effects of the transcription system having a limited vocabulary (approximately 15,000 words), and thus some words being spelt incorrectly. e.g. 'extoll', and 'prayses'.

iii) The use of the 'spellmode' command to cope with the vocabulary limitations.

iv) The effect of occasional keying errors by the operator. e.g. the first attempt at 'producing' giving 'produck con'

Many detailed results were obtained from this experiment both in terms of how the task was performed and the response of subjects to questionnaires which were administered after the completion of the experiment. Two important results were (a) how our subjects ranked a listening typewriter compared with the ranking obtained in Gould's experiment, and (b) whether there was any difference in responses from the covert and overt groups. Gould had found that his subjects were favourably impressed by the listening typewriter and ranked it very high relative to writing or (in the case of experienced dictators) relative to their favourite method of dictation. A summary of Gould's results is given in Table 1. The results from our experiment are shown in Table 2. It can be seen that, in contrast to the positive comments obtained from Gould's subjects, our subjects (none of whom were experienced dictators) were not particularly impressed by the system.

A surprising feature of Table 2 is the difference between the responses of the overt and the covert groups. The number of subjects and the potential inter-subject variation does not lend the data to statistical analysis, but the following trends can be seen.

The most noticeable difference between the data from the two sets of subjects is that those subjects who knew that they were using a simulation ranked the speech input word processor higher than those subjects who, it was believed, thought that they were talking to an actual machine. This pattern also appeared in answers to other related questions such as a ranking relative to writing, on a scale significantly worse to significantly better, and in response to the question 'Is the system a real pleasure to use?'. It should be reiterated that all the experimental conditions were identical for the two groups with the exception of whether or not the subjects were aware they were using a simulation rather than the 'real thing'.

NAIVE DICTATORS rating various types of listening
typewriter simulation relative to writing.

(1=significantly worse, 4=same, 7=significantly better)

Ranking given :   5 - 6 - 5 - 6 - 5 - 4 - 6 - 6

EXPERIENCED DICTATORS ranking two types of listening
typewriter versus other methods they used to prepare
text:

A continuous speech unlimited
vocabulary simulation: Ranked 1st.

An isolated word unlimited
vocabulary simulation: Ranked 2nd.

Table 1. Summary of Gould's listening typewriter preference ratings

(6 = highest rank,   1 = lowest rank)

	Overt	Overt With Dict. Exp.	Overt Without Dict. Exp.	Covert	Covert With Dict. Exp.	Covert Without Dict. Exp.
Handwriting	5.8	5	5.89	5.2	5.75	4.83
Dictat.Mch.	1.75	1	1.86	2.7	2.75	2.67
Secretary	2.0	2	2.0	3.3	3.0	3.5
Word Proc.	3.75	4	3.71	4.0	4.25	3.83
Typewriter	3.38	3	3.43	3.2	3.25	3.0
Speech input W/P	4.38	6	4.0	2.9	2.5	3.17
No. of subjects	8	1	7	10	4	6

(Note: none of the subjects were experienced dictators but
       some had a little experience as shown in the table)

Table 2. Preference ratings for speech input versus other methods of dictation from Newell et al.

148

6   CONCLUSIONS FROM OVERT-COVERT SIMULATION EXPERIMENTS

1) In contrast to the previous work done by Gould, our subjects found the system to be worse than writing for text composition, and were not keen to use such a system in the future.

2) Those subjects who were made aware of the operator's existence were more impressed by the speech driven word processor than those who thought that they were talking to a machine.

It should be noted, however, that the dialogue design in the Gould experiment was very primitive (Gould wished to emulate the facilities available in a dictating machine), and more appropriate dialogue structures may have found favour with our subjects.

7   DISCUSSION

The experiments with a completely unconstrained 'natural language' dialogue showed that, if no training was given, subjects had great difficulties in formatting and correcting text, and an inefficient production of written text occurred. Presumably a training session would improve the performance of subjects, but this does raise the question as to how to define 'natural' and whether or not an 'unnatural' but structured dialogue would be both easier to learn and more efficient.

In the second experiments, the subjects learnt a very structured set of simple editing commands. The transcript shown in Figure 4 provides a very graphic illustration of how much command data needs to be entered into even a simple letter in order to obtain the correct punctuation and formatting, and to correct transcription errors. Admittedly the command structure developed by Gould was (deliberately) very primitive, and could easily be improved. Nevertheless a large amount of data, which is additional to the words which appear in the text, will still need to be entered in some form or other. A shorthand typist normally does not require much of this data, and a good secretary will produce what the dictator ought to have said. (This can be substantially different from the verbatim transcript which a machine would produce!). The provision of all this additional data is hardly 'natural', and developing a dialogue structure which ensures that such commands are spoken 'naturally' will not be easy.

The overt-covert experiment indicated that it is possible to change users' perception of such equipment simply by indicating that it is a human being who is listening to the dictation. The conclusions to be drawn from such a statement for the future design of natural language and/or speech input systems, are not obvious. These results, however, raise important questions as to whether it is always appropriate or necessary to try to produce a similiar situation to that which would occur if the operator was interacting with a person rather than a machine.

The work shows that, if a human computer system such as a listening typewriter is to be successful, it must have a dialogue structure which is appropriate to the task. The design of such dialogue structures is a non-trivial task and such structures, in general, will be heavily task dependent. To suggest that the solution is a 'natural language' interface raises many more questions than it answers. Not the least of these are:

What is meant by 'natural language' in the context of the particular application, and

How 'human' should the system appear to be, bearing in mind not only the application but also the characteristics of the expected users?

Finally, and most importantly, it is clear that there is a great deal to be learnt from experiments using simulation techniques. These experiments are not easy to perform, and there are many pitfalls for the unwary. Nevertheless the data they can provide cannot be obtained any other way and can be used to lay down realistic guidelines for what is actually required for both speech recognition and natural language technology in the future.

8   REFERENCES

1   Baum, F (1900). The Wizard of Oz, pub. Wm. Collins & Sons, UK (1974).

2   Bernstein, J (1987). Private Communication, SRI, CA USA, June 1987.

3   Bridle, J, Moore, R and Johnson, C (1987). Private Communication.

4   Downton, A and Brooks, CP (1984). Automated Machine Shorthand Transcription in Commercial Applications, Proc. 1st IFIP Conf. on Human-Computer Interaction, Imperial College, London, (North-Holland), 151-156.

5   Dye, R, Newell, AF and Arnott, JL (1984). An Adaptive Editor for Shorthand Transcriptions. Proc. 1st IFIP Conf. on Human-Computer Interaction, Imperial College, London, (North-Holland), 157-162.

6   Gould, JD, Conti, J and Hovanyecz, T (1983). Composing Letters with a Simulated Listening Typewriter. Comm. of A.C.M. Vol.20, No.4.

7   Johnson, C (1987). Speech Technology and Word Processing, Prod. Intl. Speech Tech. (London).

8   Newell, AF (1984). Speech: the Natural Method of Man- Machine Communication. Proc. 1st IFIP Conf. on Human- Computer Interaction, Imperial College, London, (North- Holland), 231-238.

9   Newell, AF Arnott, JL and Dye, R (1987). A Full Speed Simulation of Speech Recognition Machines, Proc. of European Conf. on Speech Technology, Edinburgh, 410-413.

10 Shneiderman, B (1987). Designing the User Interface, pub. Addison-Wesley.

11 Underwood, MJ (1983). Intelligent User Interfaces, in The Fifth Generation Computer Project, ed. G G Scarrott, Pergamon Infotech. State of the Art Report 11.1, 135-144.

12 Underwood, MJ (1984). Requirement for Speech Input/ Output Systems. ERE Colloq. on Speech Input/Output

9   ACKNOWLEDGEMENTS

The work described in this paper was conducted under a SERC/Alvey grant, and was performed by the author and his co-workers Drs.Arnott, Dye and Carter, Messrs Cairns and Cruickshank, and Mrs. Jackson.

151

Immediate Business Systems plc
4 Knowhead, Darwill
Melton Mowbry, MK8 8DA
Telephone: 4235 621296
Telex: 268390 M

CR/kmd

1 November 1986

Dear Sir,

COME TO DESIGN '86
and see demonstrations of these
TWO NEW EXCITING PRODUCTS FROM I.B.S.
the specialists in Harsh Environment Portable Processors

IBS 3 DESKTOP BUBBLE CASSETTE SYSTEM - a new type of exchangeable, non-volatile buffer that operates reliably in the most demanding environments where many magnetic and paper tapes fail to work at all.

THE RANGEWORK SIXTY (RW60) - THE COMPLETE PORTABLE MICROCOMPUTER puts the force of a desktop computer in the span of your hand, and is engineered to withstand the stringency of field computing and data collecting operations.

So come and discuss your applications with us on

    Table 8193

    Design '86

    Alligan, Forfar.   November 19th - 30th

We look forward to meeting you.

Yours sincerely

Dominic Latto
Sales Executive

Figure 1a. A business letter used in the copy dictation task.

Right. Next letter. This is our return address which will be at the top right hand side of the page. Top line is going to be in bold. Immediate Business Systems. Small letters p l c. Opps whats happened there. Small letters plc. (laughter) No. This seems awfully narrow. Can we widen the page. If we can't don't bother. Can we widen it to about eighty? This is going to be a devellish one. That's better. Over to eighty. O.K. and then move the first line over by ten. Great O.K. Next line of that block. This is not in bold any more. Number four capital K. Sorry take out the K. I'm going to spell a word now space capital K now small letters n o w h e a d, captial D a r w a l l. Next line of the block. Melton Mowbury that's captial M e l t o n space M o w b r y which is miss spelt. Well never mind. B R Y, space this is the postal code MK8 8DA. Next line of the block. Telephone: Can we spell the whole word telephone out for this one colon space 4235 621296. Next line of the block. Telex: 268390. Back at the left hand margin up one line. Capital CR/ small kmd. O.K. Three lines down. 1 november 1986. Four lines down.

Dear Sir, two lines down.

Thirty five spaces over. O.K. make that thirty spaces. Back up five. Now this will be in bold and in caps. COME TO DESIGN '86. Next line. Twenty five spaces over. O.K. two more make that twenty seven. Now this will be in small letters and not bold, and see demonstrations. Small letters. Ah need an R in demonstrations. Ah and see demonstrations of these new line. Twenty spaces over. Now this will be in caps and in bold. TWO NEW EXCITING PRODUCTS FROM I ehm from I full stop B full stop S full stop. New line, fifteen spaces over. Now back up three. Back up two more. Now this is small letters and not bold. The specialists in capital H Harsh capital E environment capital P Portable capital P Processors. Down two lines. Bold and capital letters 'til I tell you not. IBS 3 DESKTOP BUBBLE CASSETTE SYSTEM. Need an S in system .. eh system dash. Small letters and not bold from now on. Oh take that dash out. Have it .. should read systems space dash space small letters not bold. A new type of exchangeable, non dash volatile buffer that operates reliably in the most demanding environments where many magnetic and paper tapes fail to work at all full stop

Figure 1b. The verbatim transcript of the copy dictation task using an unstructured 'natural language' dialogue.

Right this is the ah... review of the book which is number two. Eh.. could you put ah... A New Chaucer. In brackets oh no ah...no sorry cut out the brackets I don't want the brackets ah... colon. Matthew Johnston I think there's an E on the end of that thanks. Then in brackets ah... methuen M E T H U E N close brackets. Ah... a new line.

Johnstone's eh... reputation as a critic and playwright himself is considerable and well deserved full stop. Now we see him branching into what what would seem to be a new area comma namely revitalising the classics of English literature full stop. Typically he achieves with his characteristic vitality and wit comma in the case of a new Chaucer oh sorry capital letters it the title of a book a has a capital letter as well ah... brackets published this week and then put a pounds sign. 8.95. Close brackets. Full stop. New paragraph.

In his own time Chaucer was regarded as a skilled, humorous humorous has got an O instead of an E humorous yes. A skilled humorous story teller comma. Fond of the bawdy B A W D Y what was it joke dash and undeterred by whatever moral majority could you put it in inverted commas please moral majority. Might sorry scrub might which might have existed in his day full stop. For the twentieth century reader there is the problem of language to be overcome comma and Johnstone .... John .... Johnstone's is with apostrophe S translation from the middle English retains all the natural quality of the original whilst losing none of the quality whilst losing none of the ah... classical quality of the work full stop new paragraph.

For all those new to Chaucer comma Johnstone's book provides a wonderfully light hearted and readable introduction full stop. For those with memories of struggling through ah... inverted commas 'The Night's Tale' oh its K N I G H T S close commas close inverted commas at school comma the novel oh sorry the book will be a pleasurable return to a writer who comma even now even now six hundred years later comma remains one of our greatest and most enjoyed bards B A R D S. Full stop. Can I just read through that?

OK that's it thanks. Thats the end.

Figure 2. The verbatim transcript of a creative writing text with an unstructured 'natural language' dialogue.

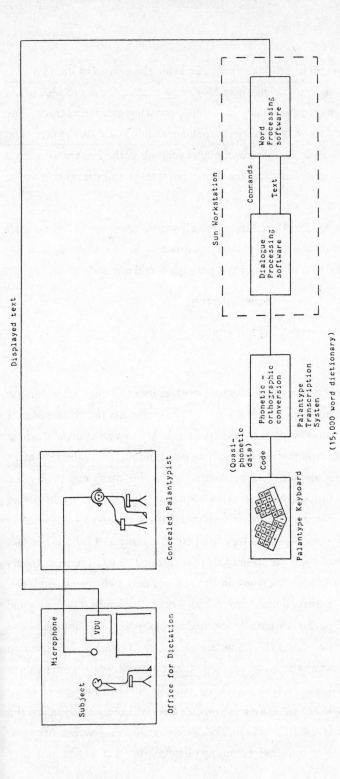

Figure 3. A Full Speed Speech Recognition Simulation System.

155

Dear Sir,

I am writing to you to extol the virtues and sing the praises of the film 'The Mission'. I saw it not long ago (having waited for many months for the chance to see it) and was very impressed by the quality of acting, producing and sound track. The story-line is not hard to follow and is very compelling, as it is based on the fact. The scenery and backgound shots are superb, though everyone in the cinema wondered where the water fall had gone;   did the Pope perform a miracle and make it disappear?(!)

All in all, it is an excellent film and well worth going to see, although I would not recommend taking younger children (say below the age of about 12 or 14) as they probably would find it distressing and perhaps would not understand.

Yours sincerely,

Wendy Hodge

start newline space capit dear capit sir comma newline indent capit i am writing to you to extoll nuts extoll nuts spellmode e e x t o l endspellmode the virtues of nuts and sing the prayses of nuts two prayses nuts spellmode p r a i s e s endspellmode of the film quotation-mark capit the mission no nuts two capit mission quotation-mark fullstop i saw it not long ago left- bracket having waited for many months for the chance to see it right-bracket and was very impressed by the quality of acting produck con nuts two comma producing and sound track fullstop capit the story hyphen line is not hard to follow and is very compelling comma as it is based on fact fullstop and seen nuts two capit the scenery and background shots were superb nuts two are superb comma though everyone in the sen ma nuts two sin ma nuts two spellmode c i n e m a enspellmode wondered where the water fall had gone semicolon did the pope perform a miracle and make it disappear question-mark bra left- bracket nuts two left-bracket exclamation-mark right-bracket newline two indent capit all in all comma it is an excellent film and well worth going to see comma although i would not recommend taking young gr nuts two younger children left-bracket see below the age nuts three below nuts nuts left- bracket say below the age of about nummode twelve endnummode nuts nummode twelve one two endnummode or nummode one four endnummode right-bracket as the nuts they

156

probably would find it distressing and perhaps would not understand fullstop newline newline indent three capit yours sincerely comma newline indent three space space spellmode capit w e n d y space capit h o d g e quit

Figure 4. The text and the verbatim transcription of the dictation of a creative writing task using the Full Speed Speech Recognition Simulation with the dialogue structure specified by Gould (1983).

Chapter 11
Alvey Initiatives
in Natural Language Processing

B OAKLEY,
Alvey Directorate DTI

1 PARTS OF THE ALVEY PROGRAMME WITH A NATURAL LANGUAGE CONTEXT

In human affairs one has to divide up or compartmentalise in order to be able to administer and control. Unfortunately we human beings very rapidly put barriers around the domains so created. In the Alvey programme we divided Software Engineering off from IKBS, and - worse - MMI from IKBS. We then subdivided IKBS, for example, into Intelligent Front Ends and Expert Systems, and MMI into Speech-and Human Factors. All these contain elements of Natural Language-indeed some would say it underpins the whole subject of advanced computing. So please excuse me if I concentrate on what, in the Alvey programme, we have called the Natural Language theme.

2 NATURAL LANGUAGE PROGRAMME

In the Alvey Natural Language theme of the IKBS part of the programme there are 10 projects - or rather more if one includes minor studies. The total value of the projects is about £2.7m but about £2.4m of this is taken up by the four major projects. I will deal with these in more detail in due course. The other six projects are Uncle projects with a cost of about £5.0k each.

The bodies taking part in this section of the Alvey Programme are many fewer in number than in almost any other part of the programme, with predominantly the Universities of Cambridge, Edinburgh, and Sussex, but with a wider set of participants in the speech projects.

We owe a great deal to Dr Karen Sparck-Jones of Cambridge University, who was the co-ordinator of this Natural Language theme in the IKBS programme.

3   NATURAL LANGUAGE TOOLKIT

The three toolkit projects are carried out by Cambridge University (Dr Steve Pulman and Dr Bran Boguraev) and Edinburgh University (Dr Henry Thompson). The aim is to provide a set of tools for natural language processing research. Each project can be used as a stand alone tool, but it is also intended that all three can be used together as a complete system running under Lisp for the grammatical analysis of a considerable subset of English.

The Dictionary Project

The largest of the three projects is the Dictionary Project - full title 'The Dictionary and Morphological Analyser for English Language Processing System'- a co-operation between Cambridge and Edinburgh Universities led by Dr S G Pulman. The aim of the Dictionary Project was to provide:

a)   A set of mechanisms for the analysis of completed word forms in English.

b)   A particular analysis of English to be used by the Grammar Project.

The system is a set of programmes which require three files:

1. A list of base morphemes   (that is individual words or affixes) with accompanying, phonological,syntactic and semantic information, into which all morphologically complex forms are to be analysed.

2. A set of 'spelling rules' governing orthographic or phonological changes when morphemes are concentrated.

3. A set of 'word-grammar' rules describing the valid contributions of morphemes in complete words.

The important point about the dictionary is that if the properties of a complex word are completely predictable from those of its components, then it should NOT be individually listed in the dictionary. Conversely, if there is anything idiosyncratic about a word it MUST be listed as a separate form. The basic list of morphemes consists of the 5,000 most common English words. It is believed that the mechanisms supplied are capable, when provided with the necessary linguistic analysis, of being used for, at least, all European languages. (I expect the Dictionary, and the Grammar Projects will be discussed by Dr Bran Boguraev in the 'On-line lexical resources' section and by Dr Steve Pulman in the 'Events and VP Modifiers' section.)

The Grammar Project

The aim of the Grammar Project is to produce a description which would provide coverage of the major syntactic constructions of English. It is written within a framework based on the Generalised Phrase Structure Grammar (Taylor et al), where each rule introducing a lexical item will be indexed to those items in the word list which may occur grammatically in the syntactic environment specified for that rule. Generalised Phrase Structure Grammar has been suitably extended and modified to offer a degree of expressiveness and flexibility required for the task of building a large grammar of natural language. The project is led by Dr Bran Boguraev of Cambridge, and is joint with Lancaster University, and, initially, Acorn. The grammar provides 'reasonably full coverage' of the following constructions:

- Most of the common verb and adjective complement types

- Yes/no questions

- Why/how questions

- Relative clauses

- Noun phrase pre-and-post modification

- Some verb phrase modifiers conjunctions

- Comparatives

and combinations of these.

160

A separate software subsystem has been implemented to support rapid and interactive lexicon development using the Dictionary Project.

The Parser Project

The Parser has been built to serve as a component of the tool set, focusing on the problems of representing grammatical knowledge in a fashion which is acceptable both from the stand-point of the grammar writer, and capable of efficient running in the computer. It has been designed as a ready-made natural language front end. The parsing algorithm is similar to the familiar chart parsing techniques but, rather than maintaining a global chart data structure, the algorithm goes through a sentence one word at a time, left to right, at each stage building a list of ways the parse could continue. These are then passed on recursively as the next word is examined, and any temporary structures which cannot possibly form part of any parse are discarded. So this 'verbivorous' parser finds all possible complete analyses of a given sentence according to the grammar.

Status of the Toolkit

The Dictionary and Parser Projects were completed some months ago; the Grammar Project ends early next year. Final versions of Dictionary and Parser are now available, together with an intermediate version of the Grammar; from the Artificial Intelligence Applications Institute of Edinburgh University.

4   NATURAL LANGUAGE AND PLANNING PROJECT

Turning now to the other three larger projects, the Natural Language and Planning Project was the last of the major projects to start, and has been running for less than a year. It is led by British Telecom (S Garrod of Martlesham), together with Cambridge and Edinburgh Universities. It aims to bring together work on natural language understanding and planning, to design a natural language interface to a general planner.

The first stage is a system to query the state of a static plan. It aims to enable queries to be answered about knowledge-based planners that will allow modifications to be made in the plans. It is hoped that advances in the interpretation of modal and temporal statements likely to arise in interactions about plans will be made. The project will have, as a focus, a natural language interface to a telecommunication planning system in the operational support domain. The project will cost about £385,000, and has another couple of years to run.

5 READ AND WRITE JAPANESE WITHOUT KNOWING IT

This rather evocatively named project aimed to develop a software package, including a dynamic English/Japanese dictionary, with modules to enable technologists speaking only English and in their own fields to

a) understand Japanese texts

b) produce simultaneous English and Japanese versions of documentation

c) teach themselves to translate Japanese texts.

The work was led by Graham Hook of ICL (now with the Alvey Directorate) together with UMIST and the University of Sheffield. As the project is being described in the Machine Translation section by Mary Mcgee Wood of UMIST, I will not say any more about it now, except to say that the Japanese/English dictionaries have now been built up to over 6,000 words. The coverage of the system is being extended by 'the building of large and robust grammar and dictionaries, resulting in a full scale working system ready for commercial development'.

6 THE RESEARCH PROGRAMME IN NATURAL LANGUAGE PROCESSING

The so-called 'NATTIE' Club is being led by SRI International's Cambridge Computer Science Research Centre, at first under Dr R C Moore, and now under Dr Fernando Pereira. The consortium members are British Aerospace, British Telecom, Hewlett-Packard, ICL, Olivetti, Philips, Shell Research and SRI supported by Cambridge and Edinburgh universities. The total cost of the three year project is £1.2m, and the project started 18 months ago, so it is about half way through. It aims to harness some of the expertise gained on the West Coast in natural language work.

The main technical aim of the project is the design and implementation of a 'core language engine' capable of producing formal representations of the literal meaning of English sentences, suitable for interfacing to a wide variety of advisory tasks. The project will also involve work on advanced topics in syntax, semantics and pragmatics.

So far the work has been largely concentrated on the design and implementation of an initial version of the Core Language Engine. This includes a parser, syntactic grammar rules for English, a semantic interpretation component, a set of semantic interpretation rules for English, and mechanisms for applying selectional restrictions for generating quantifier scopings. The design depends heavily on the use of 'unification', and handles alternative syntactic and semantic structures in a principled way based on a structure sharing technique. (For further information on this I would refer you to the report on the first year's work by the SRI Cambridge Computer Science Research Centre.)

The work will be extended to cover an extensive class of English constructions. The system will be demonstrated by applying the system and some of the work on domain knowledge and reasoning to a prototype advisory task.

7   NATURAL LANGUAGES IN THE ALVEY SPEECH PROJECTS

One of the problems in the Alvey programme is that for purely organisational reasons it was necessary to divide the programme into sections like IKBS, MMI, and Large Demonstrators. The formal natural language programme was located in the IKBS part of the programme, but the speech work was located in the MMI part - with the largest speech project in the Large Demonstrators.

Speech projects with some Natural Language content are:

i. Speech I/O An Implementation for Chinese. This project involves Sindex Speech Technology Ltd, RSRE, and UCL. The objective is the development of examples of unlimited Chinese speech-to-text and text-to-speech systems.

ii. Automatic Speech Recognition STC Technology lead this project with the University of Cambridge, and the MRC. It aims to develop techniques for the speaker-adaptive recognition of a large vocabulary 'freely-spoken' speech by the evolution of existing pattern-matching algorithms to include the use of speech knowledge. The work includes aspects of lexical access, and morphosyntactic parsing. A lexical data base management system has been developed with 50,000 entries. A model of a lexical segmentation strategy is being developed using experiments on human perception. The lexical database will be used to evaluate front ends for the recognised and suitable grammar, and will be used as a syntactic knowledge source for the evaluation of parsing algorithms.

iii. Speech Recognition and Synthesis Algorithms. This Queen Mary College project aims to provide software tools for the Alvey Speech Club, and to develop a portable software environment that provides a convenient method for expressing speech recognition and synthesis algorithms. The project involves the development of a natural language parsing enviroment for the AMT DAP510 massively parallel computer.

iv. The Speech Input Word Processor and Workstation Demonstrator. This large project involves Edinburgh University, HILSAT, and Imperial College. The withdrawal of Plessey has delayed its progress, though Edinburgh has been doing some excellent work, including the use of some AI methods and computational linguistics. But until the revised project is launched it is probably better to say no more for the moment.

8 VODIS

There is one other Alvey project that deserves attention in the natural language context, and that is the VODIS project. This is a Voice Operated Database Inquiry System, led by British Telecom Research Laboratories, with Logica and Cambridge University. The project is for four years and has about a year to run, so it is one of the largest Alvey projects involving natural language work. The aim of the project is to demonstrate a user-friendly intelligent voice operated database inquiry system which can successfully handle inquiries over the telephone from most untrained members of the general public.

Mr Jeremy Peckham discusses VODIS, so I will not say anything more on the project now, except that I feel the adaptive dialogue field - as exemplified by this project - is one of the areas of natural language work that shows most promise of early commercial pay-off.

9 CONCLUSION

There are other projects in the Alvey Programme which, perhaps, I should have covered. For example there is an IKBS project under the Expert System theme called 'Design of a Natural Language Interface for Medical Expert Systems' which should certainly have been included - even if it is very much concentrated on the Medical Expert System side. It is run by the Imperial Cancer Research Foundation (Dr David Frost, Dr John Fox), with Cambridge University, UCL and the Middlesex School of Medicine of London University, and costs £10,000. The work on Dr John Fox's team on the Oxford Encyclopedia of Medicine is - or ought to be - well known, and because it concentrates on the human-interface could be considered to have a natuaral language component.

Judging by the programme for this conference, the very interesting work by my good friend Professor Alan Newell of Dundee University, together with Possum Controls Ltd, the project 'Full-Speed Speech Recognition Simulation', is evaluating the acceptable error rates in speech driven word processors. I would not, myself, think of classifying this as natural language work, but on reflection, why not? - it is certainly concerned with the use of normal or natural language. Anyway, the organisers of this conference have classified it as natural language work, for it is the last paper in this conference - and well worth staying for.

There are, I know, other projects in the Alvey Programme to which I should have referred. In particular I have hardly mentioned the Intelligent Front-End projects. Problems of classification are very real in this subject.

In conclusion may I air one of the conclusions with which I come away from my very interesting years with the Alvey Programme? Natural language is one of those strange subjects where all but the most dim politicians - and that excludes a fair number in the UK - can see the enormous potential economic importance of the subject. At the same time, the subject is of great interest from an intellectual standpoint, and it turns out to be of very considerable difficulty, which I find very satisfying as it enhances the stature of man. There are many things we can do with computers, and as we achieve them one tends to discount them as achievements of intelligent man. With natural language, we have a field where the human being is still infinitely more capable than the computer.

Yet, the goal of achieving cost effective natural language work in a computer seems tantalisingly near our grasp. I suggest it needs a concerted push. It is, par exellence, a subject where a multidisciplinary attack is required. And, unlike almost all other Alvey topics, it is one where a concerted attack is required because the team has to learn to speak the same language - pun intended. In the USA the Centre for the Study of Language and Information, CSLI, on the campus of Stanford University, has almost 100 graduate workers drawn from a wide range of disciplines - psychologists, linguists, phoneticians, mathematicians, logicians, computer scientists and, not least as it turns out, philosophers. I feel strongly that we need such a centre in Europe, and in my view the UK would be the obvious place in which to put it, if only because perhaps the best individuals in Europe in this field are in the UK. Like CSLI it should be an academic type centre, with long range

166

goals, but should involve all firms in the UK and from the Continent who have an interest and some competence to contribute.

There are of course various candidates for its location, but in my view there are only two serious candidate locations in the UK - Edinburgh and Cambridge. I have made up my own mind where it should be, but would value your views. We do, all of us who are interested in this fascinating field, need to campaign for this centre.

Chapter 12
WH-questions and intensional logic

A RAMSAY
School of Cognitive Sciences, University of Sussex

1   BACKGROUND

Processing of natural language by machines has moved on from treating sentences one at a time to trying to deal with them in context. This is not to say, of course, that current natural language systems deal perfectly with isolated sentences - that we have correct and complete adequate grammars for any natural languages, that parsing mechanisms are as fast and robust as the human ability to process syntactic structure, that meaning representation schemes are anything like rich enough to capture the subtleties of natural languages, or indeed that any of the problems of sentence by sentence processing are really solved. They are, however, sufficiently well understood for current NLP systems to be at least useable at this level. The glaring inadequacies, the reasons why people might find such systems intolerable to work with, are currently at the level of discourse, where language has to be used in a flexible, well organised way to further any of a range of general goals. We now have NLP systems which can, to some extent, obey commands, answer questions, and store new information. The next generation of systems will be required to understand WHY they have been required to obey a command, or answer a question or store a fact, so that they can produce appropriate behaviour if they are not in fact able to do what was required, and can tailor their responses to the underlying needs of the user.

Progress in this areas has come from four main sources.

(i) To situate language use within a larger context, it is necessary to have ready access to large amounts of general world knowledge. The most significant work in this area has come from the Yale school, from Schank and Abelson's early work on scripts and plans (16), to the substantial suite of programmes based on various elaborations of Schank's theories of memory organisation (9, 10, 17, 19).

This work is of critical importance to any general theory of language processing, but it does not have much direct impact on the problems we are concerned with here, and we will not consider the matter of real world knowledge further in this paper. We will have enough problems without it.

(ii) To make sense of language use as a component of a larger behaviour pattern, we need to be able to understand utterances as actions within a general plan. To take a well known example, suppose that you know that there is a petrol station just down the road, but that you also know it is shut. If someone asks you where the nearest petrol station is, it is inappropriate for you to tell them about this one unless you also tell them that you believe it to be shut. You are not actually lying, and it would indeed be hard to understand what you were doing wrong unless you realised that their reason for asking you is likely to be that they want to buy some petrol, so that being told about a petrol station where they could not buy any petrol would not do them much good. Note that this is only one of several possible reasons for their question: they might, for instance, have been asking you because they were planning to build a new petrol station , and wanted to know about the likely competition. The earliest work on fitting linguistic actions into an overall plan in this way seems to have been done by Powers (4), though other reported work (1,4) has probably had a wider influence.

(iii) When we try to characterise the preconditions and effects of linguistic actions so we can apply our standard planning techniques to them, we find that quite a number of them concern the knowledge of the speaker and hearer. If someone asks a simple question, it is normally taken that they do not know the answer and that they believe that the person they have asked does. These conditions may be violated, e.g. if you are late for an appointment with me, and when you show up I look at my watch and say 'Do you know what time it is?', it is clear that I do know the time. But in this case I am not asking a simple question - I am expressing my displeasure with you in a way which you can only recognise because you realise I am NOT asking a simple question. To deal with this sort of issue, we need to draw on theories about how it is possible to reason about one's own and other people's knowledge. Most such theories are based to some extent on modal logic, with Moore's (12, 13) treatment, which makes it possible to link this sort of reasoning with reasoning about the effects of other actions, probably the most influential.

(iv) Finally, we need a representation language which is rich enough to capture the subtleties of natural language utterances. Although we do have NLP systems which can cope with a reasonable variety of utterances, it is becoming increasingly clear that the standard representation languages are just not powerful enough. Existing systems tend to use either some form of first-order logic (FOPC) or a variant on Schank's conceptual dependency graphs (CD). The widely used semantic network formalism is little more than a notational variant on FOPC. It has long been recognised within formal semantics that these languages simply are not capable of expressing the distinction between intensional and extensional readings. The sentence 'John seeks a unicorn', for instance, can be interpreted either as saying that there is some specific unicorn which John is looking for (the extensional reading), or that he is looking for anything which happens to be a unicorn (the intensional reading). The two readings can be invoked by follow-up sentences : 'John seeks a unicorn. He saw it in the garden this morning.' clearly requires the extensional reading of a unicorn, whereas 'John seeks a unicorn. He wants to make unicorn pie.' requires the intensional reading. For some time this distinction was ignored in AI, on the grounds that it was rather exotic and did not need to be taken into account for the construction of practical systems. It is being increasingly recognised that the distinction can have serious practical consequences. It would be impossible, for instance, to design a system which could respond to 'I want to speak to a salesman' with 'Did you have a particular salesman in mind, sir, or will anyone do?' without an account of the difference between intensions and extensions.

We see then, that any comprehensive NLP system needs to be able to deal with real-world knowledge, plan generation, reasoning about knowledge, and the distinction between extensions and intensions. The aim of this paper is to point out that although each of these is quite difficult in itself, the commbination of the last three introduces problems which are not present if you try to treat them separately. We will illustrate this by considering the difficulties involved in planning or interpreting a WH-question, i.e. a question beginning with one of the interrogative pronouns who, what, where and when. Even worse problems will arise when we come to try and deal with the other WH-questions - why and how questions. The simpler ones that we will be considering will cause us enough trouble for now. In the remainder of the paper we will sketch very briefly the models that have been used for the tasks (ii), (iii) and (iv) outlined above, and then see where the problems arise if we want to plan the sentence 'Who are you looking for?'

2 PLANNING THEORY

We start with the construction of a planner, in order to be able to relate our linguistic actions to the other actions we may carry out in order to achieve our overall goals. There is a long tradition of plan construction programs in AI. Most such programs are elaborations or adaptations of the Fikes and Nilsson's STRIPS algorithm [6]. Within this tradition, a plan is a sequence of actions, where each action is described in terms of a finite set of preconditions which must hold if the action is to be executable and a finite set of changes which it will bring about if executed. The planner constructs its plan by selecting and instantiating action schemas, usually working backwards from its overall goal to actions whose preconditions are satisfied. A typical schema from the blocks world, the schema for the action of picking up a block, might look like:

pickup(X)

preconditions: hand-empty, clear(X), on (X,Y)

effects: not(hand-empty), holding(X), clear(Y), not(on(XY))

There are plenty of variants of the STRIPS algorithm, and of the representation of actions. Many of them are quite minor, such as attempts to do away with dual predicates like hand-empty and holding (since hand-empty is true exactly when holding (X) is not true for any X, it seems wasteful to have both predicates. It is, however, often technically convenient). Others are rather more drastic, such as Sacerdoti's theory of non-linear plans [15]. They all, however, show strong traces of their ancestry - actions have preconditions, which must be true before they are executed, and effects, which will be true afterwards. The most substantial attempt so far to combine parts (ii) and (iii) of our overall model, Appelt's language generation program KAMP [2], has action summaries of this kind. Appelt's action summary for X informing Y of P looks rather like the following.

inform(X, Y, P)

preconditions: knows(X, P), not(knows(X, knows(Y, P)))

effects: mutually-know(X, Y, P)

This is not taken directly from Appelt's description of KAMP, but it does no violence to his analysis of what informing is like. The critical thing about it, from our point of view, is the presence of the operator's 'know' and 'mutually-know'. The occurrances of 'know' in the preconditions should not be too contentious. You cannot successfully inform somebody of something unless you know it, and you do not know that they already know it. There are a number of other linguistic acts you might perform which involve the transfer of the information that P is true, e.g. emphasising a fact, or confirming your awareness of it, or nagging (you still haven't painted that door), but the given preconditions seem right for informing. The reason we need 'mutually-know' in the effects, rather than just some nested version of 'knows' like 'knows(Y, knows(X, knows(Y, P)))' is that there is no *a priori* limit on how deep such nesting may have to go to explain the ramifications of a particular act of informing. It is possible to argue about the exact preconditions and effects of actions like informing. It does seem, however, as though any characterisation of linguistic acts in this way must use at least 'knows', and most probably 'mutually-knows' as well. Since all AI planning algorithms use preconditions and effects, or something so like them as to make no difference, we are going to be forced to work out how these predicates behave.

3   REASONING ABOUT KNOWLEDGE

Most AI systems that have to reason about their own or other people's knowledge use some version of modal logic [7]. Modal logic started out as an attempt to capture formally the difference between truth and necessary truth. A wide variety of axioms for the necessity operator □ have been explored [11], and a semantics has been developed for this operator in terms of 'possible worlds' [8].

172

Various people have recognised that the axioms and semantics permit alternative interpretations of □. In particular, it has been pointed out that the axioms of S4 modal logic fit the behaviour of an idealised version of 'knows', and that the 'accessibility relation' required by the 'possible worlds' semantics can be interpreted in terms of compatibility with an agent's knowledge. The axions for S4 modal logic, and the generalisations of these axioms to cover knowledge, are as follows:

K: $\Box(P \rightarrow Q) \rightarrow (\Box(P) \rightarrow \Box(Q))$ $\forall x(knows(x, P \rightarrow Q) \rightarrow (knows(x, P) \rightarrow knows(x, Q)))$
T: $\Box(P) \rightarrow P$ $\forall x(knows(x, P) \rightarrow P)$
S4: $\Box(P) \rightarrow \Box(\Box(P))$ $\forall x(knows(x, P) \rightarrow knows(x, knows(x, P)))$

These axioms, together with the inference rules of modus ponens (which derive Q from P and P $\longrightarrow$ Q) and necessitation (which says that if A is an axiom then so is □A), support most of the inferences we might want to make about what someone knows. They are clearly idealisations. They permit, for instance, arbitrary amounts of self-knowledge (from knows(A, P), repeated application of necessitation will lead to knows(A, knows(A, ... knows(A, P))) for any number of nestings), and they permit the conclusion that anyone who knows the basic rules of arithmetic also knows that there are infinitely many prime numbers, via repeated use of modus ponens with the knowledge oriented version of axiom K. They are nonetheless a good start, and we can always prevent some of the more absurd conclusions by imposing some sort of resource limit.

A number of theorem proving techniques have been proposed for modal logic, either in direct connection with its use for reasoning about knowledge or for modal logic in general. Moore [12, 13], for instance, argues for an approach which axiomatises the 'possible worlds' semantics in FOPC, using this axiomatisation to argue indirectly about the validity or otherwise of formulae involving the modal operator. Wallen [20] provides an adaptation of Bibel's [3] connection method for constructing proofs directly within modal logic. The relative merits of these and other methods are still a subject for active debate. For all of them, however, formulae involving existential quantifiers can cause problems. The difficulty can be illustrated with an example from Quine, namely the sentence 'Ralph knows that someone in this room is a spy.' This seems to have two readings if translated into a knowledge oriented version of modal logic. The 'wide-scope' reading, ∃x(location(x, Room D430) & knows(Ralph, isa(x, spy))), says that there is somebody in this room (Room D430 of the Arts building at Sussex University) who Ralph knows to be a spy. On this reading you would want to be able to conclude that Ralph knows who the spy is, whatever this itself may mean. The 'narrow-scope' reading is knows(Ralph, ∃x(location(x, Room D430) & isa(x, spy))), in other words that he knows there is someone here who is a spy, perhaps because his secret briefcase has been tampered with, but that he may not know who the spy is.

The problem here is the semantics of the wide-scope reading. In terms of possible worlds, it means that the same person is the spy in all worlds which are compatible with what Ralph knows. This makes some sense, but it does require us to have some way of referring to people (and other objects) which is reliable across accessible possible worlds. The easiest way to deal with this is to assume that all the worlds that are compatible with what someone knows are based on the same set of individuals, and that every individual has a unique name which denotes them in every world. It is recognised that real names do not work very well for this. First of all, most proper names such as Allan Ramsay or Paris, don't actually pick out a single individual even within the real world (there are many people in the world called Allan Ramsay, and there are several towns called Paris). Secondly, many names don't even pretend to pick out a constant individual - names like Miss America act like functions, picking out explicitly different people in different worlds or at different times. Finally, many things that we want to talk about just don't have names at all - there may be referring expressions that we can use to pick them out, such as the last sentence I typed, but they do not have names in any ordinary sense. The standard approach is to simply assume that everything does have a unique perfectly reliable name, and to the formal semantics of the wide-scope reading in terms of this name. The approach via such 'rigid designators' (RDs) provides a reasonable account of knowledge about things like phone numbers and combinations of safes, but completely fails to cope with discourses such as

Q: Who is Mrs Smith?

A1: She's the mayor of Brighton.

A2: She's sitting at the top table, next to the Borough treasurer.

where the questioner appears to already have an RD. or at any rate a name, and the answerer has to find out some other property which might serve the questioner's goals. A1 provides a significant fact about Mrs Smith, A2 a way of identifying her

4   INTENSIONS AND EXTENSIONS

This problem with wide- and narrow-scope quantification over 'knows' seems very like the problem we mentioned above with the two readings of 'John seeks a unicorn'. Montague semantics [5] formalises the distinction between the intensional reading of the phrase 'a unicorn' and its extensional reading. The intensional reading is something like 'any item which has all the properties which perfectly characterise what means to be a unicorn', or 'any instance of unicornhood'. The extensional reading is more like 'some specific item which has all the properties which ...'. The formal treatment of these notions does manage to sidestep the issue of R's, but only at the cost of adding the full power of the *-calculus. There is insufficient space here to go into the details of Montague's analysis of intensions and extensions. The essential point for the present argument is that it invokes an extended version of the *-calculus, and provides a possible worlds semantics for expressions of this resulting language.

If we now return to our target question, 'Who are you looking for?', we can see that it has a lot in common with John seeks a unicorn. In particular, it ought to have both intensional and extensional readings. For the first, an answer such as 'The person who stole my bike' would suffice. We have been given an exact characterisation of the object being looked for. Note that, just as with 'John seeks a unicorn', there is no guarantee that the description actually fits any real object. John can seek a unicorn even though there are no such things, and never have been, and I can look for the person who stole my bicycle even though what has actually happened is that my girlfriend borrowed it without telling me. For the second reading of this question, Rocky Roccoco would be an appropriate answer - a name, or RD, which picks out some specific individual as the one being sought.

This seems to be the right way to go. The failure of the modal logic approach to questions seems to be that it assumes that everything has an RD, and that WH-questions are always requests for RDs. RDs seem to correspond very closely to extensions - to be given an RD is to be given something which picks out exactly one individual, which is very much what an extension does. By including intensions we seem to have added the ability to have general properties as answers to WH-questions. The problem now is that our system has to contain treatments of three substantial formal theories - a theory of preconditions and effects, so we can construct plans out of basic actions, a theory of knowledge, so that we can reason about actions which depend on and affect our states of knowledge, and a theory of intensions and extensions. Furthermore, we cannot compartmentalise these theories and treat them independently. The preconditions and effects must be couched in terms of knowledge, and the knowledge must refer to intensions and extensions. This is unfortunate for us, as far as computational treatments are concerned, because it means that we have to move from first-order theorem proving to the full *-calculus. The advantage of the approaches suggested by Moore and Wallen for modal logic is that they are, essentially, both first-order (Moore's treatment is explicitly first order, Wallen's requires a fairly minor technical trick). It is well known that second order logic is fully undecidable, rather than semi-decidable as is the case for FOPC. Adding general properties, in fact, can easily lead not just to undecidability, but also to the presence of paradoxes such as Russel's paradox and the liar paradox. What we need, if we are to move on to cope with more sophisticated uses of language, is either a firstorder treatment of properties or a more robust approach to theorem proving. The first may be available in Turner's [18] theory of properties. The second looks more distant, though Bibel's recent work on problem transformations may offer a route to a solution.

5 REFERENCES

1 Allen, JF & Perrault, CR (1980), Analysing intention in utterances, Art Int 13 (3) 143-17

2 Appelt, D (1985), Planning English Sentences, Cambridge University Press, Cambridge.

3 Bibel, W (1982), Automated theorem proving, Vieweg, Wiesbaden.

4 Cohen, PR & Perrault, CR (1979), Elements of a plan-based theory of speech acts, Cognitive Science 3, 177-212.

5 Dowty, DR, Wall, RE & Peters, S (1979), Introduction to Montague semantics, Reidel, Dordrecht/Boston/London.

6 Fikes, RE & Nilsson, NJ (1971), STRIPS: a new approach to the application of theorem proving to problem solving, Artificial Intelligence 2.

7 Hughes, G & Cresswell, M (1968), An introduction to modal logic, Methuen.

8 Kripe, S (1963), Semantical considerations on modal logic, Acta philosophica fennica 16.

9 Lehnert, W (1978), The process of question answering, Lawrence Erlbaum, New York.

10 Lebowitz, M (1983), Generalisation from natural language text, Cognitive Sciences 7/1.

11 Lewis, D (1987), On the plurality of worlds, Blackwell, Oxford.

12 Moore, RC (1980), Reasoning about knowledge and action, SRI AI technical report 191.

13 Moore, RC (1984), A formal theory of knowledge and action, in Formal theories of the commonsense world, eds J R Hobbs & R C Moore, Ablex, New Jersey.

14 Powers, R (1974), A computer model of conversation, PhD thesis, University of Sussex.

15 Sacerdoti, E (1975), The non-linear nature of plans, IJCAI-75

16 Schank, RC & Abelson, RP (1977), Scripts, plans, goals and understanding, Lawrence Erlbaum, New York.

17 Schank, RC (1982), Dynamic memory: a theory of learning in computers and people, Cambridge University Press, Cambridge.

18 Turner, R (1987), A theory of properties, Journal of symbolic logic 52/2.

19 Wilensky, R (1978), Why John married Mary: understanding stories involving recurring goals, Cognitive Science 2/3.

20 Wallen, L (1987), Matrix proofs for modal logics, IJCAI-87.

Chapter 13
Events
and Verb Phrase Modifiers

S G PULMAN,
University of Cambridge Computer Laboratory

1   INTRODUCTION

Davidson (1980) proposes an analysis of adverbial modifiers (by which he means adverbial and prepositional phrases) which involves giving verbs an extra argument place describing an event. Adverbial modifiers are then predicates of this event. Where the modifier is a derived adverb, the predicate is simply the corresponding adjective. Thus a sentence like:

1   Jones buttered the toast slowly, deliberately, in the bathroom, with a knife, at midnight,

is to be partly translated as:

2   Ee butter(Jones, the toast, e) & in(e, the bathroom) & with(e, a knife) & at(e, midnight)

Paraphrased; 'There was a buttering by Jones of the toast event and that event was in the bathroom, at midnight and with a knife'. This analysis solves two problems posed by such constructions: that modifiers can be iterated virtually indefinitely, and that each successively modified version of the sentence entails the original version; if Jones buttered the toast slowly, then Jones buttered the toast. If Jones buttered the toast slowly in the bathroom, then Jones buttered the toast slowly, and so on. Both of these properties now follow from those of conjunction.

Davidson's analysis has been very influential in computational linguistics, since it leads to analyses which, being first order, are computationally tractable. However, there are several well known problems that it encounters, and some types of verbal modification that it appears unable to deal with. This paper discusses three of these and proposes some modifications and extensions to the original theory.

2   ADJECTIVES

Two modifiers in 1 are missing in 2: 'slowly' and 'deliberately'. This is because Davidson regarded adverbs like 'slowly' and 'deliberately' as not falling under his analysis: they cannot, he says, be simple predicates of events. His reason for this is that one and the same event might be slow, e.g. as a crossing of the Channel, and fast, as a swim:

3   Jones crossed the Channel slowly (by swimming quickly).

It would be nonsense to say that there was an event that was both slow and fast. A first reaction to this is that here we simply have a familiar property of many, if not all, adjectives. Adjectives are interpreted as if they have an implicit parameter referring to the relevant standard of comparison for the set of objects denoted by their subject: 'Adj for an X'. Something is not tall, *tout court*, it is tall for a man, or for a building. It is arguable that even the simplest apparently intersective adjectives behave like this: the standards of redness for a cheek are different from those for a rose or a wine.

In fact, in the case of adjectives like 'slow', it appears that all the other arguments of the verb can be relevant, not just the subject: in

4   Jones crossed the street slowly, and in doing so crossed from France into Italy,

we have an event that is slow for a crossing of the street, though possibly fairly fast for a crossing from one country into another. Davidson himself was wedded to a strictly first order analysis of English. There is a long (well, perhaps not very long) story to be told about why that cannot be the right way to go about things: here let me simply assert that the interesting features of the Davidsonian program are not compromised by ditching the first order requirement and using higher order logic. (There is of course a computational price to pay). Once we have made this

180

move, we can give these adverbials a translation which employs an extra parameter giving a full description of the type of event being considered.

5 Jones buttered some toast slowly y Textwill translate as:

6 Ee Ex (toast x) & (butter Jones, x, e) & slow(e, (\e' Ey Ez (toast y) & (butter y, z, e')))

'There was a buttering of the toast by Jones event, and by the standards of those events which are butterings of toast by someone, that event was slow'. How does something of the form Adj(e, P) get interpreted semantically? If this line of argument is correct, then understanding the meaning of such adjectives involves knowing a function which for each adjective, and for each property, divides the objects in the domain of interpretation which possess the property, into those which fall into the extension of the adjective and those which don't. No doubt many refinements for this are needed, but this will do for a first pass. We will therefore assume being given a function which enables us to use statements like this:

7 Adj(e, P) is true iff Adj-fn (Adj, P, e) = t

Of course, in an actual implementation, we can recast the effects of such a function in terms of meaning postulates, or rules of inference, at least in the cases where the property in question is capable of being dealt with in a quantitative way. So we might encode something like 'tall' as:

greater-than (height-of (x), 100ft) - tall (x, tree)

greater-than (height-of (x), 6ft) - tall (x, person)

etc.

The other adverbial present in 1 but not 2 is 'deliberately'. Davidson regards this adverbial too as not wholly extensional, since it ascribes intention to the subject of the sentence. However, now that we have moved away from first order logic, it is at least possible for us to contemplate a treatment of notions like these, and in fact, elsewhere in the paper Davidson suggests paraphrasing 'deliberately' to explicitly make reference to the intentions of the subject:

8 Jones did p deliberately = It was intentional of Jones that Jones did p

Adopting this course we might translate 'deliberately' as:

9   deliberately = \vp \x \e ((vp e) x) & intentional-of(x, ((vp e) x))

Now a sentence like:

10 Jones coughed deliberately

will translate as:

11 Ee cough (Jones, e) & intentional-of (Jones, cough (Jones, e))

'There was a coughing by Jones and that coughing by Jones was intentional of Jones'.

Of course, we still need to say what the interpretation of 'intentional' is. I have no concrete suggestions along these lines to make here, but I assume that there is a good chance that logics of the type developed by Cohen, Perrault, Levesque and their colleagues can supply enough connections between this notion and those of having goals, desires and beliefs for us to be able to make some progress here (see, for example, Cohen and Levesque 1985). The following fragment of Context Free grammar with associated semantic expressions will produce all the translations suggested so far. Notice that here, as thoughout, all functions are 'curried':

S - NP VP   : Ee NP (VP e) `

VP - Vi   : Vi

VP - Vt NP   : (Vt NP)

VP - VP Adv   : (Adv VP)

VP - VP PP   : \e \x ((VP e) x) & (PP e)

PP - P NP   : (P NP)

NP - Name   : \P (P Name)

NP - Det N   : (Det N)

Vt: $\np \e \x (np (\y (Vt\ x\ y\ e)))$

Vi: $\e \x (Vi\ x\ e)$

P: $\np \x (np (\y (P\ x\ y)))$

Det: $\P \Q\ Ax\ Px - Qx$ etc.

Adv = Adj-ly $\vp \e \setminus x ((vp\ e)\ x)\ \&\ (Adj\ e\ (\e'\ Ex'\ ((VP\ e')\ x')))$

However, there is one respect in which the suggested treament of 'intentionally' will not give the right results: if we assume that passive VPs are translated thus:

12 be arrested = $\e \y Ex$ arrest (x, y, e)

then in a sentence like:

13 The demonstrators were arrested/provoked deliberately

it will be the demonstrators who had the relevant intention. This is plausible here (more so for the 'arrested' than the 'provoked' version) but the reading on which the implicit agent had the intention is also possible. It is not clear how to contrive that this happens. One possibility might be to predicate 'deliberate' of events directly, just like other adverbs, and make the necessary ascription of intention to an agent via meaning postulates and inference in a particular context. Thus given a logical form like:

14 Ee cough (Jones, e) & deliberate (e)

and a postulate like:

15 Ae deliberate (e) - Ex intentional-of (x, happen (e))

we would simply say that if an event is deliberate then somebody had an intention that it should happen. For most verbs, this will be the agent. 'Happen' is eliminable: an event happens if there is some time that that event is at:

16 Ae (happen e) - Et (at e, t)

3   QUANTIFIER SCOPE

I now turn to a problem in the event analysis of VP modifiers concerning quantifier scope. Examples like 17a are plausibly regarded as ambiguous, between a single event that was quick, and a series of quick events. 17 b and c are biased towards one or the other reading:

17 a. Jones quickly telephoned every customer

    b. Quickly, Jones telephoned every customer

    c. Jones telephoned every customer quickly

On Davidson's original theory the single event reading can be formalised as:

18 Ee Ax customer (x) - telephone (Jones, x, e) & quick (e)

Unfortunately, this logical form entails the other reading:

19 Ax customer (x) - Ee telephone (Jones, x, e) & quick (e)

This is stronger than we want: 19 is compatible with 18, but should not be entailed by it: it might be the case that the overall event was quick even though the telephoning of one or two of the customers was slow. One suggestion is that we should try to formalise some notion of a 'minimal' event, to try to block the inference from 18 to 19. Thus adverbials might be treated thus:

20 Ax (Adj-ly P) (x) - P (x) & Adj (x) & ~ Ey P (y) & in (y, x)

18 would then translate as:

21 Ee Ax customer (x) - telephone (Jones, x, e) & quick (e) & ~ Ey telephone (Jones, x, y) & in (y, e)

Unfortunately, this still doesn't block the inference to:

22 Ax customer (x) - Ee telephone (Jones, x, e) & quick (e) & ~ Ey telephone (Jones, x, y) & in (y e)

and is in any case too strong. In a sentence involving an activity verb, we do not want to rule out the existence of subevents of the same type, which may have the same properties:

23 Jones ran quickly

24 Ee run (Jones, e) & quick (e) & ~ Ey run (Jones, y) & in (y e)

24 is too strong as a translation of 23: the defining characteristic of activity verbs is that they do contain subevents of the same type, down to a certain level, and some of these subevents might also have been quick (in fact, some of them must have been).

The problem here is again caused by the omission of the contextual parameter for the adjective meaning. If this is put in, then the readings which represent the different quantifier scopings will give rise to different values for this parameter, preventing the unwanted inference from going through - there will be different types of quickness involved. If we assume that some form of quantifier raising mechanism is in operation, operating so as to raise an NP meaning corresponding to a quantifier in the following way:

25 ... [\Q.Q---] ... = [\Q.Q---](\q. ... [\R.Rq] ...)

where the position occupied by the NP is marked by the \q variable, raised to the type of an NP by the \R, then the translation for adverbs suggested above will give us the results we need. The logical form which quantifier raising will operate on will be:

26 Ee [\P.P (Jones)] ([quickly([\np \e' \x [np](\y telephone (x, y, e'))] (\Q Az customer (z) - Qz))] e)

giving:

27 [\Q Az customer (z) - Qz] (\q Ee [\P.P (Jones)] ([quickly([\np \e' \x [np](\y telephone (x, y, e'))](\R.Rq))] e))

Given the translation of 'quickly' as:

28 \vp \e1 \x' [vp (e1)] (x') & quick (e1, (\e2 Ey' [vp (e2)] y'))

185

the first unraised form will reduce to:

29 Ee Ax customer(x) - telephone(Jones x e) & quick(e [\e2 Ey Az customer (z) - telephone (y, x, e2)])

'There was an event such that for every customer, Jones telephoned the customer, and that event was quick by the standards of those events that are telephonings of every customer by someone'. The second, quantifier raised version reduces to:

30 Az customer(z) - Ee telephone(jones z e) & quick(e [\e' Ey telephone (y z e')])

'For every customer, there was an event of Jones telephoning the customer, and that event was quick by the standards of those events which are telephonings of that customer by someone'. Now our problem is solved, for there is no unwanted inferential relationship between the two alternative readings.

4   EVENTS AND STATES

Here is another problem. The intuitive notion of event is that events are things which happen at particular places and times. But many sentences do not describe things that happen, so much as states of affairs that obtain, where the state need not be associated with any particular place and may persist through long periods of time. And these sentences seem to behave in relevant respects like our event sentences, taking VP modifiers, displaying quantifier scope ambiguities, etc.

31 Jones lived in London quietly

32 Jones owned every Hockney in London for a year (at once/in turn)

The problem of how to give a logical form for these sentences is fairly easily solved by adding to our ontology the requisite notion of state, which will behave as far as compositional semantics is concerned, exactly like events. However, this still isn't enough: there are many sentences where reference to both a state, and an event resulting in that state, seems to be being made:

186

33 Jones hired a car for two weeks

34 Jones almost ran a mile

In 33 the most natural reading is that the period for which Jones possessed (or perhaps intended to possess) the car - the resulting state - lasts for two weeks, not that the event of hiring lasted two weeks. In 34, either Jones ran, but didn't quite finish a mile, or he didn't run at all. 'Almost' can be taken to be modifying either the event or the resulting state. To account for phenomena like these we seem to need to go inside the situation described by the sentence and be able to modify components of that overall situation.

In Pulman (1977) I developed a theory within a Davidsonian framework according to which sentences described either events, actions, or events or actions resulting in states. Events were not divisible, whereas actions were: down to a certain level, actions could be seen as consisting of many instances of the same sub-action. The intention was to trade on the often observed similarity of contrast between plurals and mass vs count nouns on the one hand, and process vs punctual verbs on the other, and also to account for many aspectual phenomena in terms of restrictions on what type of ontological category particular modifiers could combine with.

Now that we have both events and states, we can help ourselves to a theory of plurality (from Link 1983) which allows us to contemplate a somewhat different formalisation of this theory on which many of the desired properties fall out from the logic itself. (See also Bach 1986 for related suggestions).

There is not space to go into all the formal details here, (even if they had all been fully worked out), but the essential features of the approach can be conveyed informally. We have atomic events, and plural or complex events. The theory put forward by Link enables us to form complex plural individuals from singular individuals of any type, events and states included. What I was calling actions now correspond to plural events. Their 'homogeneity' property then immediately follows from the nature of plurals (see Link 1983). Events, as in the original Davidson story, are just individuals like any other, whether plural or singular, likewise with states. The revised classification now looks like this:

state: own a car, live in London, like Mozart

atomic-event: blink, sneeze, cough

plural-event: run, drive a car, listen to Mozart

event + state: notice the picture, recognise Jones, hire a car,

build a house, write a thesis, recover from illness

This, as will be obvious, is similar to the well known Vendler classification, except that it is better regarded as a classification of ways people have of viewing situations, rather than of linguistic entities like verbs or sentences.

The idea now is that particular aspects and types of modifier are things which are 'sorted'; that is to say, they are functions which require their arguments (and outputs) to occupy a particular ontological slot. For example, a 'for ...' temporal adverbial requires its argument to be something capable of occupying a period of time. This requirement (although I do not know how to formalise this precisely) we will assume to be satisfied by states but not by atomic events. Thus the preferred reading of sentence 33 is that on which the 'for' phrase modifies the 'state' part of the 'hiring a car' situation, not the atomic event part. The resulting ontological category is that of another event: the event which consists of Jones having hiring a car for a week, where this retains the internal structure revealed by the interpretation of the modifier.

If the sortal requirements are not satisfied, it is possible for a process of 'coercion' to take place. (See also Moens and Steedman 1986, who take an approach which is similar in spirit). For example, we can apply an 'iterate' function to an atomic event which results in a series of such events capable of occupying a period of time, or alternatively a 'stretch' function which focuses on the normally unavailable internal structure of it, which thereby also becomes seen as extended in time.

Here is a short promissory note to illustrate how an analysis in these terms might proceed:

The progressive takes a state, or an event which it redescribes as a state, and says that the state was obtained at whatever time the sentence refers to.

188

The perfect takes an event or a state and says, to a first approximation, that whatever state resulted from that persists to the time referred to in the sentence.

This can be best illustrated informally by glossing the following examples.

35 Jones is hiring a car

The progressive takes the event part of this event + state combination, makes a state out of it and says that that state obtains now. (There is always the simple future reference use of progressives: ignore this).

36 Jones has hired a car

There was an instance of this event + state combination and the state resulting from it persists to the present.

37 Jones has hired a car for a week

There was an event consisting of an event + state combination, where the state satisfied 'for a week' and a state resulting from that event persists to the present. In cases where it is not very plausible pragmatically that events can be redescribed as states, the coercing functions might be used. Thus:

38 Jones was sneezing for a week

most naturally has the iterative interpretation. It is also possible, though desperately implausible in most contexts, to get the 'slow motion' reading induced by the 'stretch' coercing function. In fact, with ingenuity it is also possible to find similar readings in sentences like 33 and 37. The idea is that these various operators and functions build up to determine the final ontological status of a sentence in a way which, *modulo coercion*, is compositional. If this is correct, then we should be able to reduce much of the complexity of more traditional analyses to simple predications about events and states, which possibly contain reference to other events and states.

5 CONCLUSION

Clearly, much more work needs to be done before this kind of treatment could be regarded as a contender to other analyses of these phenomena currently available. However, I am optimistic about the prospects for the approach advocated here. The marriage of the Davidsonian analysis of verbs, with existing logics of mass terms and plurals, plus an intuitively quite natural expansion of our ontology to include states as well as events promises to provide an elegant and unifying approach to the semantics of these constructions, and one which does justice to the intuitions of many people that these apparently different areas of semantics actually have some deep underlying connection.

6 ACKNOWLEDGEMENTS

This is a revised version of a paper given at an Alvey workshop on Formal Semantics in Natural Language Processing, at Essex University, in March 1987, and at a seminar on 'Recent Developments and Applications of Natural Language Understanding', in London, December 1987. The work was supported by SERC grant GR/D/57713. I am grateful to Ewan Klein, Bob Moore, Henk Zeevat and many other participants on both occasions for their comments: in particular to a member of the audience on the latter occasion for pointing out that the analysis of Section 1 provided a simpler solution to the problem of Section 2 than the more complicated system I went on to develop in the original version of the paper.

7 REFERENCES

1   Bach, E 1986, The Algebra of Events, Linguistics and Philosophy, 9, 5-16.

2   Cohen, P and Levesque, H 1985, Speech Acts and Rationality, Proc. of 23rd Annual Meeting of ACL: Chicago, ACL, 49-59.

3   Davidson, D 1980, The Logical Form of Action Sentences, in his Essays on Actions and Events, Clarendon Press, Oxford (originally appeared 1967)

4   Link, G 1983, The Logical Analysis of Plurals and Mass Terms, in Meaning, Use and Interpretation of Language, ed. R. Bauerle, De Gruyter, Berlin.

5   Moens, M and Steedman, MJ 1986, Temporal Information and Natural Language Processing, Working Paper, Centre for Cognitive Science, Edinburgh University.

6   Pulman, SG 1977, Syntax and Logical Form in the analysis of Modals, Ph. D. diss, Dept of Language and Linguistics, Essex University.

Chapter 14
On-line Lexical Resources
for
Natural Language Processing

Branimir K Boguraev
Computer Laboratory, University of Cambridge

1   Introduction

Recently there has been marked interest in studying the relevance of machine readable dictionaries (MRDs) to a number of natural language processing tasks. It is clear that such sources can contain rich and variegated lexical information which extends well beyond simply defining parts of speech and is capable of supporting a wide range of activities, both of theoretical interest and of practical importance.   It is also clear, largely through the results of numerous projects, that development in hardware, as well as research in computational linguistics, offer the technology both to process lexical resources and to extract from them what is relevant to computer programs concerned with various natural language processsing applications. Data extracted from publishers' tapes has subsequently been used to support e.g. syntactic parsing, grammar development, speech synthesis, lexical disambiguation, semantic interpretation in context, robust text processing, information management, spelling correction and machine translation (Boguraev, 1986b, discusses a number of such projects).

It has been widely recognised that the Longman Dictionary of Contemporary English (Proctor, 1978; henceforth LDOCE) occupies a prominent position in lexicon-based research, due to the fact that it contains information which is not readily available in other lexical sources, organised and presented in a way amenable to formal processing by computer.

A number of research projects over the last few years, distributed between the University of Cambridge Computer Laboratory and the University of Lancaster

Department of Linguistics, have used the machine readable version of LDOCE as an online resource for studying some properties of language as well as for extracting specific data relevant to such tasks as syntactic parsing, morphological analysis, speech recognition and semantic interpretation. This paper is an attempt to bring together our experience in various aspects of dictionary use for language processing and draw some conclusions about the nature of the activities concerned with extracting data from machine readable dictionaries. In the process, I will raise some questions pertaining to principles of using MRDs as sources of lexical information for practical natural language processing.

The paper is of a predominantly descriptive nature and its structure is roughly as follows. First, I present the pragmatic background for using LDOCE by outlining some of the projects, and ultimately the utility, of LDOCE for automated language processing. Next, I discuss a number of issues concerning the placement of rich lexical resources on-line, with a view to make them readily available for use by an open ended set of diverse research projects. Specific ways in which the information in the dictionary is being used for the construction of systems with substantial coverage are described, and in the resulting context I trace some guidelines for a methodology aimed at extracting maximally usable subsets of the dictionary with minimal introduction of errors.

2 The lexical needs

The choice of LDOCE as the lexical resource underlying our research is not an accident. Ongoing work in Cambridge is aimed at extending the linguistic coverage of natural language systems: one particular project is committed to developing a substantial word list to be used, in conjunction with a computational grammar of English, by a integrated natural language parsing toolkit (Boguraev, 1986a; Briscoe et al., 1987). Concerns of different nature, under the general heading of robustness, provided the motivation for a different kind of investigation. 'Robustness' is being used here in a very general sense: thus in the context of large vocabulary speech recognition, it was taken to mean improving the performance of a system by exploiting redundancy in the speech signal (Carter, 1987); in the context of the desired functionality of a generalised natural language understanding system, it was taken to mean the ability to cope with an incomplete lexicon (Alshawi, 1987). Clearly, such projects required access to some kind of lexical resource; it was only natural to investigate the kind of information found in a machine readable dictionary.

The purely practical constraints imposed by project deadlines and limits on the manpower available strongly suggested the use of a single dictionary, if possible. The diverse nature of the work required a dictionary with certain properties; since the suitability of LDOCE for computational linguistics research has been discussed at length elsewhere (see in particular, Michiels, 1982), I will outline only briefly some of its particularly useful characteristics insofar as they are of relevance to this paper.

2.1   Requirements for syntactic data

Current formal theories of grammar place heavy demands on the lexicon. Elegant, and efficient, handling of the grammatical (and semantic) idiosyncrasies of individual lexical items can only be achieved through the massive lexicalisation of linguistic information.   This not only promotes the central position of the lexicon within a generalised architecture of a natural language processing system, but raises consequences of a very practical nature for any effort concerned with the compilation of a substantial lexical resource compatible with a particular grammatical theory.

For instance, the background for our grammar development effort is provided by the theoretical framework of Generalized Phrase Structure Grammar (Gazdar et al., 1985; henceforth GPSG). Within this theory, syntactic categories are represented as feature clusters, with individual features controlling the operations of a morphological analyser, or a sentence parser, or both. Below is an example of the syntactic component for a fragment of the complete lexical entry for *believe - as in I believe him (to be) honest and I believe (that) he has come:*

believe

[V +, N -, BAR O, AGR [BAR 2, V -, N +, NFORM NORM],

PRD -, NEG -, WORD +, AUX -, INFL +, FIN --, VFORM BSE,
LAT -, SUBCAT NP_AP]

[V +, N -, BAR O, AGR [BAR 2, V -, N +, NFORM NORM],

PRD -, NEG -, WORD +, AUX -, INFL +, FIN --, VFORM BSE,
LAT-, SUBCAT SFIN]

Details of the feature value sets used by the system need not concern us here (Grover et al., 1987, and Ritchie et al., 1987, offer more complete descriptions of the feature make up of a lexical entry, both from the perspectives of a sentence level grammar and a word level grammar). It is important to note that much of the information in the entries above is repetitive, as well as predictable - either on the basis of the part of speech assignment to the lexical item, or on the basis of the morphological rules known to the system. Thus the really essential component of a lexical entry concerns the specification of its grammatical category (via the features N and V), together with the characterisation of its subcategorisation behaviour (via a SUBCAT feature). In fact, the fully fleshed feature representations above are derived from the following abbreviated notations.

(believe ((V +) (N -) (SUBCAT NP_AP) (LAT -)))

(believe ((v +) (n -) (SUBCAT SFIN) (LAT -)))

It would seem then that the lexical requirements of a GPSC style parser can largely be met by exploiting one particular feature of LDOCE. The *grammar coding* system employed throughout the dictionary is designed specifically to represent a range of information concerning the syntactic pattern of behaviour of a word. In particular, grammar codes are capable of denoting, among other things, distinctions between count and mass nouns, differences between predicative, post positive and attributive adjectives, and subcategorisation frames for verbs. For the purposes of developing a large lexicon requiring information beyond the more conventional part of speech tagging, LDOCE seemed to offer a convenient starting point.

2.2 Requirements for phonetic data

Recent work at the Massachusetts Institute of Technology (Shipman and Zue, 1982; Huttenlocher and Zue, 1983; and Huttenlocher, 1985) has investigated an alternative model of lexical access to the one commonly utilised by current approaches to speech recognition. Typically, isolated word recognition methods utilise classical pattern matching techniques which fail to make use of any significant specific knowledge about speech and language.

However, the practical requirements of systems attempting realistic coverage impose a number of strong constraints on the model of lexical access; in particular an effective method is needed for cutting down on the large search space of possible word candidates, brought upon by the increasing lexicon size, while still making it possible to use only a crude (or partial) description of the acoustic signal. It is, in any case, unrealistic to assume that the process of lexicon lookup is similar to searches through a list of phoneme strings: not only is the full phonemic content of a word often impossible to retrieve, but speaker variations and other factors contribute to the difficulties in reliably distinguishing similar sounds.

Lexican lookup thus has to be carried out by a procedure capable of searching through the lexicon on the basis of partial knowledge of the phonetic properties of the word in question. The work at MIT proposes exactly such method, which makes considerable use of speech specific knowledge and, by employing a special representation of the speech signal based on sequential phonetic constraints, achieves the partitioning of a large lexicon into relatively small equivalence classes corresponding to phonetically similar words. The basic premise is that there are aspects of the signal, which are relatively reliably distinguished. Thus a *manner of articulation* transcription, which employs categories such as Vowel, Stop, Nasal, LiquidOrGlide, StrongFricative and WeakFricative, would assign *golf* to the class

Stop Vowel LiquidOrGlide WeakFricative

On the basis of the British English pronunciations in LDOCE, this equivalence class has only two members: golf and gulf (Carter, forthcoming). The original MIT studies indicate that at such a broad phonetic level, approximately a third of the words in a 20,000 word lexicon can be uniquely identified. The expected number of words matching a given broad class averages 25, while in the worst case it

196

seems to be about 200. This would suggest that an appropriately chosen broad phonetic representation is likely to reduce the search space of a 20,000 word lexicon to about 1 per cent of its size.

One aspect of the speech project in Cambridge was designed to investigate in detail these claims. We intended to use the *pronunciation* information in LDOCE at the basis for a study of the implications of the phonetic structure of the English lexicon with appropriately derived data from the machine-readable source, and determining the correlations between the particular combinations of partial phonetic information assumed to be provided by a front end acoustic processor and the shape of the equivalence classes resulting from partitioning of the lexicon according to this phonetic information. Some further issues of interest included questions like: how the number of words in a large lexicon (60,000 and more) affects its partitioning; what effects classification errors and variability in the speech signal might have on lexical access; and what improvements would be brought in by taking into account other factors, e.g. lexical stress.

Once a lattice of candidate phonemes was obtained, the problem of word recognition would be tackled by constructing a parser which uses information both about phoneme collocations and syntactic predictions derived from independent analyses of the phonetic and grammar coding fields in LDOCE.

2.3   Requirements for semantic data

In the model of a large vocabulary speech recogniser assumed above, a query to the lexicon would typically yield a lattice of word candidates. We intended to use additional semantic and/or pragmatic knowledge to further prune this lattice. LDOCE carries special tags, known as *subject* and *box codes,* which encode semantic notions like the overall context in which a word sense is likely to appear (e.g. politics, religion, language) and selectional restrictions on verbs, nouns and compound phrases; it was interesting to investigate the use of this information for further guidance during the word recognition process.

Quite independently, an effort of a different nature was stimulated by another distinguishing feature of the Longman dictionary. A fundamental principle underlying the definitions of all words in the dictionary is that of using *core defining vocabulary* of 2000 basic words, themselves used in their most 'central' senses, for

197

specifying word meanings across the entire dictionary. Taking this as a starting point, Alshawi set out to develop an algorithm for analysing the semantic content of the dictionary entries by converting their definition texts into fragments of semantic networks (Alshawi, 1987).

The pragmatic context of Alshawi's work was that of enhancing existing natural language processing systems with a comprehensive and robust semantic component, designed specifically to overcome problems due to incomplete or inadequate lexicons. His approach was based on generating formal semantic structures from the definitions of a suitable electronic dictionary; there are two assumptions which make LDOCE particularly appropriate for such an enterprise.

Let us imagine a natural language processing application incorporating a definitions analyser like Alshawi's. Let us also imagine that this application has access to a (hand-coded) classification of the central senses of the LDOCE core defining vocabulary together with suitable definitions of specific domain relevant concepts in terms of these word senses. Since the semantic structures output from Alshawi's analyser will, ultimately, incorporate basic defining concepts, the system would be able to carry out its application task even if a new word appeared in the input. Furthermore, and particularly true in the case of a number of applied natural language processing systems, very often even partial extraction of semantically relevant data from the definition field (e.g. only the genus term) is going to make all the difference between a system collapse or recover when faced with unknown words.

3   The software requirements

It is clear that in order to make full use of the machine readable source of LDOCE, we need a computerised dictionary embedded in a software for dictionary access with a functionality close to that offered by conventional database management systems (DBMSs). There are a number of reasons for such heavy requirements, extending beyond the obvious desire for a system capable of efficient retrieval of entries satisfying a range of selection criteria applying at various levels of liguistic description.

The alert reader may have noticed a shift in the perspective form which the premises of the projects above were described. In particular, what distinguishes the effort required by e.g. mapping the grammar codes in LDOCE into GPSG subcategorisation features from that of analysing the definition texts in the dictionary, is the presence (or, alternatively, the absence) of a fairly well defined notion of what exactly is expected at the end of the project.

I have argued elsewhere (Boguraev, 1986) that there are essentially two different modes in which MRDs can be used for natural language processing purposes. The predominant technique to date involves an arbitrary amount of pre-processing, typically in batch, of the on- line source. Those parts of the dictionary entries which contain useful data for the task at hand are extracted and suitably represented in a form directly usable by a client program. Such a model of dictionary use does not in any way rely on the original source being available at the time the language processing application is active, and thus a batch derivation of the appropriate information is a suitable way of transforming the raw data into a usable repository of lexical knowledge. To a certain extent (and I shall discuss this in more detail below) the lexical requirements of the grammar project can be met by such a development model, which can be referred to as the *deterministic mode* of dictionary use.

In contrast, Alshawi's research program exemplifies the opportunistic mode of dictionary use, also typical of a number of projects of a more experimental nature. The common denominator here is that the emphasis is on the kind of investigation focused at eliciting ways in which the availability of an MRD can aid the development of particular natural language processing systems. The assumption is that an analysis of the accumulated data in the dictionary will reveal regularities which can then be exploited for the task at hand. Alshawi took a particular property of a particular dictionary as a starting point, and, by analysing the bulk of the source, derived a 'definition grammar' together with an associated technique for parsing the definition texts into semantic structures.

Such projects (and, as I will argue below, all projects which 'push' a dictionary to its limits in an attempt to derive information which is implicitly available, but not explicitly provided) depend critically not only on the presence of a machine readable equivalent of a printed dictionary, but also on a software system capable of providing fast interactive access into the on-line source through various access routes. The placing of a dictionary on-line, for the purpose of making it accessible to a number of different research projects which need to locate and collate dictionary samples satisfying a wide range of constraints, requires an efficient and flexible system for management and retrieval of linguistic data.

3.1 Desiderata for an on-line LDOCE

Boguraev et al. (1987) discuss the major factors contributing to the difficulty of mounting a machine-readable dictionary as a fully functional database, and in particular the contradictory requirements imposed by two common properties of MRDs: the coexistence, within a single entry, of large volume of free text together with data represented by highly structured and formalised system(s) of encoding. In the long run, research on special purpose data models, capable of computationally representing a dictionary and amenable to flexible and efficient DBMS support (e.g. Tompa, 1986), will provide the functionality needed. In the short run, for the immediate purposes of our work in Cambridge, we have achieved much of the desired functionality by exploiting certain specific properties of LDOCE, which has been set up not as a database (in the computational sense of the word) but as a lexical knowledge base (LKB) with much of the desired functionality.

Target of the access This concerns the question of what is a suitable format to which fast access can be couples. The answer here lies in striking the right balance between macro- and micro- segmentation of the machine readable source. A proper database would require very detailed 'parsing' of the source, typically a highly complex task (see e.g. Kazman, 1986); however, LDOCE already provides considerable segmentation into records and fields corresponding to the natural logical units of a dictionary entry. Since it is possible to develop efficient local parsing procedures, which can be invoked after a complete entry has been retrieved from the segmented source, a convenient model of access is one where extraction of a particular datum from an entry is carried out not by the original query, but by specialist functions which manipulate the result of its execution. This saves a considerable amount of time in the process of placing the dictionary on-line.

Parameters of the access In order to be responsive to heterogeneous requests, access routes into the on-line source must incorporate knowledge about how particular kinds of lexical information are distributed across the dictionary. In order to achieve this, the local parsing functions mentioned above must be applied to all entries prior to constructing the access paths themselves, so that a complete record of the entry's explicit and implicit content is reflected into the system of routes into the source. This allows queries ranging over any combination of retrieval parameters, regardless of whether some or all of these are explicitly available in the dictionary (decompacting the formal, and often elliptical, grammar codes or imposing phonologically motivated structure on pronunciations are examples of the kind of information sought in the process of setting up the dictionary on-line; section 3 below offers more details).

Constraints on the access Efficiency of retrieval is clearly important. Since it is impossible to predict in advance the particular combinations of parameters making up specific queries, the system must be capable of dynamically constructing search paths on the basis of precompiled knowledge about the cost of satisfying individual constraints. Maximally efficient searches will then be possible by estimating the optimal order of specifying access routes into the on-line source. This happens to be a particularly important factor in interactive analysis of lexical data, as there are obvious benefits in being able to estimate, in advance, the time a query would take to evaluate.

The mounting of the machine readable LDOCE online, which follows the specifications above, is fully described in Boguraev et al. (1987). An interface system provides access to an electronic version of the dictionary. This has been restructured to provide easy coupling to client programs, but still maintains the gross format of the source, as well as preserves all information, lexical and typographic, from the original tape.

In its present form, information of six different types is analysed for the construction of access paths: semantic features classifying the meanings of words and their dependents; semantic subject area; grammatical part of speech; grammatical subcategorisation; British English pronunciations; and definition texts. Since all of these types can be mixed together in constructing search queries, individual projects can access the results of neighbouring research, thus truly sharing the lexical knowledge incorporating LDOCE. Furthermore, since the processes of any particular constraint analysis across the entire dictionary and the construction of appropriate access paths are fully automated, extending the coverage of the interface is trivial. The LDOCE access system is therefore usable by any new projects that might be set up in the future.

4 The data in the dictionary

This section is not intended to present detailed accounts of the individual projects making use of the lexical information in LDOCE; such accounts have already been given in e.g. Alshawi (1987), Carter (1987), Carter et al. (1987), Boguraev and Briscoe (1987) and Boguraev et al. (1987). Instead, I am going to examine some of the characteristics of the process of extracting and using such information.

Published dictionaries are aimed at people, consequently their computational equivalents have not been designed to be particularly easily (if at all) used by computer programs. Fundamental factors controlling to a large extent the shape of any project attempting to make use of the lexical information in a machine-readable dictionary are the *unreliability* and *incompleteness* of that information. Boguraev (1986b) makes some global remarks in this context; below I will analyse LDOCE from these particular perspectives.

4.1 Unreliability of the source

In the course of our work we have had to deal with different types of error; the methods adopted clearly depend on the severity and persistency of an undesirable property of the dictionary across the entire source.

Typographic errors This is the simplest type of error, exemplified by e.g. missing a closing parenthesis, or typesetting a field in a different font. While potentially of critical consequences, in a dictionary like LDOCE, where overall segmentation of individual entries is present at source, the scope of such errors is limited. Furthermore, they can be 'flushed out' very early during the processing and thus have virtually no effect on any subsequent activities.

Syntactic errors   More persistent, and not immediately obvious, are inconsistencies within the formal systems employed for encoding any particular type of information in the dictionary. These errors are of 'syntactic ' nature, and only become apparent during the process of retrospective analysis of such formal systems, for the purposes of developing software for local parsing. For instance, Boguraev and Briscoe (1987) discuss the 'grammar' of the grammar coding system in LDOCE, and point out a number of problems with decompacting the large number of elliptically and partially specified codes. Alshawi (1987) presents a moderately detailed evaluation of the degree to which the Longman lexicographers have adhered to the guidelines for using the core defining vocabulary. It turns out that not only the notion of 'most central sense' of a word is a very fuzzy one, but also there is no specification of the rules governing the compositionality of the defining terms for the purposes of conveying more complex notions, a situation which leads to circularities and logical 'holes' in the coverage of the conceptual core underlying the definitions in LDOCE.

In the context of the speech work, Carter (forthcoming) reports problems of a similar nature. The system employed to represent the pronunciation information in the dictionary, while seemingly formal and rigorous, makes use of a number of eliptical devices (partially specified alternative pronunciations; only stress patterns, and no phonemic information, for compound entries; no pronunciation for homophones; incomplete marking of syllable boundaries). Dealing with such problems computationally often requires not only standard techniques of data decompaction, but the application of non-trivial amounts of phonetic or phonological knowledge.

Semantic error   These concern erroneous data, stated explicitly in the source. Naturally, such errors are more rare. Unfortunately, they still occur, and are likely to throw a program working with that data off-balance. A particularly good example in the context of LDOCE is the mis-assignment of particular sub-categorisation patterns, via the grammar coding system, to particular word senses (a problem further compounded by not very perspicuous, or motivated, distinctions between the different senses within a word entry). Boguraev and Briscoe (1987) discuss the occurences of such errors and their effect on the program which attempts to use the information in the grammar codes of LDOCE.

4.2 Incompleteness of the source

This is a characteristic which can be analysed along at least two dimensions. In one sense, the term can be taken to refer to what is missing from the dictionary. An alternative way of looking at the same issue is from the perspective of the related question of implicit and explicit information in dictionaries.

Missing data Under this heading I will only consider omissions on micro scale. The fact that, for instance, LDOCE does not specify etymology is a global property of that particular dictionary. On the other hand, the lack of a particular subcategorisation pattern in an entry, either via an incomplete grammar code, or due to a word sense missing altogether, is clearly of direct concern to our effort on a lexicon for GPSG. McCawley (1986) discusses a number of ways in which dictionaries omit information; and even though he is mostly concerned with principles for writing definitions aimed at bringing out salient linguistic properties, there are quite clear consequences of the omissions at the focus of his article for a program like Alshawi's.

Implicit data This is an issue which has recently been discussed at length in a variety of contexts. Thus McCawley (1986) suggests a number of ways in which important distinctions should be made explicit in dictionaries. Atkins et al., (1986), present a detailed examination of two dictionary formats, analysing the relationships between form and meaning. They conclude that a large proportion of the information which is essential for 'knowing' the meaning of a verb is, in fact, available in e.g. the example sentences. However, it is not clear at all how to extract such information algorithmically.

This is, in fact, the central issue from the perspective of any project like the ones discussed in this paper. Not surprisingly, extracting information implicitly present, but not explicitly specified in the dictionary, is at the focus of almost all current research efforts based on machine-readable sources (the list is too big to give here; work done at IBM Yorktown Heights, Bellcore and the Center for Study of Language and Information contains a number of representative examples; see also Boguraev, 1986b, for specific references).

It is helpful to draw the same distinction here as earlier - that of seeking information in micro- or macro-scale. In the first case, the boundaries of the search are those of an individual entry. In the second case, the whole dictionary provides background data, whose analysis reveals hidden regularities about language.

An example from our work of extracting implicit information in micro-scale is the derivation of control information for verbs from the subcategorisation information carried by the grammar codes. It turns out that even though individual verb senses in LDOCE are not tagged with their semantic type (expressed by the Raising/Equi distinction in transformational grammar), it is possible to derive such information on the basis of relating grammar codes to traditional syntactic tests (Michiels, 1982). A specialised extraction procedure is fully described, and assessed for overall correctness and reliability, in Boguraev et al., 1987) produces the following output from the LDOCE definition to believe (note that while a fairly straightforward mapping can be defined, translating e.g. 'T5a' into a (Takes NP SBar) frame, there is nothing in the dictionary which specifies that *believe is* an Object Raising verb which logically takes two arguments):

believe... v1[10] to have a firm religious faith 2[T1] to consider to be true or honest: <u>to believe someone\to believe someone's report</u> 3[T5a,b; V3;X (to be) 1. (to be) 7]to hold an opinion; suppose: <u>I believe he has come. He has come. I believe. 'Has he come?' 'I believe so' I believe him to have done it. \ believe him\(to be) honest</u>.......	(believe verb (Sense 3) ((Takes NP SBar) (Type 2)) ((Takes NP NP Inf) (Type 2 0Raising)) ((or ((Takes NP NP NP) (Type 2 0Raising)) ((Takes NP NP AP) (Type 2 0Raising)) ((or ((Takes NP AP AP) (Type 2 0Raising)) ((Takes NP NP AP) (Type 2 0Raising))

For the purposes of the speech project, both in order to build a lexical knowledge base allowing, among other things, syllable based access and in order to have data suitable for large study of the phonetic structure of English, it was necessary to assign phonologically motivated structure on pronunciations, typically given as strings of phonemes and stress markers, but with no syllable demarkation. This is another instance of making explicit, by bringing linguistic knowledge into the process, the information within a particular entry: pronunciation fields are parsed into *syllables* and, within a syllable, into *onset, peak and coda*, using the phonotactic constraints given in Gimson (1980) and employing a *maximal onset principle* (Selkirk, 1978) where these yield ambiguous syllable boundaries (Boguraev et al., 1987).

205

The work on speech also provides an example of extracting implicit information ranging across the entire dictionary source. Analysis of the phonetic data in LDOCE has shed new light on the applicability, from the point of view of large vocabulary speech recogniser architecture, of certain models of acoustic front end (Carter, 1987). Furthermore, Carter et al. (1987) have been able to examine the relative usefulness of different parts of the speech signal for word recognition.

The reason for making a distinction between the micro and macro scales at which essential information is sought from a dictionary is to bring out an important consequence from any MRD-based research. While procedures for extracting information in micro-scale do not necessarily require the kind of a multi-path dictionary access system discussed in the previous section, the collation and analysis of information ranging over the entire machine-readable source, and not constrained to a single field within an entry, is almost certain to call upon the kind of a lexical knowledge base, characterised by the properties of flexibility and extensibility emphasised earlier.

In a sense, it is difficult to draw clear cut boundaries between the precise types of activity which can be facilitated by having a lexical knowledge base available and those which critically require one. For instance, the procedure for determining the semantic type of verbs was tested, tuned and evaluated over all verb entries in the dictionary. A very simple model of access, namely retrieval by grammatical category, was all that was required. This kind of need can be satisfied by writing a special purpose, 'one-off' program; indeed, if this is the only requirement from an on-line dictionary, then an effort of designing and implementing a fully functional lexical knowledge base is going to be somewhat excessive.

If, on the other hand, the particular research environment can be characterised by having to incorporate a wide range of demands from an open-ended set of projects and, furthermore, applications would have to be supported such that due to variable demands for information search strategies must be worked out dynamically every time, then a flexible knowledge base becomes a fundamental requirement for this environment; a point which is made rather emphatically by Boguraev et al. (1987) and further argued in detail by Carter (forthcoming).

5   A methodology for using the information

An obvious, and by no means an original, question in the light of the above discussion concerns the ultimate utility of LDOCE in particular, and other machine-readable sources in general, for computational liguistics. Simply asking "Was it worth it?" with reference to all the efforts of preprocessing the source, mounting it on-line, and developing the whole collection of programs which derive, digest, compile and use the lexical data in LDOCE, is going to elicit a positive reponse. The key, however, to this response is not only in the fact that LDOCE occupies a somewhat prominent position in terms of its content and format. An equally critical consideration in this context is related to the way in which the information in the dictionary is used.

It is unequivocally clear that LDOCE has been, and will be, tremendously useful for a great number of research efforts, both of predominantly theoretical nature and driven by the particular demands of natural language applications. It is also clear that after the initial stages of data analysis, pragmatic constraints come into play; and we are typically faced with the task of efficient, simple and accurate development of (some kind of a) computational lexicon from a source which cannot be regarded as providing complete, consistent and totally accurate lexical information.

It would seem then that what is required for successfully making computational use of a machine-readable dictionary is not only the development of a suite of programs which extract, or infer, whatever a client language application requires from its lexicon, but embedding these programs into an environment incorporating a particular methodology for using an on-line source on a large scale.

The critically important characteristics of such an environment are a direct consequence of the nature of the lexicon development task. First, it would be based on an interactive, rather than batch, model of use. The inherent unreliability of the source makes it unrealistic to expect that running the transformation programs 'overnight' over the machine-readable dictionary is going to result in a felicitous lexicon which is complete, correct and ready to be used by e.g. a parser. The implications of such a model of use are twofold: entries generated automatically

207

have to be checked on an individual basis; however, this should be done without slowing down the process unnecessarily.

Thus the second consequence of such design is that the lexicon development environment ought to be aimed at a linguistically competent user. The checking of individual entries is naturally done by hypothesising situations calling for their use, and the process is likely to involve grammaticality judgements. The linguist/lexicographer must always be in control; still, in order to maintain speed the system itself should embody a fair amount of liguistic knowledge (e.g. of morphology, grammar, parsing and so forth).

The environment must also be designed to be maximally supportive: from software engineering point of view in particular this means allowing the user easy access to all of the underlying functionality of the system without dramatic changes in context. For instance, editing of an entry under consideration must be possible from a point where a parser used to test the entry by parsing text with it has failed. The consideration of speed and efficiency will be further met by offering guidance at all times.

It ought to be clear by now that such methodology is based on maintaining a fundamental distinction made in the context of our research in machine-readable dictionaries, which involves the conceptual (an implementational) separation between the notions of *extracting* information from on-line sources and using this information for practical purposes.

In practical terms, this is achieved by introducing a level of 'neutrality' in the output of the extraction programs. Even if a very specific application, with clearly defined lexical requirements and format, is the client of particular extraction procedures, these procedures are defined to produce 'proto-entries' in a form which can subsequently be piped into a whole family of related applications. The intermediate specification of verb subcategorisation and control information exemplified in section 3.1 above is a case in point; Alshawi's semantic structures are also deliberately defined to be as neutral as possible with respect to a number of different knowledge representation frameworks.

Being able to posit 'theory neutral', or 'poly-theoretical', intermediate representations is not only a desirable prerequisite for true sharing of lexical data on a large scale (see Walker, Tampolli and Calzolari, 1987). In the immediate context of the transition between the processes of extraction and use of lexical data allows for softly configurable systems, in which fine tuning of both the extraction software and the shape of the back-end lexicon can proceed independently.

The design of the lexical knowledge base, presented as a stand-along system in section 2, in fact follows the guiding principles set out above. A different example of bringing all of the above considerations together is a particular design and implementation of a lexicon development environment constructed for the purposes of deriving a large lexicon for a GPSG-based system for morphological and syntactic analysis of English. The system is fully described in Bogursev et al. (1987).

6   Summary and conclusions

In this paper I have described a number of projects attempting to make computational sense of a machine-readable dictionary; I have also presented some observations stemming from our collective experiences in the process of working with a moderately idiosyncratic object. Even though our efforts have been within one framework only, namely that provided by the on-line availability of LDOCE, there are generalisations to be made concerning the use of other similar sources for the purposes of practical natural language processing.

In particular, I have argued that any such efforts are likely to require critical analysis of the source data and substantial amount of software development, necessarily incorporating linguistic knowledge.   Furthermore, in order to make interesting, and ultimately beneficial, use of the lexical data in a machine-readable source, it has to be mounted on-line in a way allowing the full utilisation of the lexical information in it, both implicitly available and explicitly specified, within an entry and across the entire dictionary. I have sketched the fundamental design considerations of such a lexical knowledge base, from the particular perspective provided by the distinguishing characteristics of LDOCE.

It is important to realise that the benefits from mounting the dictionary in a particular way are not unconditional; furthermore, these benefits arise not from having a fully functional database management system as such, but from being able to emulate such a system by emphasising the flexibility and extensibility of its interface component. The fact that the overall segmentation of the electronic version of LDOCE turns out to be additionally convenient for setting it up as a lexical knowledge base, is yet another argument in favour of the recently initiated effort to specify an interchange dictionary format (Amsler, 1987), since such a format would imply eventual distribution of machine-readable sources with similar level of segmentation.

We have experimented with a particular model of dictionary use, one where the distinction between extracting information required from an application and making that information available to the application is maintained in a strong way. Apart from promoting in-depth analysis of some (or all) aspects of the data in the dictionary, the model offers an optimal way of meeting the lexical requirements of the back- end natural language application with the particular information extracted from LDOCE. The associated methodology for making maximal use of this potentially rich, but inherently unreliable, resource is generally applicable to any effort attempting large scale utilisation of machine-readable sources.

It is clear that dictionaries are richer than they appear. It is also clear that with the right balance of linguistic knowledge, computational linguistics technology and software engineering, such sources can be pushed further and further in search of knowledge about language. Are there limits to this? How will we know when these limits have been reached? This is still an open question, perhaps best left open.

7   Acknowledgements

This paper draws on the joint work and experience of the following people: Hiyan Alshawi, Ted Briscoe, John Carroll, David Carter, Claire Grover and the author. The research has been supported mostly by the UK Science and Engineering Research Council, by means of research grants GR/D/87321 and

GR/D/4217.7 and research fellowships for Hiyan Alshawi and the author. We are particularly grateful to the Longman Group Limited for kindly allowing us access to the LDOCE typesetting tape for research purposes. A condensed version of this material was presented at a conference on 'The Uses of Large Text Databases' at the University of Waterloo.

8 References

1 Alshawi, Hiyan (1987), 'Processing dictionary definitions with phrasal pattern hierarchies', Computational Linguistics, vol. 13

2 Amsler, Robert (1987), An interchange format for machine-readable dictionaries, Record of a Working Group on Knowledge and Data Bases, Workshop on the Lexicon in Computational and Theoretical Perspective, Stanford CA.

3 Atkins, Beryl; Kegl, Judy and Levin, Beth (1986), Explicit and implicit information in dictionaries, CSL Report 5, Cognitive Science Laboratory, Princeton University.

4 Boguraev, Bran (1986a), A natural language toolkit: reconciling theory with practice, in C. Rohrer and U. Reyle (eds), Proceedings of a Workshop on Word Order and Parsing in Unification Grammars, Friedenweiler, Germany

5 Boguraev, Bran (1986b), Machine-readable dictionaries and research in computational linguistics in D. Waler and A. Zampolli (eds), Proceedings of an International Workshop on Automating the Lexicon, Grosseto, Italy.

6 Boguraev, Bran; Carter, David and Briscoe, Ted (1987), A multi-purpose interface to an on-line dictionary, Third Conference of the European Chapter of the Association for Computational Linguistics, Copenhagen, Denmark.

7 Boguraev, Bran; Briscoe, Ted; Carroll, John; Carter, David and Grover, Claire (1987), 'The derivation of a grammatically-indexed lexicon from the Longman Dictionary of Contemporary English', Proceedings of the 25th Annual Meeting of the Association for Computational Linguistics. Stanford, CA, pp. 193-200.

8 Boguraev, Bran and Briscoe, Ted (1987), Large lexicons for natural language processing - exploring the grammar coding system of LDOCE, Computational Liguistics, vol. 13.

9 Boguraev, Bran and Briscoe, Ted (1988, in preparation), Natural language processing and computational lexicology, Longman Limited, Harlow.

10 Briscoe, Tec; Grover, Claire; Boguraev, Bran and Carroll, John (1987), A formalism and environment for the development of a large grammar of English, Tenth International Conference on Artificial Intelligence, Milan, Italy.

11 Carter, David (1987), 'An information-theoretic approach to phonetic dictionary access', Computer Speech and Language, vol. 2.

12 Carter, David; Boguraev, Bran and Briscoe, Ted (1987), Lexical Stress and Phonetic Information: Which Segments are Most Informative, in Proceedings of the European Conference on Speech Technology, Edinburgh.

13 Carter, David (1988, forthcoming), 'LDOCE and speech recognition', in B. Boguraev and E. Briscoe (eds) Natural language processing and computational lexicology, Longman Limited, Harlow.

14 Gazdar, Gerald; Klein, Ewan; Pullum, Geoffrey, K.; and Sag, Ivan A. (1985), Generalized phrase structure grammar, Oxford: Blackwell and Cambridge: Harvard University Press.

15 Gimson, A.C. (1980), An introduction to the pronunciation of English, Edward Arnold, London.

16 Grover, Claire; Briscoe, Ted; Carroll, John and Boguraev, Bran (1987), The Alvey natural language tools project grammar - large computational grammar of English, Lancaster Papers in Linguistics, Department of Linguistics, University of Lancaster.

17 Huttenlocher, Daniel and Zue, Victor (1983), 'Phonotactic and lexical constraints in speech recognition', Proceedings of the National Conference of Artificial Intelligence, Washington D.C., pp. 172-176.

18 Huttenlocher, Daniel (1985), Exploiting sequential phonetic constraints in recognizing spoken words, A.I. Memo 867, Artificial Intelligence Laboratory Massachusetts Institute of Techynology, Cambridge, MA.

19 Kazman, Rick (1986), Structuring the text of the Oxford English Dictionary through finite state transduction, Technical Report TR-86- 20, Department of Computer Science, University of Waterloo, Waterloo, Ontario.

20 McCawley, James (1986), 'What linguists might contribute to dictionary making if they could get their act together', in P. Bjarkman and V. Raskin (eds), The real-world linguist (linguistic applications in the 1980s), ABLEX, Norwood, New Jersey, pp.3-38.

21 Michiels, A. (1982), Exploiting a large dictionary database, Ph.D. Thesis, Universite de Liege, Belgium.

22 Proctor, Paul (1978), Longman dictionary of contemporary English, Longman Group Limited, Harlow and London, England.

23 Ritchie, Graeme; Pulman, Stephen; Black, Alan and Russell, Graham (1987), 'A computational framework for lexical description', Computational Linguistics, vol.13.

24 Selkirk, E.O. (1978), On prosodic structure and its relation to syntactic structure, Indiana University Linguistics Club, Bloomington, Indiana.

25 Shipman D.W. and Zue, V.W. (1982), Properties of large lexicons: implications for advanced isolated word recognition systems, Proceedings of the International Conference on Acoustics, Speech and Signal Processing.

26 Tompa, F. (1986), Database design for a dictionary of the future, Preliminary report, Centre for the New Oxford English Dictionary, University of Waterloo, Waterloo, Ontario.

27 Walker, Don; Zampolli, Antonia and Calzolari, Nicoletta (1987), Towards a polytheoretical database, Preprints from a working group; Report No. 5, Instituto di Linguistica Computazionale, CNR - Pisa, Italy.

Chapter 15
Discourse Structure
in
LOQUI

T WATCHEL,
Scicon Ltd

1   INTRODUCTION

This paper is about the LOQUI system, the natural language interface being developed within the LOKI project [1]. The goal of the project is to build, in Prolog, a natural language interface to a database, in the first instance, but with a view to its being portable to other domains and also to other back-ends. A working prototype exists for English and German, and interest has been expressed in extending the software to Dutch, French and Greek outside the project.

One of the most important aspects of LOQUI is that it is intended to be more than just a question-and-answer system. It is being designed so as to have a rich dialogue capability that will allow conversations to proceed with the coherent fluidity that is characteristic of human interaction, thereby allowing both system and user the possibility of exploiting contextual information in order to minimise constraints on expressiveness. In short, LOQUI operates relative to the context that has been built up during a conversation, rather than returning to a neutral state after each exchange.

Although the title of this paper declares it to be about discourse structure in LOQUI, other aspects of the system will also be discussed, both in order to provide information about the work we are doing, and also to describe the context in which the discourse manager operates. The first part of the paper will therefore deal with parsing, world knowledge, semantic representation, generation and spelling correction. The second part will deal with discourse management, covering such points as discourse structure, discourse referents, reference resolution, and a few other minor points.

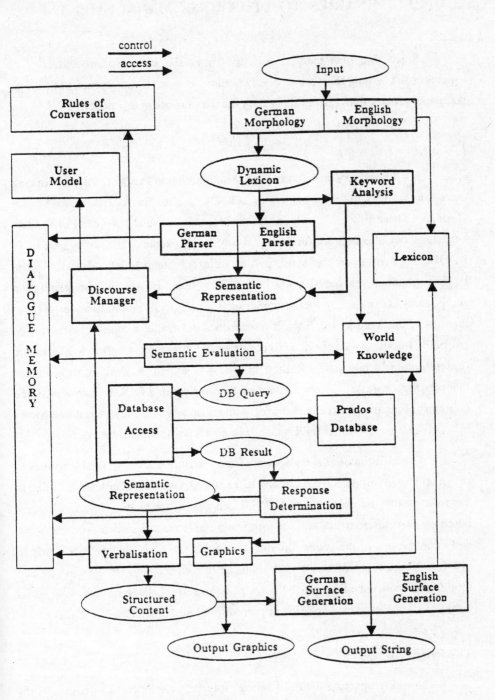

Diagram 1. Illustrates the general architecture of the LOQUI system.

2   PRELIMINARIES TO DISCOURSE MANAGEMENT

Since discourse management does not exist in a vacuum, but involves aspects of the system, this section briefly outlines some of those aspects, but without going into greater detail than is necessary for the purpose of this paper.

Parsing

I will have very little to say here about parsing in LOQUI. At the moment, there are two very different parsers in LOQUI, one for English and the other for German. These differ not only in the obvious ways required for each of the two languages, but also in more fundamental ways. For example, the two grammars in LOQUI are written in the spirit of two different linguistic theories. LFG, the English grammar, is based on GPSG. The same is true of the generation components. However, neither grammar feels ideologically bound to either of these theories. For example, the English parser does not create a syntactic structure at any point, but uses rules of syntax to constrain the direct construction of a semantic representation in one pass. Rather, the insights gained by working within these theories are expressed in the grammars that reside in LOQUI. Moreover, the German grammar is written in non-executable form which is converted into a parser by a preprocessor, whereas the English grammar is written in executable form.

These distinctions stem not only from the different theoretical learnings of the people responsible for the parsing of each language, but also from a desire to keep the system modular. Since LOQUI can operate with two different parsers based on two different linguistic theories and implemented in two different ways, and since the rest of the system operates uniformly for either language, it is safe to say that any parser whatsoever that might be introduced into the system at some future stage will not affect the behaviour of the rest of the system as long as its output is a semantic representation as currently defined for LOQUI.

The world model

No self-respecting natural language interface can operate without a world model. In LOQUI, this is written in CML (Conceptual Modelling Language), developed by SCS in Hamburg and CCI in Heraklion. (See Bibel et al (1986), Imlah (1987), Gallagher & Solomon (1986), Topaloglou (1987)). The world model is represented as a hierarchy of classes with instances and properties. In addition, rules may be defined on classes to express knowledge that can be used in inferencing, and elsewhere. For instance, rules of this type are used to relate the world model to the back-end in order to get the correct database mappings from semantic representations. Moreover, these rules, as well as other aspects of the world model, are used in error recovery, in particular to hypothesise about the user's intended meaning in the face of apparent semantic deviance or the impossibility of finding a reasonable mapping to database access formalisms. Examples of such error recovery will be given below.

A Davidsonian approach to events is adopted (Davidson, 1980). That is, in the semantic representation we find quantification not only over individuals, but also over events, states and other relations. This is reflected in the world model. In fact, the semantic representation deals only in CML objects, and a CML object may equally well be an instance of a person, an instance of a project, an instance of the possession by a person of a string as a name, an instance of the relation of temporal precedence holding between one project and another, and so on, including the classes that these instances belong to. That is, we do not take the Davidsonian position to be that of extending quantification to events, as an object is not restricted to physical object, but is taken to be any object represented in the world model, and this includes situational objects, relational objects, abstract objects, and so on, as well as physical objects.

The consequences of this are that the world model we use differs considerably from what is usually considered uncontroversial in such matters. For instance, it would be uncontroversial to introduce into the world model a root class entity with two subclasses: string and temporal, the latter of which has two subclasses: person and project. Instances of class temporal have the property name whose value must be of class string, and instances of class project have the property leader, whose value must be of class person. This could be represented as in (1), where CLASS introduces a class in the hierarchy, ISA specifies a subclass relation, and WITH specifies a property, and a restriction on the class IN which its values must be. Properties are inherited downwards. We could then represent the project called LOKI, whose leader is called John as in (2), where INSTANCE x IN y introduces an instance x of class y. XI and X2 are arbitrary names of CML objects.

In contrast, however, our world model is as in (3) (omitting certain irrelevant details, such as what is or is not a temporal). Note that the property leader no longer exists. The new properties alpha and theta are properties of instances of the class situation (which corresponds to situations as in Lyons (1977) or Comrie (1976).) The easiest first-pass way to digest them is to think of alpha as logical subject and theta as direct object. I stress that this is not what they actually are, since they are not grammatical relations at all, but abstract CML properties whose interpretation is constant only relative to each class for which they are defined, and therefore depends on the class involved, but it helps at first to adopt this fiction. There are many cases for which one fiction does not hold. We can now represent the above project as in (4).

In work in progress, we have in fact eliminated the property name, replacing it with the relation name, with properties alpha (the name) and theta (the name).

We have many reasons for adopting this approach, none of which merits lengthy elaboration here. In brief, however, the fact that the word leader exists is no subclass of the class person. The word leader is no more than a word in the lexicon, whose semantics is specified in terms of the property alpha of the class leading. Moreover, instances of the leading relation exists and can be talked about, and in particular can have other properties, such as duration, for example. The last fact alone motivates the above approach, unless one is willing to countenance properties having

(1)   CLASS: entity
         CLASS: string
                 ISA entity
         CLASS: temporal
                 ISA entity
                 WITH name IN string
         CLASS: person
                 ISA temporal
         CLASS: project
                 ISA temporal
                 WITH leader IN person

(2)

```
        INSTANCE: X1 IN person
              WITH name: John
        INSTANCE: X2 IN project
              WITH name: LOKI
              WITH leader: X1
```

(3)

```
        CLASS: entity
        CLASS: string
              ISA entity
        CLASS: temporal
              ISA entity
              WITH name IN string
        CLASS: project
              ISA temporal
        CLASS: person
              ISA temporal
        CLASS: situation
              ISA temporal
        CLASS: leading
              ISA situation
              WITH alpha IN person
              WITH theta IN temporal
```

(4)

```
        INSTANCE: X1 IN person
              WITH name: John
        INSTANCE: X2 IN project
              WITH name: LOKI
        INSTANCE: X3 IN leading
              WITH alpha: X1
              WITH theta: X2
```

properties, which we are not. Other principles of non-arbitrary world modelling, together with a dash of Occam, lead to the position we have adopted.

One of the effects of adopting this position is that LOQUI's world model may differ drastically from a domain model as LOQUI cannot be ported to a domain model supplied by an end-user for adaptation to a natural language interface. We believe that this is in fact how things should be, in that, in general, such models will support the use of natural language in that domain (those of immediate interest to the modeller), but not the semantically richer relationships and objects that are implicit in the user's use of natural language about the domain. Thus there may be many words that the user would wish to use to describe the domain which are not represented in his model adequately enough to allow an application with a natural language component. The domain mode must be rich enough to support the use of natural language about that application domain, not just the commands of a formal language of the system.

We see no actual contention between requirements modelling and modelling for natural language. A CML model for a domain application must be adequate to express what the user wants to say about the domain in natural language, if a natural language processor is to be part of the information system. However, the domain expert cannot be expected to be a natural language expert as well. Any user-defined network can be expanded so that it can represent all the same knowledge, but within LOQUI's world model.

I apologise for not providing further argumentation of the position outlined above, and fail to do so on the grounds that this is a separate topic in its own right. This section is designed only to illustrate our approach in this area, in that it impinges on other issues that are more central to this paper, such as semantic representation, reference resolution and discourse structure.

Semantic representation

The aim of this section is to provide an idea of the nature of the semantic representation formalism we adopt. The semantic representation produced by the parser is a structure represented as a list of terms which may be functors or further lists of such terms. The first terms in the list represents the speech act. Quantifiers are represented as functors at the head of a list. The restrictor of a quantifier is represented as the tail of the list of which the quantifier is the head and the scope of the quantifier by whatever follows the quantifier, at any level of list-embedding. Examples (5) to (8) should be relatively self-explanatory.

(5) the man leads a project

```
    [
      assert(exists(_3475))
    ]
    some(_3475)
    [
      unique(_3177)
      single(_3177)
      instance(_3177,person)
      propval(person,_3177,sex,male)
    ]
    [
      some(_3535)
      single(_3535)
      instance(_3535,project)
    ]
    instance(_3475,leading)
    propval(leading,_3475,theta,_3535)
    propval(leading,_3475,alpha,_3177)
    topic(_3177)
```

(6) the man that leads a project

```
    [
      supply(referent(_3303))
    ]
    [
      unique(_3303)
      single(_3303)
      instance(_3303,person)
      propval(person,_3303,sex,male)
      [
        some(_3621)
        [
          some(_3681)
          single(_3681)
          instance(_3681,project)
        ]
        instance(_3621,leading)
        propval(leading,_3621,theta,_3681)
        propval(leading,_3621,alpha,_3303)
        topic(_3303)
      ]
```

(7) does the man lead a project

```
        [
          request(affirm(exists(_3292)))
        ]
        some(_3292)
        [
          unique(_3357)
          single(_3357)
          instance(_3357,person)
          propval(person,_3357,sex,male)
        ]
        [
          some(_3732)
          single(_3732)
          instance(_3732,project)
        ]
        instance(_3292,leading)
        propval(leading,_3292,theta,_3732)
        propval(leading,_3292,alpha,_3357)
        topic(_3357)
```

(8) LOKI is led by John

```
        [
          assert(exists(_3329))
        ]
        some(_3329)
        [
          unique(_3206)
          single(_3206)
          instance(_3206,temporal)
          propval(temporal,_3206,name,str(LOKI))
        ]
        instance(_3329,leading)
        [
          unique(_4035)
          single(_4035)
          instance(_4035,temporal)
          propval(temporal,_4035,name,str(John))
        ]
        propval(leading,_3329,alpha,_4035)
        propval(leading,_3329,theta,_3206)
        topic(_3206)
```

(9) every dog bit a cat

```
[                                          [
  assert(exists(_4086))                      assert(exists(_4086))
]                                          ]
[                                          [
  all(_4616)                                 some(_4655)
  single(_4616)                              single(_4655)
  instance(_4616,dog)                        instance(_4655,cat)
]                                          ]
some(_4086)                                [
tense(past)                                  all(_4616)
[                                            single(_4616)
  some(_4146)                                instance(_4616,dog)
  single(_4146)                            ]
  instance(_4146,cat)                      some(_4086)
]                                          tense(past)
instance(_4086,biting)                     instance(_4086,biting)
propval(biting,_4086,theta,_4146)          propval(biting,_4086,theta,_4655)
propval(biting,_4086,alpha,_4616)          propval(biting,_4086,alpha,_4616)
topic(_4616)                               topic(_4616)
```

The scope ambiguity shown in (9), where two interpretations are provided, is not handled by the syntactic rules of the parser. The syntax-driven parser produces only one output for these sentences. This is presented to a module which recognises potential scoping ambiguities, and produces a number of different representations accordingly. This module is not yet complete.

Generation

For some time now, LOQUI has had the ability to generate a dialogue memory, and has had a discourse manager whose role is to maintain a coherent discourse state in respectable ordinary conversation, but also, and more importantly, in deviant or even devious conversations. However, the discourse manager has not given LOQUI any real generation component, it lacked the ability to initiate (sub) dialogues. The only mode in which LOQUI could operate was that of input-and-response. Cases of inability to respond appropriately were dealt with by declaring this to be the case, and terminating the exchange. Since LOQUI cannot initiate a dialogue, there is no possibility of the user responding in a deviant way, or, for that matter, no possibility of the user responding at all. Therefore, there is no way in which these aspects of the discourse manager's components can be invoked.

The English generation component has been designed and implemented 'outside-in'. That is, we have not yet concerned ourselves with making the link between LOQUI's database results and semantic representations, but only with arriving at suitable English strings from semantic representations. The intention is to build a generator that can handle the very general problem of expressing meanings, without yet worrying where these meanings come from, or taking into account that the generator is part of an interface to a database. The aim is to provide a general expressive component, thus ensuring the portability of LOQUI's generator.

We have used LOQUI itself as a tool to build and test the generator by taking the actual output of the current LOQUI parser as direct input to the generator. LOQUI currently operates in three modes. In normal mode, LOQUI accesses the database. In repeat mode, LOQUI parses the input to a semantic representation, which is passed directly to the generator for reproduction. In paraphrase mode, LOQUI parses the input to a semantic representation, which is passed directly to the generator for reproduction in as many different ways as possible, including the exploitation of synonyms and semantically equivalent syntactic structures. The current prototype is therefore also an indicator of LOQUI's current generation capabilities in English, including LOQUI's knowledge about semantic equivalence of various types.

The generator is decremental in that the input, a semantic representation, is scanned for fragments that can be resolved into natural language text using the syntax rules of the generator and the words that are available in the lexicon. If the resolution of a fragment is successful, then that fragment is consumed - i.e. removed from the input representation - and the rest of the input is passed to the next rule in the generator. What this next rule is depends on how earlier fragments were resolved. A generation is thus defined as successful if the input semantic representation is consumed fully by a legal sequence of rule applications, including successful lexical access for the grammatical and semantic features into which fragments of the semantic representations have been resolved.

Backtracking ensures that if failure occurs on an attempt that is, say, syntactically valid but lexically invalid, a different syntactic approach will be tried if there is one. For example, if the lexicon contains the verbs 'lead' and 'give', and the noun 'leader', but does not contain the noun 'giver', then the semantic representation of strings such as 'a man that leads' and 'a man that gives' may try to generate using an agentive nominal rather than a relative clause. This will fail at lexical access for 'giver' because it is not in the lexicon. Backtracking will then generate the relative clause solution.

The generator can perform some interesting acrobatics over the lexicon, using its rules of syntax as supports. For instance, the lexicon includes the words 'girl', 'woman', 'child', 'youngster', 'youth', 'person', 'young' and 'female'. From a single semantic representation, the generator will produce all of the examples in (10).

(10)

> a girl
> a young woman
> a female child
> a female youngster
> a female youth
> someone young and female
> a young female person

This shows its knowledge about lexical relations, and lays the foundation for a Gricean treatment of why 'young woman' means the same as 'girl', but not quite the same. The generator also knows about verbosity. That is, it can execute an instruction to reproduce 'girl' verbosely (young female person), and to reproduce 'young female person' concisely (girl).

Since the generator works in a vacuum at the moment, there is no way of generating pronominal forms, since it is obviously the case that the criteria for deciding whether to use a pronoun or a lexical noun lie in the current dialogue state. That is, it is information from the dialogue memory, which is currently not available

225

to the generator, that will decide when to use proforms. The same is true for all sorts of ellipsis.

The extended live conversation with LOQUI shown in (11) with the generator in action illustrates some of the points made above.

(11)

```
*** use repeat mode
OK.

*** the dog gave the cat a book
the dog gave a book to the cat

*** the dog gave the cat a book
the dog gave the cat a book

*** the cat received a book from the dog
the cat received a book from the dog

*** use paraphrase mode
OK.

*** the dog gave the cat a book

    the dog gave the cat a book
    the dog gave a book to the cat
    the cat was given a book by the dog
    the cat received a book from the dog
    a book was given the cat by the dog
    a book was given by the dog to the cat
    a project leader
    a leader of a project
    a task leader
    a leader of a task
    someone that heads an activity
    someone that heads a project
    someone that heads a task
    someone that leads an activity
    someone that leads a project
    someone that leads a task
    someone that runs an activity
    someone that runs a project
    someone that runs a task
    a person that heads an activity
    a person that heads a project
    a person that heads a task
    a person that leads an activity
    a person that leads a project
    a person that leads a task
    a person that runs an activity
    a person that runs a project
    a person that runs a task
```

someone that an activity is headed by
someone that an activity is lead by
someone that an activity is run by
someone that a project is headed by
someone that a project is lead by
someone that a project is run by
someone that a task is headed by
someone that a task is lead by
someone that a task is run by
a person that an activity is headed by
a person that an activity is lead by
a person that an activity is run by
a person that a project is headed by
a person that a project is lead by
a person that a project is run by
a person that a task is headed by
a person that a task is lead by
a person that a task is run by

a book was received by the cat from the dog

*** a bitch

a bitch
a female dog

*** a female puppy

a young bitch
a female puppy
a young female dog

*** a young female person

a girl
a young woman
a female child
a female youngster
a female youth
someone young and female
a young female person

*** use repeat mode
OK.

*** an english tomboy
an English tomboy

*** be verbose
OK.

*** an english tomboy
someone English boyish young and female

*** the fat boy gave the happy tomboy a new puppy
the fat young male person gave the happy boyish young
female person a new young dog

227

<pre>
*** be concise
    OK.

*** use paraphrase mode
    OK.

*** someone that leads a project

    an activity head
    a head of an activity
    a project head
    a head of a project
    a task head
    a head of a task
    an activity leader
    a leader of an activity
</pre>

Spelling Correction

Error recovery is an important part of discourse management, and spelling correction is an important part of error recovery. In conjunction with the ability to recover from the semantic deviance, and the ability to generate strings from semantic representations, it provides a useful tool in allowing a dialogue to continue in spite of errors, but at the same time alerting the user to the corrections that LOQUI has effected. Examples of this will be given in the section on error recovery, below.

Speed problems are overcome by using a deformed lexicon to minimise lookups, and a trigram array to limit the search space. This technique involves storing deformed forms of each word in the lexicon (Mor & Fraenkel, 1982). Each n-character word is stored in this lexicon n times, each time omitting one of the letters. In addition, it stores the missing character and its position in the word. The deformed lexicon and the trigram search routine are implemented in C and Pascal to further increase response time.

LOQUI's spelling corrector traps the four major types of typing error: omitting a character, inserting one, transposing one or replacing one. This accounts for over 80 per cent of spelling errors, and over 95 per cent excluding multiple errors (Damerau, 1964). It returns solutions ordered by error type probability. The four types of error that it traps occur with different frequencies, the most common being replacement and omission, followed by insertion and finally transposition (Peterson, 1986).

Problems of selectivity are tackled by ranking error types by probability and by keyboard adjacency. A model of the Sholes ('Qwerty') keyboard is stored.

Spelling corrections involving adjacent keys are more likely than non- adjacent ones. For example, *ir* would be corrected to *it* before *in* because the keys R and T are adjacent, whereas R and N are not. The parser ensures that ungrammatical alternatives are rejected, and the deformed lexicon for correction is limited to domain dependent and common words, so that irrelevant interpretations are not attempted. Peterson (1986) notes the problem exemplified by the word *sat*, which can be mistyped as 54 other words. Without contextual clues, it is impossible to trap this type of error. Conversely, an unrecognised word in the user's input may not be misspelled. It may be a proper noun, or a word that is not in the system's lexicon. All of the corrections of the word are made available to the parser, including that of being a name, ordered by the above probability rankings.

The parser uses its rules of syntax to discriminate between interpretations. This means that the same form can be given different interpretations in different sentences. For instance, 'Who lerds LOKI?' would cause LOQUI to interpret 'lerds' as a misspelling of the verb 'leads', whereas 'Who leads lerds?' would cause LOKI to interpret 'lerds' as a name.

3   DISCOURSE MANAGEMENT

Let us now turn to the discourse manager itself. In this section we will discuss the types of structures assigned to dialogues in LOQUI, the way in which discourse referents are established, and how they are used to resolve reference.

The discourse manager

The discourse manager is invoked after every user input has been evaluated, and after every response by LOQUI. It is a bottom-up dialogue parser. That is, it takes each input, and, given a current dialogue state, decides how to produce a new dialogue state that takes into account the current input. It also establishes a set of expectations as to what the next move might be, thus laying the foundation for conversational repair in the face of unco-operative user behaviour. A dialogue state consists of a hierarchical structure of move labels which refer to the dialogue memory - a permanent record of the semantic representations of all the moves in the current session, together with other information about each move. To illustrate what the discourse manager does, consider the dialogue shown as (12).

(12)

*** who leads BIM-PROLOG
   Raf Venken
*** who works on the project
   Raf Venken, Lieve Debille and Bart Demoen
*** does Lieve Debille lead any project
   No.
*** which projects does Walther von Hahn lead
   LOQUI, HAM-ANS, HAM-RPM and LOQUI2
*** doesn't he lead LOKI
   I'm afraid not.
*** who reports to him
   Helmut Horacek, Claudius Pyka, Martin Schroeder, Tom Wachtel, Bill
   Imlah, Wolfgang Wahlster, Wolfgang Hoeppner, Anthony Jameson,
   Katharina Morik, Thomas Christaller, Heinz Marburger, Bernhard Nebel
   and Stefan Busemann

This 12-move dialogue has been parsed into the structure shown as Figure 2. This is the structure actually produced by the current prototype. That is, LOQUI's dialogue memory is more than just a list of inputs. Relationships between moves are recognised, and the whole dialogue is represented as a tree structure in which certain abstract nodes are introduced. The node names used here are mnemonic for User, Conversation, Dialogue, Exchange and Move.

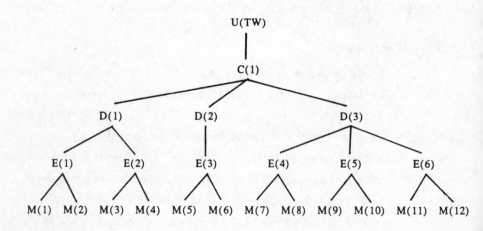

Figure 2.

This states that these 12 moves constitute a conversation with the user identified as TW, and that this is the first conversation with this user. The moves have been analysed, incontroversially, as constituting six exchanges. More interestingly, LOQUI has decided that these six exchanges constitute three dialogues. The topic of an exchange (an E-node), or of a number of exchanges, is defined at the D-node that dominates them. In the above dialogue, LOQUI identified three difference topics, with topic changes on move 5 (from BIM-PROLOG to Lieve Debille) and on move 7 (from Lieve Debille to Walther von Hahn).

The discourse manager can also identify subdialogues, where the topic of the exchange is the exchange itself, with a pop back to the matrix topic in due course, and can also introduce hypothetical moves, which are a reflex of the user failing to respond as expected. These abilities, however, are not yet integrated into the current prototype, although the discourse manager will assign the structure shown in Figure 3, which is that assigned to dialogue (13) in isolation. This shortcoming is due to the fact that the generator is not yet integrated sufficiently to allow LOQUI to produce the requests for clarification.

(13)
```
        *** when is the next IJACI meeting?
            I suppose you mean "IJCAI"
        *** yes
            Do you mean the next conference or the next
            conveners' meeting
        *** conference
            12 August 1985
```

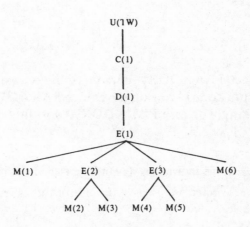

Figure 3.

Further details are available in Wachtel (1986). The point here is to illustrate the sort of thing that LOQUI does, or will do. LOQUI does them in order to establish a context of discourse to which reference can be made in subsequent parts of the dialogue.

In addition, a dialogue state includes information about the current user, the current topic of the exchange, and a set of current discourse referents.

Discourse Referents

At any point during a conversation with LOQUI, the system is aware of a set of discourse referents. These are CML objects whose existence as discourse referents has been sanctioned in one way or another.

The list of discourse referents is maintained in the following way. A CML object is sanctioned as a discourse referent either if it is mentioned by the user or by LOQUI, or was referred to indirectly during the evaluation of a user input. Discourse referents are not restricted to objects such as people or projects, but include relations, and other more abstract objects. For example, assume that there are three people on the database whose names are Achilles, Tortoise and Zeno, and that they are all working on a project called PARADOX. The exchange shown as (14) establishes the seven discourse referents shown in (15).

(14)

> *** Does anyone work on PARADOX?
> Yes

(15)

> project(PARADOX), person(Achilles), person(Tortoise),
> person(Zeno), working(Achilles,PARADOX),
> working(Tortoise,PARADOX), working(Zeno,PARADOX)

Note that the individuals do not have to be mentioned in order for them to become discourse referents. It is sufficient for the exchange to involve potential reference to them.

Furthermore, discourse referents do not have to exist on the database, or anywhere. The input 'Does anyone lead ALPHA' will generate a discourse referent project (ALPHA) even if no such project exists on the database. The justification for this is that it can still be referred to subsequently, as in this sentence.

Discourse referents are ephemeral objects in that they are created anew each time the discourse manager is called. However, since reference resolution picks up objects from among the discourse referents, they do get carried along through the conversation - but only as long as they are still being referred to somehow. That is, a discourse referent is like a ball being tossed between the discourse manager and the reference resolution component, and it is a discourse referent for as long as neither side drops it.

However, there is always one discourse referent that is salient, and that is the topic of the current exchange. The topic is determined by the discourse manager on the basis of the latest input in conjuction with the current dialogue state, and, in particular, with what the current topic is. Topics are more stable than other discourse referents, in that they do not cease to be discourse referents if they are not referred to in the subsequent move. In order for an object to cease to be the topic, there must be sufficient grounds for the discourse manager to decide that there is a new current topic which has ousted the old one. In other words, discourse referents die through neglect, unless they are the topic, which has to be killed by another topic.

Reference Solutions

The semantic representation produced by the parser for 'it' is identical to that produced for 'the thing'. That is, there is no indication that a pronoun has been used. This approach forces upon us what we see as a desirable restriction, namely, that all reference resolution is done pragmatically. That is, LOQUI does not worry about anaphors and antecedents, but only about referring expressions and referents. There is 'therefore' no such thing as pronoun resolution in LOQUI, but only reference resolution, since the resolution component operates only on the semantic representation, and cannot recognise whether a pronoun has been used, except in the case of first and second person pronouns, where the semantic representation includes a marker specifying that the addressee or speaker is being referred to.

At first glance, this approach fails to capture control phenomena traditionally associated with syntatic c-command relations. However, as Levinson (1987) points out, there are good reasons for questioning the over- grammaticisation of anaphoric phenomena, and for attempting to account on pragmatic grounds for at least some of the phenomena that have hitherto been considered the province of syntax. We support this approach, and therefore are adopting the line that all such phenomena should be so addressed in the first instance, though we have not actually done so yet. Of course, if it turns out that certain such phenomena cannot be handled pragmatically, we will not feel ideologically bound to continue to hold the radical line.

The parser therefore produces a semantic representation such as that in (16) for the input 'he hit it'. This is identical to the representation produced for 'the person hit the thing'. The sex information contained in pronouns in English is at present omitted. This is about to be remedied, but it makes no difference to LOQUI at present because the database is not itself capable of making these distinctions.

(16)

```
[
  assert(exists(_3821))
]
some(_3821)
[
  unique(_3608)
  single(_3608)
  instance(_3608,person)
]
[
  unique(_3883)
  single(_3883)
  instance(_3883,entity)
]
instance(_3821,hitting)
propval(hitting,_3821,theta,_3883)
propval(hitting,_3821,alpha,_3608)
topic(_3608)
tense(past)
```

No reference resolution is performed within the parser. Immediately after the parser, a reference resolution component scans the semantic representation for candidates for reference resolution. When a suitable candidate is encountered, an attempt is made to identify its referent from among the discourse referents available in the current dialogue state as determined by the discourse manager. If a suitable referent is found, the reference link is established, and the evaluation continues as if reference had been made to that individual explicitly. If there is no suitable referent, evaluation continues with no reference link established, which will result in the same range of potential dialogue breakdowns generated by a contextually inappropriate attempt to resolve reference relative to context.

The reference resolution component is language-independent, and requires only that the semantic representation conform to what has been specified for LOQUI. This, of course, requires that both parser and lexicon be consistent across language in the way they treat pronouns, and nouns in general. If this is done, dialogues such as those in (17) can take place.

(17)
                   *** does NO lead LOKI
                   Yes
                   *** does he work on it
                   Yes

Moreover, it is possible to refer to objects that have not been named or described explicitly, but appear only as discourse referents. In (18), the project LOQUI is not actually named at all by either party until the very end.

(18)
                   *** does CP work on anything
                   Yes
                   *** who leads the project
                   Walther von Hahn
                   *** when did it start
                   On the 15th of August 1984
                   *** what describes it
                   LOQUI-Report NLI 4711: Final Report
                   *** what is the title of the project
                   A Natural Language Interface to Databases
                   *** what is it
                   LOQUI

The dialogue in (19) illustrates the interaction between reference resolution and the topic of the exchange, and how decisions made about reference resolution affect the course of the dialogue. The list of current discourse referents is shown as a list after each exchange, with the topic as the first element of the list. The notation used for CML object names is the abbreviated class-name functor notation actually used in LOQUI. This list expands and contracts during the course of the dialogue, and the choice of topic is affected either by explicit mention of some object, or by a reference to a discourse referent. LOQUI's ability to resolve reference is not constrained by the length of the dialogue. That is, there is no constraint that the referent should have been introduced at most two moves earlier, or anything of that nature. LOQUI always operates with a set of current discourse referents, and this current set is amended as the dialogue proceeds.

Since these are pragmatic phenomena, one might expect there to be some indeterminancy about the choice of referent made in certain cases. For instance, not everyone will agree that the referent of 'he' in 'does TW work on the project he leads' should be Nick Ostler. However, this is one possible choice, and it is the one that the current limited version of LOQUI goes for, at the same time deciding that 'TW' is not the topic.

(19) *** who leads LOKI
      Nick Ostler

      [pro(LOKI),lea([pro(LOKI),per(NO)]),per(NO)]

      *** does he work on it
      Yes

      [per(NO),wor([pro(LOKI),per(NO)]),pro(LOKI)]

      *** does anyone report to him
      Yes

      [per(NO),rep([per(NO),per(VH)]),per(VH),rep([per(NO),per(JG)]),
      per(JG),rep([per(NO),per(RV)]),per(RV),rep([per(NO),per(MP)]),
      per(MP),rep([per(NO),per(KH)]),per(KH),rep([per(NO),per(WB)]),
      per(WB),rep([per(NO),per(AR)]),per(AR),rep([per(NO),per(PB)]),
      per(PB),rep([per(NO),per(JM)]),per(JM)]

      *** does TW work on the project he leads
      No.

      [per(TW),per(NO),lea([pro(LOKI),per(NO)]),pro(LOKI),pro(LOQUI),
      wor([pro(LOQUI),per(TW)])]

236

```
*** who leads the project he works on
    Walther von Hahn

[per(TW),lea([pro(LOQUI),per(VH)]),per(VH),pro(LOQUI),
 wor([pro(LOQUI),per(TW)])]

*** what is it
    LOQUI

[pro(LOQUI)]

*** what follows the project that follows it
    That has not been specified in the current database.

[pro(LOQUI)]

*** does CP work on LOKI
    No.

[per(CP),wor([pro(LOKI),per(CP)]),pro(LOKI)]
```

Donkey Sentences

An obligatory question at this point is whether LOQUI handles donkey
sentences. In short, not yet. There are several reasons for this. Firstly, LOQUI
only handles reference resolution by reference to discourse referents - i.e. exophora.
It does not, however, deal with intra-sentential anaphora. Therefore, a sentence like
'Does every person that leads a project work on it?' will be parsed, but the referent
of it will be taken to be a project that was a discourse referent before this input, if
exactly one such exists. If this happened to be LOKI, then the sentence would be
taken to be synonymous with 'Does every person that leads a project work on
LOKI?'. In the current database accessed by LOQUI this happens to be false. The
problem is complicated by the fact that LOQUI does not yet handle universal
quantification. Faced with such a problem, LOQUI gets cold feet and only checks
for existential quantification. In short, LOQUI thinks that 'Does every person that
leads a project work on LOKI?' means 'Does some person that leads a project work
on LOKI?'. In the current database accessed by LOQUI this happens to be true.
Unfortunately, it has nothing to do with whether every person that leads a project
works on it.

This also causes problems in simpler examples. With an input such as
'Does NO lead a project that he works on' an attempt will be made to determine the
referent of the pronoun by looking for the available discourse referents - but these

these may or may not include NO. These obviously major shortcomings are to be addressed shortly.

Error Recovery

We have so far been dealing with discourse situations in which there was a need to resolve vagueness in the user's input. A second type of discourse situation is one in which the user's input is well-specified semantically but contains either spelling erors, or semantic deviance, or both.

In such cases, the world model and/or the spelling corrector is invoked in order to attempt to make sense of the user's input. In addition, the generator is used to clarify to the user what corrective action has been effected.

The examples in (20) illustrate this behaviour on LOQUI's part. We have no further comment to make here, except to stress again the need for interaction between various parts of the system if smooth discourse is to be maintained.

(20)

> *** which document describes LOKI?
>
> LOKI Report 111: Results
>
> *** what describes LOKI
>
> LOKI Report 111: Results
>
> *** who describes LOKI
>
> I assume you mean "Which document is LOKI described by?" rather than "Who describes LOKI?".
>
> LOKI Report 111: Results
>
> *** which dog describes the cat that NO leads
>
> I assume you mean "Which document describes the activity that is headed by NO?" rather than "Which dog describes the cat that NO heads?".
>
> LOKI Report 111: Results
>
> *** which old bitch runs LOKI

238

I assume you mean "Who is LOKI headed by?" rather than "Which old female dog heads LOKI?".

Nick Ostler

*** who lerds LOKI

"who lerds LOKI" ...? I suppose you mean "Who is LOKI headed by?".

Nick Ostler

*** who lerds lerds

"who lerds lerds" ...? I suppose you mean "Who is Lerds headed by?".

There is no such project on the database.

*** which happy cat runs the LOKI dog

I assume you mean "Who is the activity headed by?" rather than "Which happy cat heads LOKI?".

Nick Ostler

*** which hippy chat runs hte LOKI gog

"which hippy chat runs hte LOKI gog" ...? I assume you mean "Who is the activity headed by?" rather than "Which happy cat heads LOKI?".

Nick Ostler

*** which tank does NO load

"which tank does NO load" ...? I suppose you mean "Which activity is headed by NO?".

LOKI

*** who ruins LOKI

"who ruins LOKI" ...? I suppose you mean "Who is LOKI headed by?".

Nick Ostler

Presupposition Failure

In the same vein as the preceding section, we present in (21) examples of LOQUI's ability to detect presupposition failure. Where possible, LOQUI attempts to maintain the dialogue by providing at least the information requested, but also pointing out any detected presupposition failure. At present, this is restricted to existential and uniqueness presupposition failures.

(21)

*** when do the projects of the people that report to NO start

On the 15th of August 1984, 1st of January 1981, 1st of January 1975 and 1st of January 1987

*** when did the project that preceded LOKI start

Well, it could be on the 1st of January 1975 or 1st of January 1981. There is more than one such project on the database.

*** when did the project that followed HAM-ANS start

Well, on the 15th of August 1984, but there is more than one such project on the database.

*** does anyone work on the project that follows HAM-ANS

Well, yes, but there is more than one such project on the database.

*** who

Nick Ostler, Paul Bates, Jim Madar, Walther von Hahn, Claudius Pyka, Bill Imlah, Helmut Horacek, Tom Wachtel and Martin Schroeder

*** which document describes the project that precedes the project that the people that VH reports to lead

Well, it could be HAM-RPM Final Report or HAM-ANS Final Report. There is more than one such project on the database.

Implicature

While LOQUI is not yet able to detect conversational implicatures of the type usually attributable to apparent violations of Grice's Cooperative Principle, the groundwork has been laid. This has been described above in the section on English generation, where cross-reference to the current section was also made.

LOQUI now has a concept of prolixity. That is, LOQUI knows not only that 'girl' means the same as 'young female person' at one level, but also that these two expressions of the same semantic representation involve different levels of prolixity. Therefore the information on which to base a derivation of an implicature based on apparently unwarranted over-proxility has been laid.

We will, however, say no more on this point here, firstly because there will be more to say once actual implicatures are being derived, and secondly because LOQUI is at the stage where the interaction of generation and discourse management is becoming crucial, as we noted in the introduction to the section on English generation.

Response Determination

This brief section is intended merely to illustrate another ability that LOQUI has which depends on the interaction of several independent modules. In the very vague requests shown in (22), LOQUI combines its knowledge of the world together with its knowledge of possible database mappings, as well as using reference resolution, in order to discover what sorts of things it can say about a given individual. It then finds those particular things in the database, and uses the generator to express the semantic representations created as a result.

We do not claim subtle text generation here. You will note that there is an obvious need for stylistic improvement, particularly in the use of anaphors and ellipsis.

*** describe MS

> The name of the person is Martin Schroeder. The
> alias of the person is MS. The costcode of the person
> is 1234. The id of the person is 471142. Martin
> Schroeder works on LOQUI. Martin Schroeder reports to
> Walther Von Hahn.

*** describe the project he works on

> The name of the project is LOQUI. The title of the
> project is A Natural Language Interface To Databases.
> The project LOQUI is described by LOQUI-Report NLI
> 4711: Final Report. LOQUI is run by Walther Von Hahn.
> The LOQUI project starts on 15/08/84. LOQUI ends on
> 15/02/87. Walther Von Hahn works on LOQUI. Claudius
> Pyka works on LOQUI. Bill Imlah works on LOQUI. Helmut
> Horacek works on LOQUI. Tom Wachtel works on LOQUI.
> Martin Schroeder works on LOQUI. LOQUI precedes LOQUI2.
> LOQUI succeeds HAM-RPM. LOQUI follows the HAM-ANS
> project.

4 CONCLUSION

The LOKI project is due to end in July 1988. The main thrust of the work in the remaining period will be to integrate the full abilities of the discourse manager by improving in particular the relationship between it and the generator, and thereby increasing the power of LOQUI'S response determination in general. Other major aspects of the work include the addition of a large lexicon held in secondary storage, and the integration of the graphics facilities being developed by the Fraunhofer Institute in Stuttgart to give combined direct manipulation and natural language input.

Footnotes

LOKI is ESPRIT project P107, with a consortium of partners from Britain, Belgium, West Germany and Greece. The natural language work is being undertaken by Scicon Ltd (Bill Imlah and Tom Wachtel), the University of Hamburg (Walther von Hahn, Helmut Horacek, Claudius Pyka and Martin Schroeder), the Fraunhofer Institute (Jaap Hoepelmann) in Stuttgart and BIM (Jean-Louis Binot and Lieve Debille) in Brussels.

5 REFERENCES

1 Bibel, W J Gallagher & Venken, R, 1986, PROLOG Support for high-level knowledge representation formalisms.

2 Comrie, B, 1976, Aspect London: Cambridge University Press.

3 Damerau, F J, 1964, A Technique for Computer Detection and Correction of Spelling Errors. Communications of the ACM 7:171-176.

4 Davidson, D, 198,. Essays on Actions and Events. Clarendon Press, Oxford.

5 Gallagher, J and Solomon, L, 1986, CML Support System. User's Guide. Unpublished paper, SCS Technische Automation und Systeme GmbH.

6 Imlah, W G, 1987, CML in LOQUI. Unpublished LOKI working paper BI-30, Hamburg University, 1987.

7 Levinson, S C, 1987, Pragmatics and the grammar of anaphora: a partial pragmatic reduction of Binding and Control phenomena. Journal of Linguistics 12.2.379-434.

8 Lyons, J, 1977, Semantics. London:Cambridge University Press, volume 2.

9 Mor, M & Fraenkel, A S, 1982, A Hash Code Method for Detecting and Correcting Spelling Errors. Communications of the ACM, 25:935-938.

10 Peterson, J L, 1986, A Note on Undetected Typing Errors. Communication of the ACM, 29:633-637.

11 Topaloglou, T, 1987, Final report on CM (Conceptual Modelling). Unpublished paper, Institute of Computer Science, Research Centre of Crete.

12 Wachtel, T, 1986, Pragmatic sensitivity in NL interfaces. Coling 86.

Chapter 16
Communication Failure in Dialogue Implications for Natural Language Understanding

R REILLY
Educational Research Centre, St Patrick's College, Dublin

1   INTRODUCTION

The purpose of this paper is to highlight some of the theoretical and technical issues involved in getting computers to engage in non-spoken natural language dialogue with a user. An additional concern of this paper is the issue of robustness in natural language communication.

If one conceives of dialogue as a mechanism for ensuring robust communication, the topics of dialogue understanding and robustness can be seen to be closely related. The content of a dialogue can be divided into two components: one dealing with the purpose of the dialogue, and the other concerned with effecting this purpose. The role of the latter component is to manage the smooth exchange of information between participants. It is this component that makes dialogue more than just a sequence of exchanges. If this source of information could be tapped, it would greatly increase the robustness of natural language understanding systems.

It is generally accepted that the proper interpretation of utterances in a dialogue requires that participants go beneath the surface of linguistic exchanges to their underlying intent. Within a computational framework, this means adopting a plan-based approach to dialogue understanding. Planning as a general problem-solving technique is well understood within artificial intelligence, and has been applied to the areas of discourse and dialogue understanding with some success [1,7].

The main theoretical assumptions of this paper can be summarised as follows: It is argued (1) that the best medium for robust natural language

244

understanding is dialogue; and (2) that the best basis for a computational dialogue system is a plan-based one. In the following sections the range and type of dialogue miscommunication will be discussed. This will be followed by an outline of a dialogue model intended to form the basis for a robust natural language understanding system.

2   SOME DEFINITIONS

Before proceeding, some terminological clarification is required. In some of the literature in this area, the terms discourse and dialogue are used interchangeably. Nevertheless, it is often useful to distinguish between extended monologue, both spoken and textual, and true dialogue involving one or more participants. The term dialogue as used in this paper will refer to the latter form of communication.

In subsequent sections, reference will be made to miscommunication and ill-formed input. These terms need some elucidation. By miscommunication is meant any form of misunderstanding or misinterpretation that ultimately leads to a disruption in the flow of dialogue and to explicit corrective action by the dialogue participants. The definition of ill-formedness, on the other hand, entails computational considerations. Ill-formedness usually refers to any input which the language understanding system cannot deal with in a straightforward manner. An utterance can be anything from lexically ill-formed (e.g. involving a misspelled word) to pragmatically ill-formed (e.g. a database retrieval request for information to which the user is not entitled). An ill-formed input can be defined as any utterance which requires modification in order to be interpreted. Obviously, not all ill-formed input will lead to miscommunication. Misspellings and mispronunciations, for example, can often be processed without any disruption of the dialogue. In contrast, all miscommunications are caused by, or manifested as, ill-formed utterances (semantically and pragmatically ill-formed utterances in the main).

Notwithstanding this definition, it is possible for dialogue participants to communicate at cross-purposes without either of them realising it. This is indeed a form of miscommunication, but it must be excluded from the definition given here,

245

since one cannot be privy to the mental models that the participants have of their dialogue and its content. A measure of miscommunication must be grounded on the empirical evidence provided by the utterance.

3   A TAXONOMY OF MISCOMMUNICATION

Ringle and Bruce [11] identify two main categories of miscommunication in ordinary conversation which have some relevance to miscommunication in the person-machine context: input failure and model failure. Since we are primarily interested in the computer implementation of dialogue systems, in the following description of the taxonomy the recipient of the utterance will be referred to as the system, and the sender as the user.

An input failure occurs when the system is unable to obtain a complete, or at least a coherent, interpretation for an utterance; a model failure occurs when the system is unable to assimilate inputs to a coherent belief model, as intended by the user.

<u>Input failures</u>

Within the broad category of input failure it is possible to identify the following sub-types: identify the following types:

(a) Perceptual failures;   A word or phrase is not clearly perceived and no interpretation results, or a word or phrase is misperceived and an inconsistent interpretation results. An analogue of this in the context of the person-machine interface would be a failure to understand lexically ill-formed input, i.e. a mistyped or misspelled word.

(b) Lexical failures: A word or phrase is clearly perceived but the system either fails to produce the correct semantic interpretation or is unable to produce any interpretation at all. The ill-formed input giving rise to this type of failure might be a word that is not in the system's lexicon. In the context of keyboard input, the distinction between type (a) and (b) input failures is not clearcut.

(c) Syntactic failures: Individual words and phrases are correctly perceived and interpreted, but the user's intended meaning is misconstrued. Such failures are likely to be due to a combination of poorly phrased input on the part of the user and an inadequate coverage of possible utterances by the system's parser.

(d) Dialogue failure: A given utterance can be understood in isolation, but cannot be integrated into the ongoing dialogue representation. This might be due to an unresolved anaphoric reference, or to the violation of some norms of well-formedness for dialogue structure (e.g. a question being replied to with another question).

A closer look at syntactic failures. Carbonell and Hayes [2] distinguish between a number of classes of ill-formed utterance that can give rise to syntactic failure. The following is their categorisation: (i) missing words (e.g. copy new files my directory); (ii) spurious words (e.g. copy if you would be so kind the new files to my directory please; delete I mean copy the new files to my directory); (iii) out of order words (e.g. new files to my directory copy); and (iv) constraints violation (e.g. copy the two new files to my directory).

Case (i) is a good example of the commonly observed phenomenon that people communicating with a computer via a natural language interface employ a form of 'computerese', leaving out function words, articles, and so on [2, 3, 15]. This is probably in the belief that a telegraphic form of input is easier for the computer to understand. Case (i) also covers ellipses and other fragmentary inputs. Ellipses are linguistically entirely legal phenomena, but they must be treated computationally by the same mechanisms that treat sentential ill-formedness, as they have the same appearance as ill-formed sentences. Utterances containing ellipses can only be understood in the context of preceding utterances. Take, for example, the following fragment of dialogue:

A: John can walk and chew gum.

B: Mary can 0 too.

The notation 0 is used to indicate an elliptical reference to the phrase 'walk and chew gum'. Utterance B is incomprehensible without reference to utterance A

Case (ii) illustrates the opposite problem to that of missing words, the occurrence of spurious words. In some cases these may be valid phrases that cannot be dealt with by the parser, as in the example provided, or as in the following one from Carbonell and Hayes [2]:

Add if you would be so kind two fixed head and if possible
dual ported disks to my order.

However, spurious words can also result from the user breaking off an utterance and starting a new one. In some cases an explicit warning is given that a phrase is being restarted, such as the phrase 'I mean' in the second of the two examples given above. A more complex example of this phenomenon is the following (again from [2]):

Add a high speed tape drive, that's disk drive, to the order.

The type of recovery strategies required to parse utterances containing spurious words are surprisingly similar to those needed for utterances with missing words. The input will contain recognisable as well as unrecognisable words. While in some cases the unrecognisable elements may be noise phrases such as 'please' and 'if you would be so kind', in others they may be important information carrying elements that are critical to a successful parse. In the latter case we must parse what fragments of the utterance we can recognise, as if the unrecognisable words were indeed missing.

Out of order constituents (iii) are similar from a parsing point of view to sentences in which the functions words, or the 'syntactic glue' of the utterance is omitted. Since much syntactic information is carried by word position (although this is true of English more than, say, Italian), a strategy designed to deal with missing syntactic constituents is also the best one to adopt when dealing with words that are out of order.

Constraint violations (iv) cover a range of ill-formed input, from the violation of number and gender agreement to the inappropriate use of tenses.

In general, methods for dealing with syntactic-level input failures are relatively well-developed. Where progress needs to be made is in the area of dialogue input failures and the much more problematic area of model failures.

A closer look at dialogue failures. An important class of dialogue failure is the inability of a participant to resolve references in the domain of discourse. This form of miscommunication, and techniques for its repair, are discussed in some detail by Goodman [4].

Goodman studied the instructional dialogues used by Grosz [6] in which an expert tells an apprentice how to construct a toy water pump. He noted that a frequent source of error in this type of dialogue is the description used by a speaker to identify an object in the domain of discourse. The description can be imprecise, confused, ambiguous, or overly specific. Goodman proposed that the primary means for repairing faulty description is by reducing the specificity of (relaxing) parts of the description.

The perceptual features of an object are used in a description to provide a means for distinguishing one from another. Goodman has observed that the features most likely to be relaxed are those that require the most active consideration, for example the colour or shape of an object. Features that require more active consideration on the part of the listener (such as relative size, distance or weight) are usually the last feature to be relaxed. According to Goodman people tend to be casual with less active features and more careful with active ones. As a result, the main cause of reference failure is found to be the inaccurate use of less active features.

The main aim of Goodman's work is to try and incorporate in a computer-based system the tolerance for inaccurate description which he has observed to be used by human participants in dialogue. He considers one of the main techniques used by humans to be a relaxation of certain parameters of the description in a principled way.

Model failures

Whereas input failures are local in origin model failures tend to be global in nature. They involve misconceptions which can lead to a breakdown in the structure or content of a participant's belief model. Unfortunately, model failures are extremely difficult to study in naturalistic dialogue because there is no way to accurately assess a participant's belief model.

Webber and Mays [15] provide a further sub-classification of model failure in the context of a natural language interface to a database. They suggest that there are two main classes of misconception which a user can have when interacting with a database: (1) misconceptions about what is the case, and (2) misconceptions about what can be the case. This distinction seems to be analogous to that made between

249

assertional and terminological knowledge in many systems of knowledge representation. The work of Webber and Mays suggests that it is not enough to rely on a simple collection of facts to deal with model-level misconceptions, but that this needs to be augmented with a much richer representation of the entities in the dialogue domain.

Although most categories of input failures can be dealt with at the sentential level, model failures require a solution at the dialogue level. The next section will outline a dialogue model which could provide a framework for such a solution.

4   SKETCH OF A DIALOGUE MODEL

The purpose of the model described here is twofold: to provide a framework within which to encompass a wide range of dialogue phenomena, and to provide the basis for robust communication. However, as has been suggested in the introduction, the provision of a computational model of dialogue is a major step towards a robust natural language understanding system.

<u>Dialogue in Context</u>

In research on natural language understanding, when the focus of attention is shifted from the sentential to the dialogue level, the role of context assumes a central importance. Take, for example, the following exchange:

Q: What time does the train to Cork leave?

A1:[Context: In a railway station] 11 o'clock, Platform 5.

A2:[Context: In a travel agency, planning a trip] 11 o'clock; but there's another at 11.30 if you miss your connection.

Although, both A1 and A2 are co-operative responses, they could be inappropriately co-operative if the contexts were switched. Therefore, aspects of the context as well as the meaning of the communicative act determine a participant's interpretation and response. Consequently, the structures used in computationally representing dialogue must not only represent the linguistic content of the utterance, but also go some way to representing the relevant facets of the situation in which the act was uttered. Of course, determining what are relevant and

250

irrelevant facets of a situation is another variation of the 'frame' problem, and as such is one of the several hard problems of artificial intelligence.

Apart from the external context of the utterance, there is also the utterance's internal context. This refers to the cognitive state of each participant, and encompasses such things as their intentions and their representation of the preceding dialogue. It will be assumed that each dialogue participant is never intentionally obstructionist, and that their overall aim is to engage in co-operative dialogue. For any computational model of dialogue, therefore, data structures are required that can adequately represent the contextual and linguistic aspects of dialogue. More importantly, algorithms are required that can construct and manipulate these data structures.

Components of the Model

Much of what follows is derived from the work of Grosz and Sidner [6] and some implementation details have been inspired by the work of Zweben [16] on the Grosz-Sidner model.

Grosz and Sidner distinguish three main components in their model: a linguistic structure, and intentional structure, and an attentional state. The linguistic structure represents the segmentation of a dialogue as units which can stand in relation to other dialogue segments.

The intentional structure of a dialogue relates to the purpose of each dialogue segment. The intentional components of a dialogue can be related to each other by two structural relations: dominance and satisfaction precedence. The dominance relation, as its name suggests, represents the subsumption of one intention by another. The satisfaction-precedence relation indicates that satisfaction of the purpose of one segment is necessary, and prior to, the satisfaction of another. In Grosz and Sidner's paper [6], they propose a stack system to represent the dynamic unfolding of the intentional structure of dialogue.

The concept of attentional state in the Grosz-Sidner model is used to represent those elements in the dialogue that are currently in focus. In the Grosz-Sidner model the attentional state is parasitical on the intentional structure, in that the discourse segment purpose (DSP) at the top of the stack is also the one on which attention is being focused.

251

A number of modifications to the original Grosz-Sidner model are proposed. Rather than using a stack system, the model outlined here constructs a number of tree-like structures, reflecting both the linguistic and intentional structure of the dialogue. It was felt that the act of stack-popping, where an element of the intentional structure is removed from the stack and effectively thrown away, is too final. The capability should be preserved for re-activating a previously popped discourse segment. This can be done by preserving the tree-like structure of the dialogue as a whole, and by allowing an attentional pointer to traverse the elements of the tree. Traversal, however, would be limited in a number of ways. Details of the proposed structure will be given below.

An additional modification to the Grosz-Sidner model is that the attentional state is tied more closely to the linguistic structure than to the intentional structure of the dialogue. However, as will be discussed below, the intentional and linguistic structures are closely linked.

It is proposed to extend the Grosz-Sidner model by elaborating on the notion of discourse segment. In keeping with our focus on the role of context in the interpretation of an utterance, it is felt that an important element of

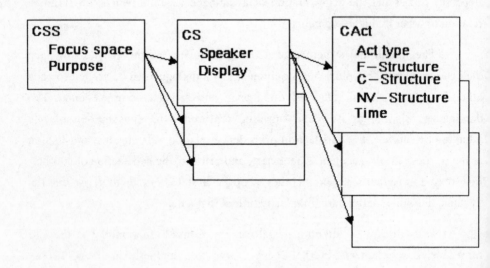

Figure 1. The constituent elements of the dialogue structure.

252

the linguistic representation should be the representation of the situation in which the utterance takes place. Therefore the data structure used to represent the linguistic utterance is also used to represent relevant aspects of the context in which the utterance was made.

The following sub-sections will outline the main components of the dialogue model.

Dialogue structures. Figure 1 represents the main dialogue structures of the model. The Communicative Situation Structure (CSS) is equivalent in level of analysis to the discourse segment of the Grosz-Sidner model. As mentioned above, it was felt necessary to represent contextual as well as linguistic information within the one framework. The three components of CSS are the communicative act component (CAct), the communicative situation component (CS), and certain properties specific to the CSS itself. A CSS can consist of a number of CSs, and these in turn can consist of a number of CActs.

The CAct is not quite equivalent to the utterance level, although in most dialogues it will be. Provision is made for gestural information accompanying an utterance, such as a deictic gesture involving a mouse or some other pointing device. A deictic gesture is considered to be a separate communicative act, though part of the same communicative situation. The facets of the CAct contain information about the fine-grained structure of the verbal or non-verbal act. In the example in Figure 1, the slots of the CAct refer to the structures of Lexical Functional Grammar; C- and F-structures. They could just as readily contain information derived from other grammatical formalisms.

A number of factors serve to distinguish one communicative situation from another. These can involve any change in the context of the dialogue; for example, a change of location or a change of speaker. In the case of person-machine communication it is most likely to involve a change in the speaker or a change in some aspect of the computer's visual display.

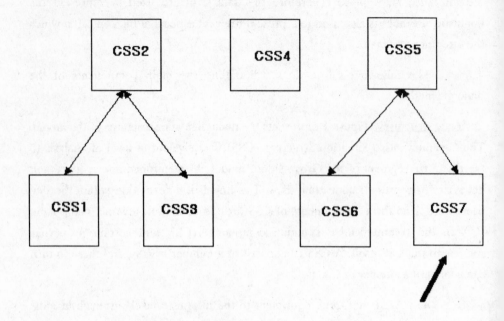

Figure 2. A set of communicative situation structures (CSS).

A number of communicative situations go to make up a CSS. What distinguishes one CSS from another is a change in the purpose of the CSS. In addition to the purpose slot, the CSS also has a slot containing information about the entities in the dialogue that are currently the focus of attention. This element of the model will be discussed below.

Structural relationships. A CSS can be related to another CSS in a limited way. The relationship can only be hierarchical, and it represents a route through which information relating to the focus of attention can be transmitted. If the focus of attention is on one CSS, definite noun phrases and anaphora in general can be resolved either from entities in focus within the current CSS or from the focus space of a CSS that is connected to the current one.

Figure 2 represents a structured collection of CSSs. As can be seen, they consist of a number of tree fragments, rather than one large tree. Such a situation can occur if the purpose of a dialogue is to achieve a number of distinct goals, which cannot be integrated under a dominating CSS.

254

Attentional state

      The disembodied arrow in Figure 2 represents the current focus of attention. The focus of attention sets bounds on what are valid targets for anaphoric reference within a CSS. This focus shifts automatically as a new CSS is created. It can also be shifted by one or another of the dialogue participants explicitly requesting a shift of focus back to a previous topic in the dialogue. However, there is a constraint put on this shift. When moving from one tree fragment to another, the focus of attention can only shift to the top-most node of the target tree. From there, it may traverse the subordinate nodes of the tree to locate the appropriate CSS. This restriction reflects the fact that when a dialogue participant returns to a previously active topic in the dialogue, he or she tends to proceed

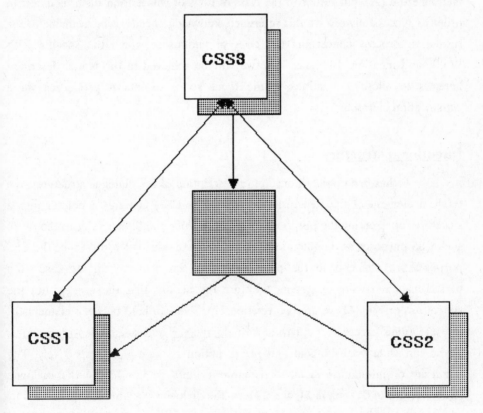

Figure 3. The relationship between dialogue and intentional structure.

from the general to the specific aspect of that topic. Traversal of the CCS tree from top to bottom represents such a transition.

The component of the model operated upon by the attentional mechanism is the focus space. This consists of a list of items that have been topicalised in the dialogue. Topicalisation can be effected by a number of syntactic devices [9]. The entities on the list can either have properties in their own right, or can inherit them from higher up in a classification hierarchy. The reason for having highly structured objects in the focus space, is to allow for the resolution of anaphoric references of the following type (after Sidner [14]):

A: I saw John's Irish Wolfhound yesterday.

B: Yes. They're really big dogs.

In (B) the phrase they're does not refer back to any specific entity mentioned in (A), but rather to the class of dogs of which John's is a member. In order to successfully resolve this reference, knowledge needs to be available to the resolution process concerning the class of entities to which the specific Irish Wolfhound mentioned belongs. The way this is achieved in the model described here, is to allow the entities in the focus space to inherit properties via a classification hierarchy.

Intentional structure

As has been pointed out in the description of the dialogue structures, the topmost element of the structural hierarchy (the CSS) contains a pointer into a structure representing the purpose of the CSS. Grosz and Sidner refer to the set of such CSS purposes as the intentional structure of the dialogue. In essence the CSS purposes are elements in the plan underlying the dialogue. In the case of a person-machine dialogue system, they are the actions that the user wishes the system to perform. There are two relationships that can hold between elements of the intentional structure, and these are dominance and satisfaction-precedence. These represent goal/sub-goal and pre-condition relationships, respectively. The hierarchy of intentional elements is more or less isomorphic to the dialogue structure, as can be seen in Figure 3. Here, the dialogue structure is represented by white boxes and the underlying intentional structure by shaded boxes. Also note that the intentional structure may be expanded by an inferential process, without there being a corresponding node in the dialogue structure. The slots of the intentional structure components are dependent on the dialogue domain, unlike those in the

256

dialogue structure. In the following example of an application of the model, the domain is that of database interaction with the user performing the specific task of tabulating data about students' ages and courses. Each intentional component represents an action of tabulation, and the place that the action has in the intentional hierarchy is determined by the complexity of the table requested (or inferred).

A sample application

The following dialogue (except S8) was collected as part of a corpus of simulated person-machine dialogues in which the user communicated with a human expert via keyboard, screen and mouse. S8 is inserted to illustrate how an inferred intention can be used by the system to direct the dialogue.

U1: How many students, both male and female, under 16 or younger in the three year degree course?

S 2: There are no students of that age group in the College.

U3: Again in the three year degree course, how many male and female students in the following age groups: 18 19 20 21 22 23 24 25 or older?

S 4: Here is the table.

U5: Total number of both male and female students in this course of study.

S 6: 153 males and 559 females.

U7: Please supply a breakdown of both male and female students in the graduate course.

S 8: Do you wish to see a complete sex by age by course breakdown?

Figure 4 illustrates the unfolding of both the dialogue and intentional structures (the numbers in the boxes correspond to utterances). The intentional structure underlying S8 is inferred on the basis that if the user has asked for the same breakdown for two courses, he or she may wish to have a three-way breakdown for all courses. This inference then gives rise to utterance S8, which is incorporated into the dialogue structure. The left of Figure 4 represents the state of the dialogue and intentional structures up to and including utterance U7. The right of the figure represents the structures after S8.

257

In U5, the reference to an unspecified course (underlined) requires that a referent be found. The bi-directional links in the discourse structure allow information from the focus spaces of the connected nodes to be accessed in the resolution process. Thus, the anaphoric reference in U5 can be resolved by accessing the focus space of utterances 3 and 4.

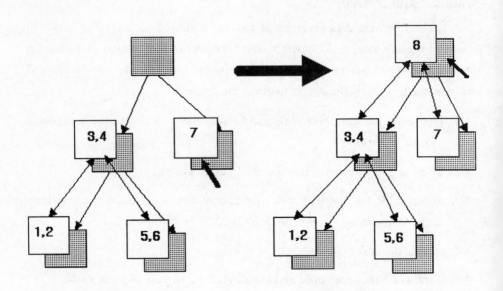

Figure 4. A structural analysis of the sample dialogue.

Note that the small disembodied arrows in Figure 4 indicate the current attentional state of the dialogue.

5 CONCLUSION

The dialogue model outlined above is underspecified in a number of important aspects. Firstly, no algorithmic description has been provided that can generate and utilise the data structures of the model. Secondly, no explicit indication has been given of the way the model might deal with miscommunication and ill-formedness in dialogue. These issues are addressed below.

Implementation

The research programme, of which the work described here is a part, is still in the early stages of implementation. However, a number of implementation decisions have already been made which give some indication of what the final system will look like.

Both the dialogue and intentional structures are to be represented using a version of FRL [12]. The frames will be connected in a network. The instantiation and interconnection of the frames will be the job of a general control algorithm, while the filling of many of the slots in the various frames will be demon driven. That is, associated with each slot will be a function that is activated when data is required for the slot, such as when the frame containing the slot is instantiated. Very limited use will be made of the inheritance mechanism of the frame system. Inheritance will be mainly used for the inheritance of focus-space information. The feature of frames that will be most utilised is that of demon-driven slot filling.

Robustness

As has already been argued, providing a dialogue framework within which to interpret natural language utterances is a form of insurance against miscommunication. The dialogue system described above, with its linguistic, contextual, and intentional components, provides, to some extent, an intrinsically robust communication framework. Nevertheless, this is not the full story; miscommunication will still occur.

In the taxonomy of miscommunications described above, a distinction was made between input and model failures. Apart from the dialogue category, input failures are the responsibility of the parsing system. Techniques for dealing with them are reasonably well understood (e.g. semantic grammars, parsing meta-rules). In addition, techniques for dealing with some types of dialogue input failure are fairly well developed (e.g. the reference relaxation technique [4]). Other types of dialogue input failure, such as structural ill-formedness, are more problematic.

259

However, something like a dialogue grammar [10] may be a useful tool for detecting this type of ill- formedness.

Model failures, by definition, tend to be domain dependent. Their detection and repair is the concern of the model's intentional component. Pollack's [8] work on the detection of faulty domain plans suggest some avenues that might be pursued in dealing with them. Her theses provides a useful general framework for inferring and judging the validity of domain plans, albeit simple ones. The possibility of incorporating versions of her axioms into the intention inference component of the dialogue model is being considered.

Finally

It is hoped that this paper has given some indication of the advantages of dealing with natural language understanding within a dialogue framework. Although the computational complexity of a dialogue system is considerably greater than a sentence-based one, there are significant benefits in terms of robustness in taking this route. Furthermore, since a dialogue-based system is a more 'natural' natural language understanding system, it should also have a greater degree of user acceptability.

REFERENCES

1 Allen, JF, Perrault, CR (1980), Analyzing intention in utterances. Artificial Intelligence, 15, 143-178.

2 Carbonell, J & Hayes, PJ (1983), Recovery strategies for parsing, 123-146.

3 Eastman, CM, & McLean, DS (1981), On the need for parsing ill-formed input. American Journal of Computational Linguistics, 7, 257.

4 Goodman, BA (1987), Repairing reference identification failures by relaxation. In R Reilly (ed.), Communication failure in dialogue and discourse. Amsterdam: North-Holland.

5 Grosz, B (1977), The representation and use of focus in dialogue understanding. Unpublished PhD thesis, University of California, Berkeley.

6 Grosz, BJ & Sidner, CL (1986), Attention, intentions, and the structure of discourse structure. Computational Linguistics 12, 175-204.

7 Litman, DJ (1985), Plan recognition and discourse analysis: An integrated approach for understanding dialogues. TR 170, Department of Computer Science, University of Rochester, New York.

8 Pollack, ME (1986), Inferring domain plans in question answering. MS0CIS-86-40, Department of Computer and Information Science, University of Pennsylvania, Philadelphia.

9 Reichman, R (1985), Getting computers to talk like you and me. Cambridge, MA: MIT Press.

10 Reilly, RG (in press), An ATN-based grammar for the structural analysis of dialogue. In N E Sharkey (ed.), Review of cognitive science. Hillsdale, NJ: Ablex.

11 Ringle, MH & Bruce, BC (1982), Conversation failure. In W G Lehnert, M H Ringle (eds), Strategies for natural language processing. Hillsdale, NJ: Erlbaum.

12 Roberts, RB, & Goldstein, IP (1977), The FRL manual. Memo 409, MIT AI Lab, MIT.

13 Thompson, BH (1980), Linguistics analysis of natural language communication with computers. In Proceedings of the Eighth International Conference on Computational Linguistics, Tokyo, Japan.

14 Sidner, CL (1979), Towards a computational theory of definite anaphora comprehension in English discourse. Technical Report 537, MIT AI Laboratory, Cambridge, MA.

15 Webber,BL & Mays,E (1983), Varieties of user misconceptions: detection and correction. In Proceedings of IJCAI ' 83, Karlsruhe, Germany.

16 Zweben, M (1987), Using intentional and attentional structure for anaphor resolution. In Proceedings of CogSci '87, University of Washington, Seattle, Washington.

Chapter 17
Conceptual and Semantic Co-ordination in dialogue:
Implications for Interactive Natural Language Interfaces

S GARROD,
Glasgow University

> 'Communication' comes from the latin 'communico' meaning 'to share' . . . Communication is essentially a social process. Sharing does not mean simply passing something, some sign, from one person to another, it implies also that this sign is mutually accepted, recognized and held in common ownership or use by each person.

> Colin Cherry, 1971

1   INTRODUCTION

While it is fair to say that much has been learnt about the nature of human languages from treating them as sign or code systems analogous to the artificial languages invented by man, many aspects of human linguistic communication depend upon principles not often encountered in artificial systems. For instance, when we design machines to communicate, we ensure that they do so in a 'language' whose structure and interpretation is predefined, so that the machines will not have to establish a mutual acceptance or recognition of the signs they are using. In encoding or decoding messages each machine simply refers to the same manual for the 'language'. However, effective human communication, at least in the framework of natural dialogue, depends upon the speaker and listener being able to co-ordinate their respective use and interpretation of the language, within the context of the particular exchange. In effect, they must establish that they 'share' the same overall conception of what is being discussed and agree upon how each utterance should be understood in relation to this shared conception. To this extent human communication can be seen as an exercise in semantic and conceptual co-ordination [1, 3]. Furthermore, any truly effective dialogue interface between a human language user and a machine will also have to come to terms with such problems in co-ordinated language use.

In this paper, I will be discussing some of the ways that dialogue partners seem to collaborate to solve these inherent problems in communication. But I will take this analysis of human dialogue as a starting point for deriving interactional principles which should be of relevance in designing effective natural language interfaces and which may even lead to a simplification of their design.

The first section of the paper therefore explores co-ordination in the context of a particular conversational setting amenable to laboratory investigation. I start by illustrating more clearly what is involved in such co-ordination and the various co-operative strategies that speakers seem to be using to effect it. Out of this analysis emerges the notion that speakers are more concerned with modelling the interaction between each other than they are with building an explicit model of their partner, and it is this principle which may be of importance in designing effective interactive interfaces.

2   AN EMPIRICAL STUDY OF CO-ORDINATION IN HUMAN DIALOGUE

At Glasgow we have developed an experimental technique for eliciting natural dialogues, but within a controlled setting [3]. The technique involves pairs of subjects playing a co-operative computer-controlled maze game, which is so designed that the players will regularly produce descriptions of their location within the maze.

The essence of the game is as follows: each player is seated in a different room confronted with a VDU on which a maze is displayed. The mazes consist of small box-like structures connected by paths along which the players can make alternate moves (see Fig. 1). The goal of the game is to move their respective position markers through the maze one path link at a time until they both manage to reach a predefined finish position. Although the basic structure of the two mazes is identical, each player can only see his or her own start position, finish position and current marker position.

The co-operative nature of the game arises from two additional features of the mazes. First, each maze contains obstacles in the form of gates, which block movement along the paths, and secondly there are certain nodes marked as switch positions, both of which are distributed differently for each player. It is in overcoming these obstacles that verbal co-operation is required, since the fundamental principle of the game is as follows. If a given player (say A) moves into one of the switch nodes marked on the other's (B's) screen, then the entire configuration of B's gates will change. All paths previously blocked will be opened and all previously open ones blocked. Thus whenever a player requires the gates to be changed they have to enlist the co-operation of the other player, find out where the player is and guide him into a switch node only visible on their own screen.

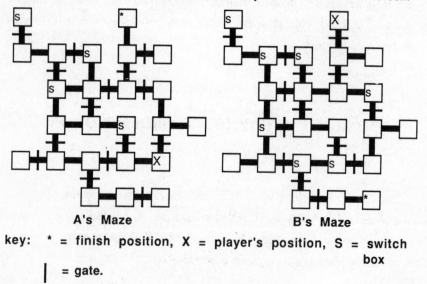

A's Maze   B's Maze

key: * = finish position, X = player's position, S = switch box

| = gate.

Figure 1. Example of mazes used in the maze game task.

264

Typically a game will consist in players moving through the maze with dialogue intervening between moves, where the dialogue contains recurrent descriptions of the players' positions in the maze, switch node locations and finish positions. These dialogues can then be recorded and transcribed along with exact information about the actual positions being described.

Such transcripts provide a useful record of how the players collaborate to establish mutually acceptable description schemes. First, it is possible to analyse the range of different types of description which emerge in such a situation and then determine the extent to which the speakers within any dialogue develop particular idiosyncratic schemes. Thus, Garrod & Anderson [3] have reported an analysis of 56 such dialogues from 29 pairs of players which yielded 1396 descriptions of positions within the mazes. On the basis of this analysis a wide range of distinct schemes could be identified, each depending upon one of four different 'conceptual models' of the overall maze configuration which could be combined with a particular 'language' of description, that is set of interpretation rules for expressions used in the description.

The four basic models which we were able to identify consisted in the following:

(1) A Path network model, where the nodes are treated as being in a network whose links are the actual paths in the maze (similar to an underground map). So, for instance the point marked '1' in the Figure might be described in the following fashion:

'See the bottom left, go along four and up one, that's where I am'.

36.8 percent of all descriptions were of this type.

(2) A co-ordinate model, which depends upon treating each node in the maze as lying within a notional grid of intersecting horizontal and vertical lines. Thus the point marked '1' in Figure 1 might be given the following co-ordinate descriptions:

'I'm on the third row and fifth column'

'I'm at D five'.

23.4 percent of all descriptions were of this type. (3) A line type of model, where the nodes were treated as lying on a system of lines oriented in some particular way, e.g.

vertically, horizontally or even diagonally. Thus point '1' in the Figure might be described as:

'I'm on the third level second from the right.'

23 percent of the descriptions were of this type. Finally, there was a fourth model:

(4) The figural model, in which the maze as a whole was broken down into distinct patterns or figures of nodes, such as 'T shapes' , 'limbs', 'rectangles' etc. Thus position '2' in Figure 1 was described in the following fashion:

'See the middle right indicator, well I'm right out at the end of it'.

17.3 percent of the descriptions were of this figural type.

Of course, there was a wide range of different schemes which could be associated with any particular type of model or conception of the maze structure. Thus, even within the 'horizontal' linetype of model four, distinct description schemes were used to represent the way in which the lines might be discriminated from each other (see Garrod & Anderson [1] for details). At the same time, there was considerable variation in the different terms that pairs of speakers would use to designate components in the model. For instance, in giving 'horizontal' line type descriptions, the lines might be described as 'lines', 'rows', 'levels', 'layers', 'columns' or even 'floors'.

However against this background of variation, individual dialogue partners were extraordinarily consistent with each other in the schemes being used. For instance, we were able to demonstrate that 98 percent of the pairs were producing a more similar pattern of description schemes across the dialogue than would be expected by chance [3]. In other words, there was evidence that the speakers entrained each other in description choice. However, this similarity in description schemes between speakers did not simply arise through convergence on a single preferred scheme. As the dialogue proceeded there was also evidence that speakers tended to adopt more abstract schemes. For instance, there was a general trend to shift from path network or figural schemes to line and co-ordinate ones. Nevertheless the degree of entrainment in description choice actually increased as this development of new schemes occured.

266

This analysis of human dialogue therefore indicates that our choice of language in production is critically dependent on what are essentially interactional factors. It comes both from an attempt to converge on a mutually acceptable conception of the domain as well as a mutually acceptable construal of the language in the domain. This raises a number of interesting questions about how speakers are able to establish such a co-ordinated dynamic system for communication. In the next section some suggestions will be made about mechanisms underlying co-ordination in the maze game dialogues. On the basis of these a general interactional modelling principle can be derived which can then be explored in relation to HCI design.

3   CO-ORDINATION MECHANISMS

The most obvious way in which interactants could solve co- ordination problems of the sort presented by the maze game dialogues is to negotiate explicitly about the description scheme to be used, and on occasion such negotiation can be observed in these dialogues. For instance, in one such game the players began by setting up a scheme in the following fashion:

A: . . . o.k. right: make an imaginary grid: starting from the bottom left : that's one, two three, four you know?

B: Bottom left.

A: Bottom left and along.

etc.

However, it does not seem to be either a popular or effective means of achieving co-ordination in practice.

Two observations from the dialogues highlight the problem with explicit negotiation of this sort. First, explicit negotiation, when it did occur, only happened after many descriptions had already been given, and then only after the conversants had experienced considerable problems in establishing a mutually satisfactory

267

scheme. For instance, of the 15 games where such negotiation could be identified, in nine cases it was only after the pair had already completed one game and in the remainder it occured after an average of seven descriptions had been produced.

The second observation is that, even in cases where speakers have gone to the trouble of negotiating a description scheme, they very often do not stick to it for long, letting the descriptions wander from the scheme as soon as any problem arises. Thus in games where explicit negotiation was identified, the negotiated scheme only predicted 59 percent of the subsequent descriptions used by both players. Explicitly negotiated semantic plans do not therefore seem to play a major part in determining what is actually said in such a task (see Suchman [7] for an interesting discussion about the role of interactional planning in other tasks). In practice, our conversants seem to solve the co-ordination problem in a more flexibile and cost-effective way.

As Clark & Wilkes-Gibbs [2] have pointed out, a major factor in the economy of conversation is the minimisation of what they call collaborative effort. This means that conversants should formulate their utterances in such a way that they do not have to spend unnecessary time or effort in ensuring mutual intelligibility. In the context of the maze game dialogues this can be achieved by following a very simple interactional principle which we have termed the output/input co-ordination principle [3]. This principle may be stated as one of formulating your utterances (i.e. output) according to the same interpretation rules (i.e. model and semantics) as those assumed in interpreting the most recent relevant utterance from the other (i.e. input). In effect such a principle requires speakers to be locally consistent with each other in the use of the language, and so long as both abide by it in contexts such as the maze game, they should quickly come to establish a mutually satisfactory description scheme with a minimum of collaborative effort.

Co-ordinating output with input is an efficient means of hunting out the minimal common ground needed to support effective communication. It serves this function in the process of fulfilling the primary purpose of the utterance (e.g. describing locations in this case), without requiring a special additional interaction of the sort underlying explicit negotiation of a semantic scheme. Furthermore it does so without the speaker having to build up an explicit model of his or her audience, the only model required is one which captures the co-ordinated system which the speaker is presuming at the time of utterance. Finally, output/input co-ordination has processing utility to the extent that it minimises the joint pool of resources which a speaker/listener has to call upon when alternately formulating and interpreting utterances within the same dialogue, since both processes will refer to the same set of interpretation rules.

Garod, Anderson & Sanford [4] constructed a computer simulation of two conversants generating and interpreting maze location descriptions which incorporated just such a principle of co-ordinating output with input. The general control structure of the simulation model for a single player is shown in Figure 2. While it is beyond the scope of the present paper to report the details of the simulation, the basic principle behind it is one of attempting to generate and interpret descriptions through access to a limited focused knowledge representation, incorporating a particular model and set of semantic interpretation rules. Any failures in interpretation can then be used to instigate shifts in focus and hence lead to a new model and/or set of semantic interpretation rules to be tested against the input. At the same time, focus shifts could be used to instigate appropriate feedback from the listener by running the description generator to produce a repeat or possibly restatement of the original description, according to the listener's new focus specification.

While this model did quite a good job of simulating the exact form of many description sequences taken from actual dialogues, it also highlighted some of the inherent limitations in the rigid application of the output/input co-ordination principle. The most obvious limitation concerns its inflexibility. In most of the maze game dialogues the conversants develop new, more elliptical, forms of description as the games proceed, and in many cases these new forms depend upon rather different models and 'languages' from those used previously. However, it is not possible to introduce such changes without violating the basic output/input co-ordination principle, since it requires one of the speakers to be locally inconsistent. But closer observation of the actual dialogues suggested a simple way of augmenting the model to capture these dynamic aspects of description choice, while retaining the basic notion of co-ordinating output and input.

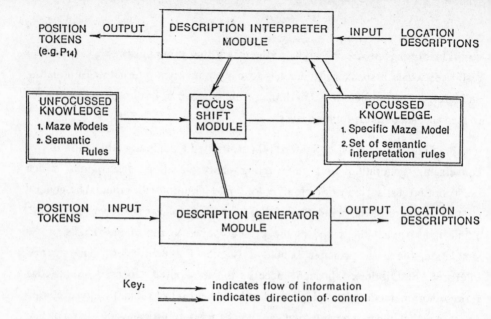

POSITION OUTPUT **DESCRIPTION INTERPRETER** INPUT LOCATION
TOKENS **MODULE** DESCRIPTIONS
(e.g. P_{14})

UNFOCUSSED
KNOWLEDGE
1. Maze Models
2. Semantic
   Rules

FOCUS
SHIFT
MODULE

FOCUSSED
KNOWLEDGE.
1. Specific Maze Model
2. Set of semantic
   interpretation rules

POSITION INPUT **DESCRIPTION GENERATOR** OUTPUT LOCATION
TOKENS **MODULE** DESCRIPTIONS

Key: ———▸ indicates flow of information
       ═══▸ indicates direction of control

Figure 2. Flow chart for the dialogue description simulation

Lewis [6] has pointed out that dialogues often rely upon an implicit division of labour and power such that one of the participants is recognised to hold epistemic control over the others. The controller (or master in Lewis's terminology) can be thought of as arbiter of the common pool of presuppositions underlying the dialogue. Hence whenever a master says anything it is incumbent of the other participants (the slaves according to Lewis) to alter their current conceptual and linguistic assumptions in order to make the master's statement true. On the other hand a master may choose to accept or reject a slave's statement if it in some way violates his or her current assumptions.

In fact we observed just such a role discrepancy in many of the maze game dialogues, whereby one participant would effectively lead in the development of new description schemes, while the other followed. Thus it was common to observe dialogues where each of the descriptions produced by one participant was questioned if it did not conform to the partner's immediately preceding scheme, while no such corrective questioning occured in the other direction [3].

This suggested introducing a similar control asymmetry into the simulation models. Basically, the model of one participant would be given master status while the other was given slave status, and at times the master could introduce a novel, more elliptical, description (through a manipulation of the focus state). The slave

270

simulator would then have to attempt to interpret this new description by shifting its focus structure, which in turn affected all the subsequent descriptions generated. This augmented model does a good job of simulating many of the actual description sequences arising in the maze game task.

4 IMPLICATIONS FOR INTERACTIONAL HCI DESIGN

In the literature on design of human-computer interfaces it is commonly argued that one should try and incorporate a model of the user. However, in dynamic interaction between two rational agents such modelling of the other is fraught with real problems. As Lewis [5] among others has argued, any attempt to establish the relevant beliefs and expectations of your partner will have to take into account that they too are going to be engaged in modelling yourself, including your beliefs and expectations about them, so quickly one encounters an infinite spiral of higher order expectations and beliefs and the excercise seems doomed to failure.

Therefore it is not surprising that conversants in our laboratory setting do not behave as if they were trying to model their partner directly. Instead they seem to be attempting to model the relevant intersection between each other's beliefs on the basis of the immediately preceding interaction. In effect, they are operating on conservative presumptions about what is mutually known. If your partner produces an utterance which can be satisfactorily interpreted by making a minimal set of assumptions about how they view the domain and construe the language then you presume that these assumptions correctly model their presumptions about what is mutually known. Should any problem arise through a failure to interpret an utterance correctly, then it is always possible to try and rectify the problem through some form of negotiation.

It might seem that the role discrepancy between master and slave discussed above makes the modelling process one sided, but this is not really the case. The decision of labour only concerns who is the arbiter over what is essentially a single model which reflects the overlap in relevant beliefs. Thus slaves are not expected to model the master's beliefs but rather his or her contribution to the prior interaction.

Such a co-ordination approach therefore treats the process as one of modelling the interaction as opposed to modelling the partner, and it is this aspect of the analysis of the dialogues that suggest a general principle in designing flexible interactive interfaces.

Quite apart from this general principle our analysis of human dialogue also suggests that interfaces that capitalise on what the user has actually said and how it was said (i.e. utilise some form of output/input co-ordination) will probably prove much more convincing for the user. The extraordinary verisimilitude of Weizenbaum's famous ELIZA program may well be due to the way it builds on what the user has said rather than trying to construct intelligent novel comments and expressions.

5   REFERENCES

1   Clark, HH (1985), Language Use and Language Users. In G Lindzey & E Arponson (eds) The Handbook of Social Psychology. 179-231. New York, Harper Row.

2   Clark, HH & Wilkes-Gibbs, D (1985), Referring as a collaborative Process. Cognition, 22, 1, 1-39.

3   Garrod, S Anderson, A (1987), Saying what you mean in dialogue: A study in conceptual and semantic co-ordination. Cognition, 27.

4   Garrod, S, Anderson, A & Sanford, AJ (1984), Semantic negotiation and the dynamics of conversational meaning. Technical Report, 1. Glasgow University.

5   Lewis, DK (1968), Convention: A Philosophical Study. Cambridge, Ma. Havard University Press.

6   Lewis, DK (1979), Scorekeeping in a Language Game. Journal of Philosphical Logic, 8, 339-359.

7   Suchman, LA (1985), Plans and Situated Actions: The problem of Human Machine commumnication. Palo Alto, Xerox Corporation.